Praise for *Leading Through Disruption*

"Andrew Liveris offers a set of principles, lessons, and skills any leader should learn—and they come with all the more authority and insight given his illustrious career across industries and around the world for many decades." —TONY BLAIR,
former prime minister of the United Kingdom

"To master systemic transformation goes far beyond managing change. Andrew Liveris's book equips the reader with the intellectual and pragmatic framework to succeed in the new corporate environment, where permanent disruption is the prerequisite for success." —KLAUS SCHWAB,
founder, World Economic Forum

"Throughout his career, Andrew Liveris has been adept at building multisector collaborations to benefit the private sector, the not-for-profit sector, and the planet. *Leading Through Disruption* distills his lessons into an indispensable guidebook."

—INDRA NOOYI,
former CEO and chairperson, PepsiCo

"In a world full of uncertainty—political, economic, and environmental—Andrew Liveris shows that, under the right leadership model, we can bring all stakeholders across the global spectrum to the table to plan out a better future." —HENRY KRAVIS,
cofounder, KKR & Co. Inc.

"Leaders in today's volatile world have much to learn from this book. Andrew Liveris transformed Dow into a global market leader while placing a major emphasis on sustainability. He is truly a citizen of the world with an ability to transcend cultural differences. He is able to work with heads of state, regulators, customers, and stakeholders around the world while maintaining a relentless, results-oriented management focus."

—HANK PAULSON,
former US secretary of the treasury

"Andrew Liveris has written an insightful primer on a new kind of leadership that is urgently needed in this era of disruption. This book is essential reading for anyone interested in how business must change and collaborate to create a future that works for all." —JULIE SWEET,
chair and CEO, Accenture

"*Leading Through Disruption* offers a real-world perspective about some of the most pressing challenges future business leaders are certain to face. It's a critical read for the next generation of leaders seeking to learn from a range of perspectives on how we might address them." —LARRY FINK,
chairman and CEO, BlackRock, Inc.

LEADING
THROUGH
DISRUPTION

A Changemaker's Guide to Twenty-First Century Leadership

Andrew Liveris

HarperCollins
Leadership

An Imprint of HarperCollins

Published by HarperCollins Leadership, an imprint of HarperCollins Focus LLC.

Any internet addresses, phone numbers, or company or product information printed in this book are offered as a resource and are not intended in any way to be or to imply an endorsement by HarperCollins Leadership, nor does HarperCollins Leadership vouch for the existence, content, or services of these sites, phone numbers, companies, or products beyond the life of this book.

This book is written as a source of information only. The information contained in this book should by no means be considered a substitute for the advice, decisions, or judgment of the reader's professional or financial advisors. All efforts have been made to ensure the accuracy of the information contained in this book as of the date published. The author and the publisher expressly disclaim responsibility for any adverse effects arising from the use or application of the information contained herein.

ISBN 978-1-4002-3385-4 (eBook)
ISBN 978-1-4002-3383-0 (HC)

Library of Congress Control Number: 2023931460

Printed in the United States
23 24 25 26 27 LBC 5 4 3 2 1

CONTENTS

INTRODUCTION

The twenty-first century is complex and blindsiding in ways no one could have predicted or prepared for even two decades ago. To be sure, global volatility goes back to the Dutch tulip crisis of 1637, when a single flower ended up being worth twice the amount of a Rembrandt, and earlier if you like, to the Greek and Roman Empires. But as the economist Milton Friedman said, "The one thing about history is we don't learn from history." In the early 2000s, an acronym surfaced to describe the instability of this century: VUCA, short for *volatile, uncertain, complex,* and *ambiguous.* Think the internet bubble collapse of 2000, 9/11, the global financial crisis, the COVID pandemic in early 2020, and Russia's invasion of Ukraine in early 2022.

No country or company was equipped for any of these events. COVID especially offered a discouraging education around the failures of modern-day leadership. None of these first-time crises were easy to catalog, nor were they in any business school manual. How many *other* upheavals are waiting for us in the decades ahead?

Since VUCA appeared, the rate and pace of change has become even more feverish. In 2020 alone, the world experienced the worst public health threat since the 1918 Spanish flu; the global economy saw its sharpest downturn in decades; and the US witnessed the largest social disruption since the 1960s, triggered by the racially charged murder of George Floyd. Zoom became a verb, telehealth a new medical norm, QR codes ubiquitous. The travel industry imploded. China saber-rattled. Disinformation collided with facts. Capitol Hill was assailed by a mob.

This isn't to say that many business and leadership lessons or skills from the twentieth century aren't relevant. They are. But the business landscape today is so foreign from that of two decades ago that figuring out how to deploy those lessons and skills needs to be reimagined and retaught. Business leaders lack a toolbox for *this* century, one that details the context and the issues that CEOs and enterprises need to focus on to create an impact from their place in time today. How can you make your business work today for tomorrow—and not yesterday, or the day before? How can you engineer your company, and country, to be both resilient and agile, to better arm yourself against VUCA in the decades ahead? How can you immunize yourself against future crises and ideally extract opportunity from them?

The good news is it's not too late. We can't change the times in which we do business, but as the Austrian psychiatrist and writer Viktor Frankl wrote, "When we are no longer able to change a situation, we are challenged to change ourselves."

To explain how we got here, let's go back to 2004.

IN THE MONTHS BEFORE I was chosen to be the eleventh CEO of the Dow Chemical Company, I hired a business coach, a fellow Aussie with a deep understanding of corporate boards and board processes. Together, we created a manifesto of all the things I wanted to accomplish if I got the top job. Vision. Strategy. Milestones. The makeup of my team and board. What was working at Dow at the time and what could be improved. My five- and ten-year goals (one of which was to acquire, or merge with, DuPont, which would happen thirteen years later, proving that good things sometimes come to CEOs who wait). My manifesto was systematized and analytical. I left nothing on the field. A few months later, I was told the CEO job was mine.

I've always been a diligent preparer—even an overpreparer. Every time I got a new assignment, I tracked down every last piece of background material and studied it in depth. I did the same after being named CEO, spending the next two months interviewing nearly two dozen business leaders, including Sam Palmisano at IBM, A. G. Lafley at Procter & Gamble, Jack Welch at General Electric, Jim McNerney at 3M, Sandy Weill at Citigroup, and Lee Thomas at Walmart, among other CEOs I admired, and who were willing to give me the time of day. I digested as much of their wisdom and experience as possible. Each CEO had a strong take on one or more of the subjects that mattered most to me, whether it was boards, growth agendas, crisis management, or multistakeholder engagement. I was especially taken by the four-part management axiom championed by P&G's A. G. Lafley—*Embrace your reality; choose among your options; build the team to execute; lead the charge.* These are words I still quote today.

With my coach's help, I filled a memo pad with notes about what the greatest CEOs of my time did and how they did it and what they didn't do and why not. Armed with the lessons, principles, and advice of my peers and predecessors, and anticipating piecemeal progress, and a straightforward geopolitical backdrop—there being no reason to expect anything else—I got to work.

I still have that memo pad. It's the nearest thing I had to a twentieth-century business and leadership toolbox. If anyone had told me that two decades later it would be mostly obsolete, I wouldn't have believed them. I also would have been wrong.

As a former CEO with more than four decades of global experience, I've spent most of my career at the intersection of business, government, academia, the nonprofit sector, and civic society. In addition to the fourteen years I spent running Dow, I'm also a scientist and engineer who believes that my training and knowledge base gives me the right and even the duty to solve the biggest problems humanity faces. That knowledge base has allowed me to gather insights about the multiple fault lines I see across the world and come up with solutions about what businesses and leaders must do to ensure their survival and success in the upcoming decades.

Wanting to create a new toolbox to educate a generation of younger leaders about the core issues of the twenty-first century, a few years ago I endowed the Andrew N. Liveris Academy for Innovation and Leadership at the University of Queensland, Australia. Our mission is to provide the environment, programs, and curriculum to deliver a pipeline of effective, creative, empathic, problem-solving future leaders who can make the difficult decisions necessary to bond a siloed, fragmented world and ensure a more equitable, sustainable future for everybody.

Underlying the philosophy of Liveris Academy are urgent questions: How can today's leaders step up to provide societal, financial, and human benefits at a time when we all recognize this is the only planet we have, and we need to protect it? How can today's businesses create common platforms of understanding that elevate everyone? How can today's leaders master not only the content of their businesses but the context of their operating environment, while also creating a culture that guarantees their success?

Liveris Academy is a work in progress. With the physical construction completed, we opened our doors in early 2022. Our goal of equipping the next generation of business leaders with a set of navigational tools for *this* century is zooming ahead. More than anything, I want the graduating classes of Liveris Academy to gain confidence in assessing and solving problems so that no matter where their careers take them, they'll be able to draw on a handful of considerations and principles that are relevant for today.

This book is an opportunity to audit some of the same material Liveris Academy faculty gives our students. Don't worry—there are no grades, or even pass-fail. So roll up your sleeves. There's a lot to do (which, I might add, is music to an engineer's ears.) If the twentieth century brought us think tanks, now is the time for *do* tanks.

The Case for a Twenty-First-Century Leadership Toolbox

VUCA or no VUCA, why does the business world need a new toolbox? What makes this century so atypical that it can't be negotiated using traditional business or leadership models and methods? The answer is found in an intersecting set of tectonic, permanent fissures that have come together to reorganize what it means today to do business. Most have taken place simultaneously and, to use a favored expression of mine, at the speed of *live*. Each one intersects with and amplifies the others.

Among them are the retreat of leadership around the globe; the failed promise of globalization; the prioritizing of short-term business goals over long-term strategies and vision; an ever-mutating geopolitical chessboard;

and the mission-critical urgency of environmental, social, and governance (ESG) factors that come together under the heading *sustainability*.

We are living in a new normal or, rather, a new abnormal. Let's look more closely at the shifts that have convinced me that last century's business toolkit is in need of revision.

THE RISE OF THE G-ZERO WORLD

In the years after World War II, the US and other leading nations came together to create the liberal international order (LIO). Anchored by the UN, the World Bank, the International Monetary Fund, the World Health Organization, the G7, and eventually the G8, the LIO had the mission to resolve conflicts, maintain peace, and elevate global prosperity. Today, beset by numerous challenges, both external and self-inflicted, these institutions can no longer do what they set out to do. With their influence waning, countries and companies have no choice but to fend for themselves. G-Zero is the term that public policy guru Ian Bremmer coined to describe today's landscape. No leadership. No direction. No one in charge. Every business and country for itself.

Leadership today comes from where? Who, for example, stepped up to lead the global response to the COVID pandemic? No one. The institutions of last century that might have once connected the world's most sophisticated medical offices with the foremost global disease institutions to create practical, best-in-class measures and outcomes around managing COVID-19 were noticeably missing. Ask a group of people to name the leaders they admire most, and what names come up? Angela Merkel, before she stepped down, followed, maybe, by Emmanuel Macron. That's it. In the US especially, leadership has taken a big step backward, a void that has certainly contributed to the rise of power mongers around the world. Donald Trump's election in 2016 was a symptom of deeper changes taking place in America, marked by introspection and retreat from the global stage.

THE FALSE PROMISE OF GLOBALIZATION

Globalization had almost everything going for it, including prioritizing the free movement of capital and goods, and prizing deregulation. After all, when had markets overseen by governments ever led to anything good? Everyone assumed globalization would elevate everybody, not just Western economies but nations across Latin American and Asia too.

The global financial crisis of 2008–2009, and the job loss that followed, offered a sober reality check. Governments bailed out banks and insurance companies and ignored workers. Companies found themselves competing against *countries*—China, Inc.; Germany, Inc.; Israel, Inc.— and those countries' strategies, meaning that a level playing field was never going to happen. These nations and others established top-down programs focused on their own present and future capabilities, including government-run R&D strategies, labs, and tax and regulatory policies hospitable to overseas companies and their best-in-class technologies. The US doesn't do that—it's seen as interfering with markets—leaving it the responsibility of companies to manage and oversee their own development and growth, without any accompanying government-led instruments around taxation, regulations, and infrastructure.

Naturally, with countries like Japan and Germany providing these advantages, imbalances occurred. If a trade deal was struck in, say, Germany, to open markets between that country and another, with Germany offering governmental or policy-related instruments to make itself competitive in new technologies, from batteries to solar cells, *countries* were now in the position of beating out *companies*. A good example? Airbus versus Boeing. Airbus is supported by three countries in the EU. Their policies, which included making airplanes in three different countries, via three different government-run companies, and employing workers in Spain, Germany, and France, meant Airbus could easily beat out Boeing, a publicly listed US company.

Today, the open system of global fair trade is in pieces. Countries worldwide have failed to provide equal spoils for their citizens. The result has been an increase in economic nationalism, a rise of autocracies worldwide, and a retreat by most nations to the safety of their own borders. Globally, most people have come to realize that the distribution of wealth is patently unjust and that the top earners of society are the only ones with access to quality health care and education, and wasn't it always that way?

THE PROBLEM OF SHORT-TERMISM

As a species, we seem to have lost our long-term planning mechanisms. How can anyone talk about where humanity will be in 2030, much less 2050, if the only thing politicians care about is getting reelected four years from now? How can businesses, with their single-minded focus on quarterly earnings, redirect their efforts by focusing on longer-term thinking, vision, and strategy?

To many companies, balancing the short term with the long term feels unworkable. Sure, younger growth companies like Amazon—or Apple and Microsoft when they were starting out—could be forgiven for a lack of profits, given their almost infinite potential for expansion into new spaces. For more established companies, I know from experience how hard it can be to wean shareholders off their monthly dividend checks. But it can be done, and it's one of my proudest accomplishments at Dow.

In the 125 years since its founding, Dow has had five successive transformations. When I became CEO, the company was mired in the fifth one, petrochemistry (for those who don't know the term, petrochemistry involves the transformation of crude oil and natural gas into products or raw materials). Sandwiched on one side by the needs of our financial owners, and on the other by the conservative mindset of many employees, Dow found it impossible to innovate. In response I created a mini–Silicon Valley *within* Dow, which proved to be key in repositioning us for the twenty-first century (more about this later).

Bottom line: combining short-term goals with longer-term visions and building an engine for the future, versus one that's fixated only on the near-present, requires sustained resiliency and an ability to bring your board along with you. Short-term and long-term planning aren't *either/or*; like most solutions today, it's a question of *and*.

DIGITALIZATION RUN AMOK

Along with everything else, the COVID pandemic made it clear the extent to which digitalization and automation have overtaken our lives. (In fact, a 2020 study by McKinsey predicted that by 2030, anywhere between four hundred and eight hundred million individuals could be displaced by automation.)[1] Today, no matter who we are or what we do for a living, big data surrounds us. Technology is a game-changer, of course, but it also brings up issues around privacy, cybertheft, and conduct that no twentieth-century leader could ever have predicted, in addition to the ADHD-intensifying nature of social media and online browsing.

Digitalization today has lapped our ability to understand and saddle it. As a species, we haven't caught up yet with the changes it has created, much less with those the future will bring. Technology will steamroll us unless we gain control of it, especially considering that the digital world is still in its primitive Model T and Wright Brothers era.

UNSTABLE GEOPOLITICS

In the twentieth century, everyone could agree what the world order looked like. There were big nations, small nations, stronger nations, weaker nations, and developing nations. There were two superpowers, the US and the USSR. The European Union didn't exist. China seemed content to continue in its role as the workshop of the world.

That physical map still exists, of course, but it's been shaken and rearranged. We are in the early stages of witnessing the remaking of world order. Today there are two dominant nations: the US and China. An older geopolitical chessboard has been replaced by newer, more intricate ecosystems that reflect the rearrangement of regional alliances based primarily on trade. With traditional global alliances less feasible now that China has surfaced as a world leader, countries must figure out whom they trust— *trust*, in this case, meaning economically, politically, and even militarily— and whose value systems are most closely aligned with their own.

PLANET, INC.

The audiences I speak to around the world are always surprised when I refer to myself as an environmentalist. *But Andrew, you're the former CEO of Dow!*

Labels can be hard to resist. As someone who has spent his career thinking about big subjects (or trying to) and listening to as many viewpoints as possible, early on in my life I got comfortable being uncomfortable—and in the end, I'm proud to say I was the CEO who made Dow's sustainability strategy central to our business operations.

Today, companies, governments, and societies around the world are literally incapable of putting into place any protections around our planet's survival. Missing are any global institutions able to manage issues around climate change, automobile emissions, or future pandemics. Most countries can't even handle these things at national levels. Nonetheless, I still believe businesses and governments can work side by side to create a low-carbon future en route to a zero-carbon future by 2050.

DOES THIS SOUND LIKE too many things at once, and too much to think about? The sheer number of conversations taking place in this century is dizzying: the global-climate-emergency conversation (which is not unrelated to the COVID pandemic conversation); the geopolitical conversation; the-retreat-of-global-leadership conversation; the conversation around short-termism versus long-termism; not to mention others. Welcome to the twenty-first century, where leaders and businesses have no choice but to address all these conversations simultaneously *now*.

As I said, I come to this book as someone who has spent his career at the intersections of business, government, academia, the nonprofit sector, and civic society. I bring with me the benefit of four decades of global business experience and four decades of coming up with solutions—solutions that come from lessons I learned in the boardroom, lessons about management, handling risk, and leadership.

I grew up a raw, introverted, unconfident outback boy, the grandson of a Greek immigrant who emigrated to Darwin and found work in a slaughterhouse.

My own father died unexpectedly when I was fifteen. I was devastated. Overnight I became the head of the family, the sole provider for my mother—who was very much a first-generation Greek immigrant and not a great English speaker—and my two sisters. I was always ambitious and curious, eager to expand myself. I eventually earned an academic scholarship, becoming the first person in my family to go to university, in my case the University of Queensland in Brisbane, where I got my degree in chemical engineering—a new field of study back then—learned *how* to learn and *how* to be a leader, and many years later had the opportunity to run a multibillion-dollar multinational. I also eventually outgrew my shyness! Decades later, after retiring from Dow, I wanted to give back to my university a fraction of what it gave me.

Like the Northern Territory abutting it, Queensland is a rugged, pioneering state in northern Australia. It may be relatively isolated geographically, but the joint mission of the University of Queensland and Liveris Academy is farsighted in its reach and ambition. By the time they graduate, our students will have completed a curriculum that allows them to go forth into the twenty-first century and . . . work in finance. Or venture capital. Or manufacturing. Or government. Or academia. Or in an NGO. Their education will have also given them a mindset, and a training, that they can apply to solving just about any problem they will face in their lifetimes.

An earlier genesis for this book was my experience working with Asian governments, especially China, between 2004 and 2007. As a new CEO, I was frustrated by how little control I had over some of the things that were boxing in our company. Dow had no power, for example, over how the Environmental Protection Agency chose to adjudicate and regulate us, or how the discussions taking place in the Department of Commerce could affect our trade agenda and our ability to move goods from one location to the next, not to mention the amount of revenue we would have to pay in taxes. In short, we had almost no control over numerous important items on our company's balance sheet and P&L.

But when I took my concerns to our tax experts, they would invariably point their finger at Washington or Beijing. "Wait a second," I said. "So who's telling Washington and Beijing what to do?" No one knew. I was advised to take my questions and concerns to the Business Roundtable, the influential lobbying organization made up of business CEOs. Then one day, I had an epiphany.

The rulebook around digital, geopolitics, and ESG practices was changing so fast that no one, neither the regulators nor the regulatees, knew what was going on. The people elected to office, mostly lawyers, bankers, and political wonks, had almost no basis for understanding the companies that were being regulated, whether the issues were around science, technology, or the environment. (This is still a problem today, with governments mostly at a loss about how to regulate the world's biggest tech companies.) Businesses and their regulatory frameworks simply weren't being as effective as they could be.

This frustration led to my first book, *Make It in America*, which set out a list of practical policy solutions that President Barack Obama (whom I worked with for eight years) among others acknowledged to be an invaluable contribution to the economic resurgence and revitalization of America's manufacturing sector. With the goal of rebuilding manufacturing in the US, I detailed ten policies to get businesses from here to there. Along the way I realized, "Hey, rules aren't so bad. I want rules." But not last century's rules—*this* century's rules. This set me off on a quest to figure out what exactly those new rules *were*, whether I was speaking at the World Economic Forum, chairing the Business Council or the American Chemistry Council, creating partnerships with the Nature Conservancy and with NGOs, or forming new entities focused on long-term capital.

In addition to being a handbook for twenty-first-century businesses and leaders, *Leading Through Disruption* draws on my own experience as Dow's chairman and CEO—from surviving a boardroom coup attempt in 2006, to coming this close to bankrupting Dow during the global financial crisis, to surviving an attack from an activist investor (and turning it into a win-win for everybody), to the evolution of Dow's and my own thinking around sustainability, to Dow's game-changing merger with DuPont in 2017, a marriage engineered to ensure Dow's relevance and profitability in the century ahead, one that brought together 320 years of combined corporate history. Not only did three viable enterprises come out of that alliance—Dow, DuPont, and a new company, Corteva—but the architecture of the deal was a harbinger of the splits and spin-offs that have taken place in recent years at General Electric, United Technologies, Johnson & Johnson, IBM, and elsewhere. Ultimately, though, *Leading Through Disruption* argues that the twenty-first century requires businesses and business leaders to broaden their bandwidth and begin operating in multidimensional spaces that challenge and redefine traditional comfort zones.

My background in science made me a natural problem solver and a good match for Dow, a problem-solving company that continually set the highest standards in our industry. Communicating my passions across multiple areas and applying purpose and focus to identifying and solving problems has always been my drug of choice. I never see problems; I see only solutions. It was a big part of my management style at Dow, where I urged everyone around me to develop a solution-oriented mindset versus a problem-amplification one. I wouldn't agree to a one-on-one meeting unless the person requesting the meeting (a) defined the issue and (b) showed up with a solution. I might disagree, or ask for more work, but if someone appeared with just a problem, it would be our last meeting until they came up with a fix.

This book, then, highlights the biggest issues businesses and business leaders face today, along with a few possible solutions. Whenever I address Liveris Academy students, it's clear they are seeking both guardrails and lighthouses to help them navigate the next few decades. My message to them, and to all young leaders, is invariably, "Make an impact but first have all the information you need, so you know what you're talking about!" This book, I hope, provides that information. Strewn among the chapters are also a handful of twenty-first-century leadership lessons I hope readers will find relevant as well. The chapters can be read alone, but you'll find that the subjects of greatest concern intersect with all the others. In fact, I would advise anyone to read this book using a lens that combines breadth and perspective along with a granular attention to detail. The final chapter lays out what the world might look like in 2050 if we accept what is being asked of us and do what we know is right and necessary for business, society, our communities, and our planet.

Creating a more equitable society that benefits both business and humanity won't be easy—nothing in this century so far is easy!—but I know we can get there.

The New Role of ESG

The weather in Glasgow was overcast and rainy in contrast to the animated, hopeful mood inside the UN Climate Change Conference, otherwise known as COP26. For two weeks, world leaders, government officials, diplomats, and policy makers had been engaged in discussions with former and current business CEOs and the occasional well-known face from film and fashion, while outside Glasgow's Scottish Event Campus, tens of thousands of younger protesters marched along the streets and sidewalks, chanting, "What do we want? *System change!* When do we want it? *Now!*"

I was at COP26 in my role as a member of the B Team, a collective of global business and civil society leaders, systems experts, sustainability pioneers, and entrepreneurs. Paul Polman of Unilever, an early member, brought me aboard when I was still at Dow, noting that the public perception of Dow as a straightforward chemical company was at odds with our leadership in sustainability. Where environmental, social, and governance (ESG) metrics were concerned, Paul told me he believed Dow was one of the greatest business stories never told.

The B Team was founded in 2013 by Sir Richard Branson and Jochen Zeitz of Harley-Davidson and operates side by side with the Elders, the human rights organization Branson also founded, whose original members included Nelson Mandela and Desmond Tutu. But instead of addressing dozens of issues, the B Team has focused on three critical ones: climate change, social justice, and gender equality.

The B Team is plainspoken in our belief that the current economic model is broken and can't be fixed, and that plan A—the idea that business should be motivated exclusively by profit—is a model that no longer works. Plan B, and the core mission of the B Team, is to help create new and improved norms of corporate and governmental leadership that result in environmental, social, and economic benefits for everyone.

Over the years I've been to my share of UN Climate Change Conferences. Most are characterized by lengthy, spirited conversations that end up in half measures, but few tangible or measurable actions. A long-standing gulf exists between those who are determined to stop climate change and those who continue to deny its existence. This divide exists between political parties and between developed and emerging economies.

Despite the absence of China and Russia, the Glasgow COP26 felt different from its predecessors. By the time it was over, more than a hundred nations had committed to ending deforestation and reducing methane emissions by 30 percent by 2030. The leaders of nearly two hundred countries had signed their names to the Glasgow Climate Pact, the first-ever UN deal articulating the worldwide need to move away from fossil fuels and fossil fuel subsidies and "phase down"—though not "phase out"—unabated coal usage ("You can't let perfect be the enemy of the good," noted John Kerry, the US Climate Envoy[1]). Governments also agreed to return to next year's COP with more robust pledges to reduce greenhouse gas emissions and to contribute more aid to poorer nations.

Leaders were left with one last important takeaway: governments were too slow and ungainly to take the lead on addressing the climate crisis. If they could do something, they would have by now, and they haven't. To achieve a zero-carbon future, *business had to take the lead.*

In practical terms, this means that the successful stewardship of a twenty-first-century enterprise needs to exist alongside the stewardship of our communities and the Earth. It also means that our prosperity and well-being as a society are possible only when a diversity of voices is at the table. If they haven't already, today's enterprises need to go beyond compliance and adopt forward-looking ESG metrics that create sustainability and social standards for the rest of the world. Society today demands nothing less.

"What do we want?" came the voices outside.

"*System change!*"

"When do we want it?"

"*Now!*"

DURING MY FORTY-PLUS YEARS in business, inevitably I've found myself putting together a taxonomy of people. One (favored) category I've come up with is "natural problem solvers." These are people intent on finding solutions, instead of, say, relitigating issues or proving they understand every last nuance and dimension, a condition known more informally as paralysis by analysis. With apologies to humanities majors, in my experience the best problem solvers have a background in either technology or engineering. In the main, they are mathematicians and scientists whose studies have trained them to identify, test, and solve the issue before them. Nowhere is their expertise needed more than in addressing and solving the issues inherent in ESG.

What Is ESG?

As we've seen, ESG stands for three separate pillars—environmental, social, and governance—but it's also widely used as a synonym for sustainability. ESG has had a deepening imprint in business since 2009, when a widely read *Harvard Business Review* article promoted sustainability as a driver of innovation. Noting that our global economic system has overburdened our Earth, "while catering to the needs of only about a quarter of the people on it," the article noted that if these issues remain unaddressed, "traditional approaches to business will collapse, and companies will need to develop innovative solutions."[2] Little wonder that after the article was published, CEOs and enterprises took notice.

The *E* of ESG refers to the impact a business has on the environment (energy use, manufacturing processes, disposal of waste, conservation of natural resources, and so on). The *S*, or social aspect, focuses on a company's relationships and values. Who are your suppliers? What are your hiring practices? How much do you care about your employees' workplace health and safety? Lastly, the *G*, or governance, side, has two definitions. "Small *g*" governance refers to a company's leadership, executive pay, internal controls, accounting methods, and relationships with stakeholders. "Big *G*" governance goes wider and is focused on making sure that developing nations have the highest, most equitable standards in hiring, social and human rights, and gender and racial equality.

Two decades into a new century, we are at a cultural, social, and demographic inflection point. Younger generations who have lived through the decisions made by older generations are demanding that companies (and countries) take responsibility for the world they have created. Companies are under growing pressure to establish sustainable enterprise-wide visions and strategies that benefit the environment and society, while maintaining ethical and transparent corporate governance. From the perspective of all its stakeholders, whether they're owners, regulators, governments, or NGOs, a company's focus on sustainability, diversity enhancement, and exemplary governance affects its license to operate in this century.

Why Is ESG So Important?

Businesses today need to calculate their long-term cost of ownership as a return metric to create the business solutions that minimize their own impact on the planet. At the same time, most boards and stakeholders would demand the heads of their leaders if CEOs sacrificed short-term profits for a quixotic, longer-term "good." No company can move overnight from mercantile capitalism to one that takes into account all levels and layers of society. To those enterprises that have yet to adopt ESG metrics, or use them as window dressing without any edge or accountability, or who haven't yet followed through, let me take you through each letter of ESG.

Before doing that, remember that leaders need to consider E, S, and G as standalone concepts. Make sure you get the individual pillars right. The sum of the parts will define the whole. Inside each vertical should be metrics that force behavioral changes for each.

ENVIRONMENT

Environmental action must be grounded in collective action led by responsible leaders who are thinking ahead to 2050 and even 2100. As a company, how do you put "preserving our planet" on your balance sheet? How can you make your business more accountable for overseeing the Earth, not as a philanthropic gesture but in recognition that your company's well-being is inextricably linked to the well-being of society and the future of our planet? The prospect of ten billion people inhabiting the Earth by 2050 makes it clear that future metrics and accountability must be led by purpose-based enterprises. *Someone* needs to own the environmental issue—and it's not going to be governments. The entities that need to step forward today are those who have the most to gain from humanity's survival fifty or a hundred years from now, that is, enterprises that hope to create ongoing stakeholder returns.

SOCIAL

The "social" component of ESG has been blended into a mix alongside words like diversity and inclusion. Social means *all of us*—and it's clear that we have a long way to go before everyone on our planet is afforded equal treatment and opportunities. Whether because of corruption, the rich enriching themselves, or the suppression of women and minorities, the human economic experiment still lacks social justice parameters. What about the promise of democracy, you might ask? Unfortunately, we have seen that democracy overlaid with crony capitalism defies its own efforts to create lasting equality, as the rights of the individual (especially in the US) always seem to override those of the larger society.

GOVERNANCE

Good governance is at the heart of good business *and* good countries. "Small *g*" governance means that leaders and boards comply with their fiduciary duties. It means that compensation practices are in line with SEC laws and Foreign Corrupt Practices checks and balances—all the things ensuring that the voice of the shareholder (represented by the BlackRocks, State Streets, and Fidelitys of the world) is present in the boardroom. A company might ask, "What do you want to see from us that is missing around executive compensation or the attention we are giving to climate change? If you are reluctant to invest in companies that don't achieve net-zero emissions by 2030, what metrics do you expect from us?" All that is "small *g*" governance.

"Big *G*" governance is about a company's license to operate provided by society *and* governments. The elected representatives of any country, or nation-state, exist to ensure that fairness, equality, and the checks and balances that accompany them, are provided. Those government-led policies and systems did a serviceably good job in the second half of the twentieth century. There were no world wars, and a lot of countries, including China, rescued large numbers of people from poverty. Unfortunately, those decades also saw the global decline of institutions like the UN, the WTO, and WHO, meaning that "big *G*" governance metrics in countries around, say, supply chain transparency don't yet exist. Within *companies* they do. At Dow, for example, our internal auditors perform spot checks around the world to ensure that no exploitation or slave or child labor exists in developing nations. But those are internal metrics. Where are the metrics in *countries* that ensure that the right checks and balances exist within the supply chains of multinationals? They have yet to appear.

In their absence, good governance must be set by one of the few systems that is already working: the global enterprise. It won't be perfect. A lot of people dislike big business and are against the idea of large enterprises controlling governance templates. But until governments in developed nations step up to match first-world practices around transparency and the elimination of corruption, it will have to suffice.

The Relationship between ESG and SLO

The social license to operate, or SLO, refers to the ongoing acceptance of a company's methods, practices, and procedures by employees, stakeholders, and society. A company's SLO builds up incrementally over time. At its foundation is trust, and consistent values and ethics. At Dow, we took our SLO very seriously. Our existence as an enterprise was given us *by* society *through* government. Not once did we assume our present and future were automatic or assured. This meant, among other things, that instead of sitting around complaining about governmental laws and regulations, it was our responsibility to meet with agencies and officials and collaborate on regulations that would benefit not just Dow but society, too. (We never self-identified as a featureless multinational but as a company with operations in 150 distinct communities. Dow employees lived, shopped, volunteered, went to school, worshipped, and voted in these communities. Any harm done there affected Dow employees and their families as much as it did everyone else.)

Today, companies' SLOs are under close review. The era of shortcuts and abstract promises is over. Society is demanding zero carbon, zero fossil fuels, and more equitable global access to education and opportunity. The transformation that society is asking for may not be as speedy as younger generations would like, but the demands they are making are entirely reasonable. Today's businesses in turn need to respond more aggressively than they would if those demands were more incremental.

Along with the divide between younger and older generations, another divide exists between newly emergent economies and the developing world. China, along with Nigeria, Angola, Zimbabwe, Kenya, and other African nations, feels excluded, often at their own expense, from many of the resources the developed world has been accumulating. Some of these countries are urging developed nations to establish a level playing field for the future and repair any broken models from a century ago. In short, in a world where our survival as a species is under threat, societies around the world are fed up that the only outcome ever measured by business is money. The consequences of climate change threaten everybody's future.

In short, this century's businesses won't thrive unless society and the Earth also thrive. The global enterprise I call Humanity Inc. needs to evolve aggressively for everybody's survival, which is why adopting and embedding ESG metrics is minimal table stakes of a business's license to operate in the twenty-first century.

The Four *D*s: Corporate Responses to ESG

Despite ample photographic evidence, my children still find it hard to believe that when I was in college, my hair came down to my shoulders, and my classmates and I marched against the war in Vietnam. (Obviously, none of us wanted to get drafted.) I even protested against Dow for its part in manufacturing napalm for the US government. (At the time Dow had gone from being the creator of Saran wrap, Ziploc bags, and Styrofoam into a kind of war machine.) When I graduated, cut my hair, and began interviewing for jobs, I remember telling the Dow recruiter that one reason he should hire me was that I belonged to a generation that wanted to repair the less-than-ideal public perception of chemical companies. I got the job, and for the next few decades, I did everything I could to burnish Dow's reputation, especially around sustainability. With a nod to author and management consultant Andrew Faas,[3] who has written about "The Five *D*s of Engagement," in some ways my trajectory paralleled the evolution of corporate thinking about ESG, a progression made up of its own four *D*s: denial, defiance, debate, and dialogue.

For most American companies, the sixties and early seventies were like the Roaring Twenties. Profits were huge. Growth and expansion were unstoppable. It took a while for corporations (and countries) to say, "Hold on a second. That river over there is in flames. There are dioxins in the mudbanks. Shouldn't we slow down this momentum and consider controlling the impact we have on society and the environment?" Throughout the 1960s, most management teams were trained to defend an enterprise no matter what, which led to the first of the four *D*s, denial. But with the EPA's founding, and the passage of the Clean Air Act in the early 1970s, denial soon gave way to defiance.

The defiance era, which lasted throughout the 1980s, was marked by belligerence and confrontation. In one well-known incident, Dow's then CEO threatened to sue the EPA after the agency conducted aerial surveillance over Dow's factory in Midland—Dow scientists knew more about our business than the government did, after all. In hindsight, corporate resistance was in some ways understandable. The EPA mostly set its sights on the Dows, Exxons, and Shells of the world and didn't bother with small- or medium-sized businesses that would find it harder to pay penalties or whose local communities wouldn't roll out the welcome mat to federal agencies.

In the late 1980s, when the federal government began to hire experts from the same industries and sectors it sought to regulate, defiance transitioned into debate. If defiance was combative, debate was measured and science based. What were the effects of chemical X on air pollution? Did chemical Y contribute to acid rain? Dow was an early leader in the debate stage. Then and now, our goal was to promote "smart regulation" (a favorite oxymoron of mine, considering that nine times out of ten, the agencies that do the regulating don't consult early enough with the enterprises being regulated). With Washington agencies getting savvier and better organized, Dow and other companies in our sector responded by creating and joining groups like the Chemical Manufacturers Association and the American Plastics Council.

In the 1990s, debate transitioned to the fourth D. Dialogue surfaced largely in response to a new government agency, the Council on Sustainable Development, which was focused on helping the US develop "bold, new approaches to achieve our economic, environmental, and equity goals."[4] If 1970s- and 1980s-era environmental protection was driven by businesses complying with EPA laws and regulations, under President Bill Clinton, regulations would now be developed in consultation with industry. If government was going to regulate business anyway, why wouldn't business want to collaborate with Washington around what environmentally sound business practices looked like?

A new phrase, *sustainability*, took hold. So did a new business standard known as Responsible Care, which established quality standards in manufacturing, distribution, and consumption, and the effects they had on the environment and people. (David Buzzelli, Dow's head of Environment, Health, and Safety, was one of its earliest adopters.) Dow was even inspired to create its own council, made up of former EPA officials, NGO heads, and business and academic leaders who met with our board two or three times a year to offer directors input around sustainability. Members of the council, later redubbed the Sustainability External Advisory Council, regularly visited Dow facilities worldwide while continuing to create sustainability goals for the company.

Clinton's Sustainability Council also helped give birth to the "triple bottom line," a term coined by business author John Elkington, referring to a business's economic, environmental, and social impact. The first bottom line was *profit*, of course, but equally important were the environment and society. The widespread adoption of the triple bottom line in companies led to additional ESG considerations at Dow. Dow, in fact, was one of the first American companies to publish an accountability report describing the impact our products had on the environment and society, and how we planned on minimizing that impact. Along with appointing board members from the environmental community, in 1995 Dow launched its first set of ten-year sustainability goals, a practice we renewed in 2005 and 2015—but I'm getting ahead of myself.

The Fifth *D*: *Do*

It was 2004, and I'd just been named CEO. From my perspective, business was done with denying, defying, debating, and dialoguing. It was time for a fifth *D*—*do*—but first Dow had to take stock as a company, which meant acknowledging both the good and the areas where we could do better.

The fact was, some of Dow's scientific and technological advancements, while benefiting humanity in unnumbered ways, had come at a price. Now and again, our environmental impact had been less than exemplary. Dow had never *not* complied with the regulations of the era in which we operated, but we *had* done things that had damaged the environment. Some had happened a hundred years ago, at the turn of the twentieth century, and

Dow had been oblivious to others. After the First and Second World Wars, for example, when the public sought out jobs, affordable housing, clothing, and medicine, Dow focused exclusively on meeting those needs. Employee safety was our major concern, sustainability less so. But times had changed. As CEO, my job was to respond to the moment by embedding sustainability into our company for a new century—which is how we came up with the concept of Dow's Blueprint.

Blueprints didn't come out of nowhere. It was the third in a progression that began when Dow launched its Footprint goals in the mid-1990s. Accompanying our first set of ten-year sustainability goals, Footprint asked: What products and emissions is Dow sending into the world from our asset footprint? What is their impact on the earth's resources?

A decade later, Footprint grew to include Handprint. If Footprint focused on sustainability goals in and around Dow's preexisting assets, Handprint was anchored in our assets *and* our products. What were the effects of a Dow product or ingredient on human skin, hair, or clothing? What effect did a Dow product or ingredient in foods, beverages, or pharmaceuticals have on human health and well-being? Footprint and Handprint weren't just slogans; they were embedded deeply in our vision and strategy. (Dow, for example, partnered with Unilever to create an affordable soap to improve personal hygiene across India and Africa and minimize the spread of viral diseases.)

By 2011, our thinking around sustainability had evolved further. Footprint and Handprint were critical steps forward, but did they really address the needs of society and humanity in *this* century? Multinationals like Dow were regulated by governmental laws and regulations. It was our responsibility to comply with them, and we always did, of course. But societies aren't perfect in communicating their needs to governments, and governments aren't perfect in developing and enacting regulations that benefit societies. That means (and still does) that Dow and other companies had to take responsibility for closing the gap between where society was and where it needed to go. Blueprint filled that gap.

Blueprint was the clearest possible articulation that Dow's license to operate meant we needed to create best-in-class standards for society and the planet. Yes, it would cost us money in the short term, but in the long term it would generate returns—financial, social, and environmental. My conviction around Blueprint was so strong that I even added a new company value.

Values are a part of a company's DNA in a way practically nothing else is. Ignore or revoke a company value, and you risk alienating employees and consumers, or even destroying your reputation. Adding a new company value isn't a small thing either. You need board approval, followed by a lengthy bottom-up process to embed that value throughout your employee base and organization. Dow's two preexisting values, Respect for People and Integrity, had been in place almost since H. H. Dow founded the company. Our newest value, which debuted in our 2009 report, was Protecting Our Planet.

With Blueprint and Protecting Our Planet, Dow made it clear that our focus was on having zero impact on the environment and zero prison labor or modern slavery in our overseas supply chains. Building on our Blueprint sustainability goals, Dow launched a new aggressive target in line with the Paris Agreement to become carbon neutral by 2050, along with setting ambitious targets to help eliminate plastic waste. (In 2020 alone, Dow tripled sales of products made with renewable bio-based feedstock, ensuring that our packaging applications were reusable and recyclable. We also increased our agreements to purchase cost-competitive renewable energy while continuing to invest in technologies that can help provide a path to decarbonization.) We still lead the conversation today on how to reach net zero and begin removing greenhouse gases from the environment via carbon neutrality, carbon recycling, and/or the replacement of carbon entirely.

More than a decade ago, our commitment to sustainability was strengthened even further by the first-of-its-kind partnership that we created with the Nature Conservancy.

A lot of the ideas I've had as a leader come from an unexpected place. *Anger*—the kind I feel when science is minimized or overlooked. For 125 years, Dow has been at the forefront of science. Our products serve as core components in energy, transportation, health, nutrition, infrastructure, agriculture, and construction. But decades after the Vietnam War ended, our public reputation was uneven. Some members of the public saw us as a bad actor, a giant smokestack that made obscene profits from degrading the environment. Left out was our legacy of scientific, engineering, and technological advancement and invention.

It was our own fault. We hadn't communicated who we were in a clear, simple way. I had devoted my whole life and career to the company. Using chemistry to make a positive difference in the world was always my North Star. I saw chemistry as a noble science, the combining and recombining of 118 elements to create something new, powerful, and miraculous. Chemistry was Alfred Nobel's pursuit, Niels Bohr's business, Marie Curie's passion. Chemistry explained *everything*. How could I not get angry when chemistry, the basis of life itself, was undermined?

My thinking was also influenced by my childhood in Northern Australia.

I was born and grew up in Darwin, a coastal city in Australia's Northern Territory. It's a rough, macho, sparsely populated region of Australia. Imagine a hybrid of west Texas and Central America. Ethnically and geographically diverse—over a third of the population are First Nations Australians—it has rain forests, mountains, deserts, pasture lands, ranches the size of Oklahoma, and Kakadu National Park, which is as big as Wales and teems with crocodiles, flatback turtles, deadly snakes, and poisonous spiders. What's past is prologue, as Shakespeare said. We are all shaped by history and by the memories of our early environments. Though I've always disliked labels, I thought of myself as an "environmentalist" and a "naturalist" before those two words became popular.

During my first few years as CEO, the board and I were in ongoing dialogue about transforming our strategy and innovation engine. We kept coming back to the idea that Dow and nature were partners. No one would ever describe nature—a desert, an ocean, the sky—as "free." So why hadn't we ever thought to price nature into our business decisions and strategies? Soon we had entered into a partnership with the Nature Conservancy. The goal was to show that by embedding the "values" of nature into our business strategy, Dow could produce better outcomes for our company *and* the environment.

What is the value of air, water, trees? Whenever Dow built a factory, we disrupted forests or wetlands. What was the *price* of that disruption, and what was the *price* of restoring those trees or wetlands to their original condition? Take water, for example. In some parts of the world, water is difficult to access, and in others, it is abundantly available. In developed countries, water is either notionally "free" or so low-priced it might as well be free. The price of water is set artificially by municipal authorities who seldom if ever pause to consider where that water comes from. Whether it's a mountain range, a river, or a dam, no thought is given to restoration, meaning that no incentive exists to price the water that comes out of a hose or sink tap. This is true for everything in the natural world. No causal relationship exists between "nature" and the enterprises and individuals who make use of the "inputs" that nature represents. By collaborating with the Nature Conservancy on an algorithmic financial model to measure the "value" of nature, Dow sought to change that.

Some people may balk at the idea of "valuing" or "pricing" nature or see it as the peak of hubris. But when you consider that our world has been consumed, subsumed, divided, and dominated by capital since the beginning of time, it makes sense. Like it or not, currency and cash top the list of humanity's reasons for being, and the degraded condition of our planet today is an unfortunate illustration of what happens when humanity *doesn't* value nature. Creating an ROI for oceans, rivers, trees, water, and arable and nonarable land elevates everyone's standards. If nature "costs" something, businesses and people are that much more likely to take the steps necessary to protect it.

In 2020, we celebrated the ten-year anniversary of our partnership with the Nature Conservancy. To date, Dow has achieved $530 million in savings toward an original $1 billion target of uncovering economic value in nature-related projects that are good for business *and* the environment. We have seen some spectacular results too.

A few years ago, Dow realized we needed to construct wastewater treatment plants to treat the water coming from one of our Texas facilities. The projected cost was almost $300 million. But instead of building new *gray* infrastructure, we invested in *green* infrastructure by reconfiguring the waterways surrounding the factory. Run-off water could now sift itself through neighboring swamplands and wetlands. No chemicals were produced or emitted. Choosing green over gray infrastructure meant that Dow's decision was both economical and, by creating wetlands for local animal life, environmentally beneficial.

Thousands of miles away, Brazilian, Chilean, and Peruvian farmers also saw their operating costs cut in half. Deforestation in the Amazon was often the result of fallow local soil caused by the runoff of nitrogen in fertilizers that local farmers use to maintain their land and grazing areas. If the soil was fallow and crops couldn't grow, farmers had no choice but to cut down trees to create new farming and grazing areas. In response, Dow scientists came up with a process, nitrogen fixation, to prevent the nitrogen in the soil from running off. This process allowed farmers to reuse their land over and over, eliminating the need to destroy forests to plant new grass to generate new food supplies for their cattle. Dow's nitrogen-fixation technology aligned with our goal of getting affordable fertilizers, chemicals, and even pharmaceuticals to the people and nations least able to afford them.

I ALWAYS MADE IT A point to emphasize the importance of diversity from the board level down. I ensured the Dow board reflected the communities we served. I added women and minorities to the Dow board and created a management committee to establish metrics around gender, minority equality, and minority representation. This ensured Dow's financial and behavioral commitment to addressing systemic racism and inequality, and it ultimately resulted in our being recognized as a leader in inclusion and diversity by organizations ranging from Great Place to Work to *Forbes* to the *Financial Times*.

The governance side mattered just as much to me. In most American corporate boards, the chairman and CEO roles are combined. Early in my tenure, I did studies to determine whether we should separate the two. In the end, we kept the chairman role but reinforced independence by appointing a strong lead independent presiding director. To increase diversity of thought across Dow, and a range of perspectives around governance,

I chose directors with deep experience and expertise in other sectors and industries, including appointing finance experts who had knowledge of the inner workings of the Federal Trade Commission and the Department of Justice to Dow's audit committee. The goal was to create a multilayered board with a diverse spectrum of directors, each one bringing in different motivations relating to risk management.

That said, as any company knows, maintaining superior, ongoing ESG leadership is a story line that never ends. An enterprise can always do better. Over the years, Dow has built up a formidable corporate audit team that is committed to carrying out ongoing checks to ensure that our ESG metrics are undertaken by all our regional offices from Bogotá to Mumbai. Considering our size, and the scope of our operations, occasionally we will stumble. But overall, I'm very proud of what we have accomplished.

ESG Strategies in Other Corporations

When people ask, I tell them that during the fourteen years I spent as CEO, I don't remember having any interaction with any financial analyst, or any of the institutional owners of the company, in which I was asked about ESG factors. Not once. No one brought up the environment or climate change or a company's license to operate.

It's a different era today. Profit and purpose have converged. Doing well *and* doing good is—or should be—in the DNA of what it means to be a leader. That means that one challenge of present-day leadership is combining "doing good" with more pragmatic concerns, including ensuring profits and finding science-based solutions that benefit humankind on a planet that is home to 7.8 billion people, and where eight hundred million of those people go hungry every day.

It took Dow and other companies nearly three decades to pass through the five *D*s, from denial to defiance to debate to dialogue to do. Three decades is a luxury that's missing for businesses today. Today, various factors—a changing geopolitical stage, failing global leadership, the internet serving as a 24-7 judge and jury—mean that the fortunes and reputation of businesses lacking strong ESG metrics can change overnight. With society and investors measuring the impact businesses have on the world, companies in this century need to ask: Are our practices sustainable? How well do we treat our stakeholders? How equitable are our hiring practices? What are our strategies around climate change?

Value and *increasing value* are integral to every business model. *Any* enterprise can increase its value and profits by reducing costs related to energy, water, and waste. Dow's first set of ten-year sustainability goals returned $4 billion to the company on a $1 billion investment in projects and sharply reduced both our energy costs and carbon emissions. Sustainability is also a robust revenue driver. Consider the influence Tesla's electric automobiles have had on industry rivals. Noted the *New York Times* in 2020, "Wall Street investors think Tesla is worth more than General Motors, Toyota, Volkswagen and Ford put together. And China, the world's biggest car market, recently ordered that most new cars be powered by electricity in just 15 years,"[5] news that prompted Mary Barra, the CEO of General Motors, to announce that GM plans to sell only zero-emission vehicles by 2035.[6]

Sustainable business practices are also critical if enterprises want to attract and retain best-in-class employees and raise investment. Few twenty-first-century businesses will survive or thrive without ESG measurements being front and center. Nor can those companies be confident about gaining access to capital. Climate change is central to the investment strategy of BlackRock, the private equity firm with $9.5 trillion under management. In his 2021 "Letter to CEOs," chairman and CEO Larry Fink wrote that in the future BlackRock will require companies "to disclose a plan for how their business model will be compatible with a net zero economy—that is, one where global warming is limited to well below two degrees Celsius, consistent with a global aspiration of net zero greenhouse gas emissions by 2050." Added Fink, "We are asking you to disclose how this plan is incorporated into your long-term strategy and reviewed by your board of directors."[7] In his 2022 letter, Fink made it a point to clarify his belief that an enterprise-wide focus on ESG metrics should not impede the pursuit of profits, writing, "Make no mistake, the fair pursuit of profit is still what animates markets; and long-term profitability is the measure by which markets will ultimately determine your company's success."[8]

State Street, whose Global Advisors division manages $3.1 trillion in assets worldwide, is another influential private equity firm that announced its plan to vote against company directors that lag the firm's targets for ESG changes.[9, 10] State Street's website advises investors to "define and develop specific ESG investment objectives and goals, based on their vision, mission, and investment goals. Common investor objectives can include alpha generation, risk mitigation, adhering to ESG regulations, or aligning the portfolio to the investor's values."[11]

With more and more investors aligning their investments with ESG values and metrics, companies that haven't yet fallen into line are feeling the pinch. In the next few years, I expect all investment firms will follow BlackRock's and State Street's models. Until then, responsible, purpose-based enterprises should tell investors hoping to milk the cow in the short term that their companies have a responsibility to invest in zero emissions, modernize their factories, and decarbonize and eliminate plastics from the environment. In other words, ESG metrics must become core to companies' business strategies. Everyday activities must be contained to create zero negativity on companies' ecosystems, whether it's products, communities, or the planet itself. This is a potentially costly proposition—I get that, and so does everyone. There is no evident short-term return. But it is the cost, and *the license afforded you as an enterprise*, of doing business in the twenty-first century.

Dow isn't the only company with best-in-class ESG metrics. In 2021, Salesforce announced it had achieved net zero energy usage across the full range of activities involved in transforming raw materials into finished products (otherwise known as the value chain) by using 100 percent renewable energy—and Salesforce is determined to help other big businesses accelerate to net zero.[12] The company also launched the Salesforce sustainability cloud to track emissions reductions strategies in categories ranging from infrastructure to supply chain. The company is also taking action to sequester carbon from the atmosphere and is working with lawmakers and regulators worldwide to support policies that positively affect employees, customers, communities, business, and the planet.

Coca-Cola's ESG goals are embedded in how the company operates globally. Even at the height of the COVID pandemic, Coke maintained its "World Without Waste" efforts, offering 100 percent recycled plastic packaging options in at least one brand across markets representing 30 percent of the company's global volume. Coke supports a vision to be net zero carbon by 2050 and has set a 2030 science-based target to lower its greenhouse gas emissions by a quarter relative to 2015 levels.[13]

Yet no company has promoted positive ESG metrics as aggressively as Unilever has under the leadership of my B Team colleague Paul Polman. Under his watch, Unilever set out to eliminate deforestation in the company's palm oil, paper, tea, soy, and cocoa supply chains, while pushing Unilever to transition to renewable energy across all its operations, expanding its plant-based product array and developing cleaning and laundry products free of fossil fuels.[14] Unilever is in the lead in pushing for a fairer, more socially inclusive world, decent standards of living, greater access to opportunity, and a planet where human rights are celebrated and no one is left behind.

Making ESG a Corporate Reality

Why isn't every company rolling out ESG metrics? What's taking them so long?

Well, one answer is that many businesses aren't willing to stick their heads over the parapet. Other companies may believe passionately in ESG but choose to remain silent. They follow the example set by industry leaders while declining to take the risks that real leadership requires, because those leadership genes aren't in the corporate DNA or in that of the CEO, the board, or the sector. That said, companies and CEOs that haven't created ESG reports must realize that they will eventually be forced to comply because of government policy (or financial institutions that are unwilling to lend them capital). Rather than being forced to comply, companies should get ahead of their governments and make ESG central to their business strategy *today*.

Bear in mind three things. First, change will happen only if corporate leadership, directors, owners, and policy makers find consensus on how to act on climate-related risks and opportunities. Companies must lead the way forward by going *beyond* government compliance. Again, if you don't step up, who will? Wouldn't you rather do it before your government *makes* you?

Second, companies must double and triple down on R&D and technology to reduce to zero their overall impact on the environment. Enterprises must ensure that they are using sustainable technologies and fuels, whether it's new nuclear energy, hydrogen from fossil fuels, or water renewables.

Third, companies need to begin hunting for acquisitions and mergers with enterprises that are already expert recyclers. There is an entire waste management system out there eager to find partners with resources. Identify these enterprises and track them down. Double and triple down on the technology and recycling world to eliminate everything from our environment, and profits are certain to follow.

For me, the hope, *and* the opportunity, for an expansion of ESG measurements and sustainability becoming central to all businesses comes from the entrepreneur class. I once gave a speech in which I reminded the audience that the periodic table is made up of 118 elements. The 119th element is *humanity*. Our role is to figure out the interactions among those other 118 and apply them to solving the world's problems. BlackRock's Larry Fink echoed this during the 2021 Future Investment Initiative in Saudi Arabia. He predicted that the "next 1,000 unicorns—companies with a market valuation over a billion dollars—won't be a search engine or media company. They will be businesses developing green hydrogen, and green agriculture, and green steel, and green cement."[15]

This century has already given birth to a new wave of entrepreneurs who aren't reliant on venture capital wealth or subject to the legacy gatekeeping systems that helped grow the entrepreneurs of last century. The barriers to entry are as flat and hospitable as they've ever been. Today, anyone can come up with a transformative idea, whether it's a Peruvian farmer using the internet to predict the weather or his counterpart in India using technology to reorganize crop rotation for his plots in the Maharaja state. Across science, education, and business, technology has opened the gate to all varieties of entrepreneurs, making it that much more likely that solutions can ultimately be found to some of humanity's most pressing issues.

Sustainability will always be a noun. But in the future, ideally, its adjectival form, *sustainable*, will become commonly used. We will see *sustainable* business. *Sustainable* technology. *Sustainable* strategy. *Sustainable* communities. *Sustainable* urbanization. *Sustainable* wind farms. *Sustainable* oil and gas companies. All these things will be driven by sustainability drivers, along with other ESG metrics. Over time *sustainable* will become so embedded in corporate thinking and strategy that the word will vanish. There will be no doubt that everyone's actions and behaviors are being carried out in a sustainable way.

Which leads me back to Glasgow and the tens of thousands of protestors marching outside the Scottish Event Campus. The crowd was all ages, but most protestors were in their teens and twenties. Why weren't the protestors invited inside the conference hall? Because most of the people inside were too busy protecting their positions. Few understood that the people on the sidewalks outside were delivering a message: "You're not moving fast enough—and no amount of posturing on the political level will provide answers to solve the issues around climate change." These "protestors" intuitively understood that our collective future requires going beyond philanthropy to social responsibility—which means creating leadership ethics that bring social and economic benefits to everyone. They understood that citizens need to get fair and accessible education to equip them for this century's jobs, along with the skills and training to ensure that they can succeed in those jobs.

Raised voices have a role to play, as my own did back when I was in college. That said, voices raised repeatedly in protest that go no further, or that refuse to work toward solutions, are at risk of creating resistance and even backlash. That was another part of my university education. Those protestors might consider doing what I ended up doing. I put down my bullhorn and placard. Instead of protesting outside, I chose to go inside. I took a seat at the table. Across from me were people I disagreed with. I didn't talk—I listened. I learned why others thought what they did. I participated. I got uncomfortable early on. I grew that much closer to uniting all sides of the issue—and helping come up with a solution. Enterprises today that haven't yet adapted forward-looking ESG metrics for this century should consider doing the same, the emphasis being *do*.

Takeaways and Tools

- Leading a company in this century means administering and overseeing the health and well-being of society and our planet, while ensuring greater levels of equity, diversity, and inclusiveness.

- Adopting and embedding ESG metrics is a baseline requirement for an enterprise's social license to operate now and in the future. Society quite simply demands it.

- The *E*, or environmental side, of ESG describes the impact a company has on the environment. The *S*, or social side, refers to a company's relationships and values. The *G*, or governance side, has two parts: small *g* governance concerns internal leadership, executive pay, and stakeholder relationships; and big *G* governance ensures that emerging economies adopt the highest, fairest standards in hiring, social and human rights, and gender and racial equality.

- Today's enterprises must go *beyond* compliance and take the lead in accomplishing a zero-carbon future by 2050.

- Sustainable business practices are critical for (a) driving revenue, (b) raising outside investment, and (c) attracting and retaining best-in-class employees.

- Today's businesses need to double and triple down on R&D spend and technology to reduce to zero their overall impact on

the environment by using sustainable technologies and fuels
(new nuclear energy, hydrogen from fossil fuels, water
renewables, and so on).

- Corporate responses to ESG in the twentieth century evolved
  through four stages: denial, defiance, debate, and dialogue. The
  fifth stage, applicable to all enterprises today, is do.

- The first step in incorporating ESG metrics and practices is to
  benchmark—immediately—what every one of your stakeholders
  is saying about ESG. Study the metrics coming from the range of
  places that control where capital gets allocated and understand
  how the capital allocation process affects your share price.

- Begin the ESG conversation at the board level. Bring in external
  experts, as we did at Dow when we created the Sustainability
  External Advisory Council. Include your biggest critics, whose
  job it is to meet with your management team and board and push
  you to take an honest look at what they are proposing. Listen
  carefully, remembering that these individuals represent *society*.
  Next, make sure you can implement their proposals in a
  meaningful time frame.

- Work closely with external regulators to ensure that you comply
  with emergent ESG rules. These rules change quickly, so it's
  important to get ahead of them.

- Consider emergent ESG regulations as your company's baseline
  minimum. Now, work with your internal team and subject-matter
  experts to determine your *optimum*. After all, a decade from now
  your business will have evolved from meeting today's emergent
  rules to dialing these same rules forward.

- The most heated topic in the climate change discussion today
  concerns scope 1, scope 2, and scope 3 emissions. (Scope 1 is
  direct emissions from entities owned or controlled by your
  business; scope 2 refers to indirect emissions via heat, electricity,

cooling, and so on; and scope 3 means all other emissions linked to corporate activity.) Every business today is targeting scope 1 and scope 2 factors—but only companies with their heads in the sand could fail to see scope 3 on the horizon. Identify which future-based rules apply to you—and bring them into your practices as soon as possible.

- Having consulted with outside experts and regulators, don't reveal what you have planned, and don't share critical information too freely. Instead, apply these new metrics internally and, depending on your latitude, experiment with them for one or two years. This will help ensure employee buy-in.

- Last but certainly not least, study your supply chains, both the input and the output. See how they are raising the bar on ESG metrics. Make sure these behaviors are congruent with what the input and output sides of your enterprise are doing. This will bring them into the conversation so you can proceed together.

2

The New Common Good

Inclusive Capitalism

Only a few days after President Biden was sworn in as president in 2021, my cell phone rang. On the other end was a longtime friend, a very senior Democrat, who wasted no time in getting to the point.

I had a long, successful history in working both sides of the aisle, he pointed out—and Joe Biden and I were old acquaintances, having collaborated on manufacturing policies when he served as vice president under Obama. Would I be willing to cochair an initiative of CEOs focused on persuading Republican senators and House members to get behind a Democratic infrastructure bill that was in the works? The Biden administration wanted the bill put to a vote as soon as possible. Could I pull this off in six months?

I'm a longtime believer in Country Before Party. It probably comes from growing up in a Greek household in a largely Anglo-Saxon country, and in a northern port city, too, where most of my friends were from other cultures and ethnicities. Early on I learned how to adapt to different people, places, and things, whether I was at home with my Greek-speaking mother and two sisters, out in the community, or visiting the homes of Chinese,

Malaysian, Italian, or Serbian classmates after school. Whenever people ask me the best way to learn about other people, my advice is always to walk in their shoes.

That flexibility, and the politically agnostic stance I adopted as Dow CEO, shows up in the work I've done with the government over the years. I've been privileged to work with four US presidents—Bill Clinton, George W. Bush, Barack Obama, and Donald Trump, who asked me to chair the US Manufacturing Council. Biden would be my fifth president. My friends in the CEO community tell me I'm a good, possibly radical, example of a business leader who can put aside his own political beliefs for the sake of the country and the greater good. Doing my part to help accelerate the passage of the Biden infrastructure bill was an extension of that work.

Republicans and Democrats were as polarized as they had been for a long time, but most could agree on one thing: coast to coast, American infrastructure was decaying and in urgent need of repair. By replacing pipes, ports, bridges, and highways, the US could better equip itself for a new century and economy, one centered on the digital age and future forms of energy.

In America's favor was a fruitful history of collaboration between government and business. Roosevelt's New Deal programs played a significant role in making the US the preeminent twentieth-century economic power. America came together to build bridges, roads, hydroelectric dams, power plants, sewage systems, air transport, pipelines, irrigation systems, levees, and more. Biden's proposed infrastructure bill sought to do the same. But before anything, first I had to call on a group of CEOs whose businesses and sectors the bill would influence *and* who had credibility with both parties. Only then, working entirely behind the scenes, I might add, could we begin slowly pushing the bill forward.

Two weeks later, I had convened a group of business leaders, including GM's Mary Barra, Nike's John Donahoe, AT&T's John Stankey, and Brian Moynihan, the chairman and CEO of Bank of America. The next six months were spent in a marathon of midnight and early morning phone calls and Zoom meetings. (I was in Australia, in quarantine, sixteen hours ahead of everybody else.) The CEOs first needed to sign off on elements of the infrastructure bill that had an impact on their industries. One or more of the plan's provisions might compromise their sector, but those had to be weighed against the bill's overall benefit to the American economy. This took us a while, and once we were all aligned, it was time to begin reaching out to Republicans in the Senate and House.

None of this, I should also add, could have been accomplished without the support of the president's team, a handful of key Democratic senators, and the Business Roundtable, chaired at the time by Walmart's Doug McMillon, who was also a member of our CEO group. Eventually we secured the approval of the Republican lawmakers; our momentum stalled only when the extreme left faction of the Democratic party tacked a larger social-spending reform onto the infrastructure bill, putting in jeopardy the Republican votes we'd already wrangled and delaying passage for two months. But finally, President Biden's bipartisan, $1.3 billion Infrastructure Investment and Jobs Act was signed into law in November 2021.[1] The money would be set aside to improve US roads, railways, pipes, ports, public transit, airports, water infrastructure, broadband, and power grids. It was, said the *New York Times*, "the most important step in a generation toward upgrading critical infrastructure . . . and could soon begin to pay dividends for a wide range of businesses and people, from electric vehicle manufacturers to rural web surfers."[2]

More to the point, every single stakeholder—business, government, the public, the country, the US economy—was the beneficiary. The Biden infrastructure bill was a near-perfect example of a concept and movement, Inclusive Capitalism, that will continue taking hold in the decades ahead. Inclusive Capitalism is a policy movement focused on creating long-term value not just for shareholders but for *everybody*. Its premise is that business has a critical, if not the *most* critical, role to play in creating equality of opportunity and access across all levels of society, regardless of people's backgrounds, genders, ethnicities, races, religions, ages, or economic standing.

What Is Inclusive Capitalism?

Corporate jargon, students at Liveris Academy probably think when they are first exposed to the term Inclusive Capitalism. It sounds necessary, overdue in fact, but maybe quixotic, too, short on specifics and as yet unsupported by any measurable steps or practices. If Inclusive Capitalism were less abstract and more real (so their thinking might go), then surely businesses and governments would already be building and investing in new and transformative institutions, programs, practices, and regulations, and to date most have not.

Younger generations would be right to infer that Inclusive Capitalism is a Rorschach test of sorts, whose meanings and definitions vary depending on who you're talking to. Is Inclusive Capitalism the same thing as Moral Capitalism or Conscious Capitalism, to throw in two other, pot-muddying terms? Even more confusing, *Inclusive Capitalism* is sometimes used interchangeably with a related concept, *Stakeholder Capitalism.* They're not the same. Stakeholder Capitalism refers to businesses that manage for all the individuals or entities that directly influence a company and play direct roles in ensuring the success of a business along its value chain—employees, customers, shareholders, local communities, and the planet—as opposed to managing exclusively for shareholders. Nor, despite some overlaps, is Inclusive Capitalism the same as adopting ESG metrics and practices. (Confusing Inclusive Capitalism with ESG, in fact, risks blurring and weakening the value and meaning of both.) So now that we have a better idea of what it's *not,* what *is* Inclusive Capitalism?

Inclusive Capitalism starts with the notion that capitalism, and the business world in general, has for way too long been narrowly and selfishly focused on profits and the enrichment of a single entity, that is, the shareholder. In an era of widening inequality between the rich and everyone else, society is insisting that an enterprise's license to operate means distributing wealth more equitably across all levels of society. Business is being asked to address the bigger role capitalism plays, redress past mistakes, and do better in serving *all* levels of society, so that capitalism works not just for the few but for the many. How and why we got to this point is another question.

The short answer is that capitalism and democracy aren't coexisting as well as the ancient Greeks (and Milton Friedman) believed they would. The benefits of capitalism—growth, prosperity, improvements in standards of living all around the world—are well known and commonly acknowledged. Still, no one could have foreseen the level of inequality capitalism has ended up creating if they subscribed, as so many businesspeople did in the 1970s and 1980s, to the so-called Friedman Doctrine.

Milton Friedman was a popular University of Chicago economist who published a seminal, widely read article in the *New York Times* in 1970. Its title—"The Social Responsibility of Business Is to Increase Its Profits"— was pretty blunt. The role of business, Friedman wrote, is "to use its resources and engage in activities designed to increase its profits so long as it stays within the rules of the game, which is to say, engages in open and free competition without deception or fraud."[3] In Friedman's view, the free market was the ultimate authority and shaman. Business needn't concern itself with society, social injustice, the environment, or anything else other than the relentless pursuit of profits. Anyone who believes "business has a 'social conscience' [emphasis Friedman's] and takes seriously its responsibilities for providing employment, eliminating discrimination, avoiding pollution and whatever else may be the catchwords of the contemporary crop of reformers . . . [is]—or would be if they or anyone else took them seriously—preaching pure and unadulterated socialism."[4]

Fifty years later, the *New York Times* called Friedman's article "the essay heard round the world,"[5] and his philosophy "arguably the most consequential economic idea of the latter half of the 20th century."[6] The Friedman Doctrine, as it was known, was an open summons to corporate combat, one that, according to Salesforce's Marc Benioff writing in the *New York Times* in 2020, "brainwashed a generation of CEOs who believed that the only business of business is business."[7] Benioff added that he had always disagreed with Friedman's philosophy, adding, "And the decades since have only exposed his myopia. Just look at where the obsession with maximizing profits for shareholders has brought us: terrible economic, racial, and health inequities; the catastrophe of climate change."[8] Nonetheless, Friedman's ideas helped usher in an era of spectacular wealth accumulation in the 1970s and especially the 1980s, when *Wall Street*'s Gordon Gekko—"Greed . . . is good"—was seen by audiences less as a villain than as an aspirational ideal.

In the early 1990s, with the end of the Cold War and the fall of the Berlin Wall, most of the world rightly celebrated the victory of capitalism over communism. At the same time, minus the reference point of Eastern Europe, capitalism had to confront its worst consequences, which it would do repeatedly over the next few decades.

Given that capitalism's moments of self-reflection generally haven't led to much, what makes today different? Capitalism is thriving, after all. A recent McKinsey study notes that while US GDP growth has slowed in this century, the US is still outperforming other G7 nations and leads the world in research and development.[9] The study adds that "many of the breakthroughs fueling 21st century growth, from digitalization and artificial intelligence to innovations in the life sciences, have emerged from its ecosystem."[10] Moreover, US firms rank among the most widely known and the most profitable globally, comprising "38 percent of the top 10 percent of firms, and two-thirds of the top 1 percent of firms globally."[11]

But the world today finds itself at an inflection point. Society is demanding that capitalism take an honest look in the mirror. In the wake of globalization, the global financial crisis, and the COVID epidemic, it has become obvious, again, that capitalism as it exists serves to benefit the few, while leaving most people feeling dispossessed and excluded. It appears the top tiers of Maslow's hierarchy of needs, beginning at the bottom with the physiological (food, water, sleep) and culminating at the top with self-actualization (achieving one's full potential), are accessible only to the few. What happened to education, health care, and good jobs for everyone? Why is economic mobility stalling for the middle classes, who have seen their living standards drop and higher education become unaffordable? At the same time, millions of manufacturing jobs have disappeared overseas, leaving behind a generation of middle-aged workers who lack the skills and qualifications necessary for this century's digital and tech-related jobs. Capitalism, it seems, is all about preserving the incumbency of those who already have access to capital, education, and health care, further stratifying social and economic class systems for which no developed country was ever designed.

Between 1970 and 2007 in the US alone, for example, the after-tax income of the top 1 percent of earners grew by 275 percent.[12] CEOs have always been well compensated. But if the average CEO earned roughly 40 times more than the average American worker between 1970 and 1979, that same CEO in 2020 earned 351 times more.[13]

The pandemic worsened this trend, with vaccine access in Western democracies accelerating the already-wide divide between richer and poorer nations. In late 2021, the *Wall Street Journal* reported that "just 7 percent of people in Africa [were] fully vaccinated, compared with 42 percent of the global population."[14] Not only did COVID impede global economic growth, it pushed countless employees out of work. Lower-wage workers, disproportionately women and people of color, found themselves more likely to be laid off, find their hours reduced, or be at higher risk of contracting COVID. As for the already well-off, they did just fine. According to an Oxfam report, during the pandemic "the world's ten richest men more than doubled their fortunes from $700 billion to $1.5 trillion—at a rate of $15,000 per second or $1.3 billion a day—during the first two years of a pandemic that has seen the incomes of 99 percent of humanity fall and over 160 million more people forced into poverty."[15] The *Washington Post* noted that 2021 was "the best time in history to be one of America's 745 billionaires, whose cumulative wealth has grown by an estimated 70 percent since the beginning of the pandemic even as tens of millions of low-wage workers have lost their jobs or their homes," adding, "Together, those 745 billionaires are now worth more than the bottom 60 percent of American households combined."[16] In the past five decades, the economic division between poor families and the top 0.1 percent has risen "more than tenfold,"[17] with children today having only a "43 percent chance of out-earning their parents."[18] Democracy and capitalism are going through a divorce, a decoupling resulting from the failure of the capitalist model to distribute wealth more equitably, which has arguably led to the rise of autocracies around the globe.

But what's the solution? Regulating an economy by raising taxes or enforcing egalitarianism is untenable. Countries need to grow and maintain capitalism by allowing entrepreneurs to access finance to create new goods, products, and services. But governments and businesses also need to provide access, latitude, and greater opportunity to citizens around the world who through no fault of their own were born into the bottom half of the social and economic ladder. If the Earth has any plan on hosting sustainable life in 2050, it's very clear we need to pivot in how we distribute wealth. Let me contradict Milton Friedman: Inclusive Capitalism isn't a synonym for socialism. It's a system for evening out a historically skewed playing field.

Spreading the Wealth 2.0

In 2019, the Business Roundtable broke with longstanding corporate dogma—and two decades of principles—by issuing a statement signed by nearly two hundred CEOs, including the leaders of Walmart, Apple, and Amazon. Instead of focusing on shareholder profits, the organization's "Statement on the Purpose of a Corporation" proposed "a fundamental commitment to all of our stakeholders," meaning employees, suppliers, customers, and small and large communities.[19] The BRT's statement was widely seen as a repudiation of the Friedman Doctrine and a tipping point for businesses of the twenty-first century.

Around that same time, Salesforce's Marc Benioff wrote an op-ed in the *New York Times* titled "We Need a New Capitalism." While acknowledging the historic success of free markets in launching new industries and unleashing global prosperity, Benioff wrote, "As a capitalist, I believe it's time to say out loud what we all know to be true: Capitalism, as we know it, is dead."[20] Asserting what is plain to anyone paying attention—that the markets' obsession with maximizing shareholder profits has led to dramatic levels of global inequality—Benioff added, "Globally, the 26 richest people in the world now have as much wealth as the poorest 3.8 billion people,"[21] and noted that economic inequality in the US is currently at its highest level in half a century, "with the top 0.1 percent—people like me—owning roughly 20 percent of the wealth while many Americans cannot afford to pay for a $400 emergency. It's no wonder that support for capitalism has dropped, especially among young people." Concluded Benioff, "It is time for a new capitalism—a more fair, equal, and sustainable capitalism that actually works for everyone and where businesses, including tech companies, don't just take from society, but truly give back and have a positive impact."[22]

But why should Inclusive Capitalism be the responsibility of business? Shouldn't government step up? As is true with climate change, if governments had any ability to act, they would have by now, and they haven't. There is a widespread and growing realization that governments lack the tools and the leadership to solve our most challenging issues. Nor do most people even trust their governments. The 2022 Edelman Trust Barometer of thirty-six thousand people in twenty-seven countries revealed that business again leads the list as the most trusted institution worldwide, whereas government and media were in "a distrust spiral," chasing "exaggeration and division to gain clicks and votes."[23] The Trust Barometer also showed that respondents wanted business to play a larger role in addressing climate change, economic inequality, racial injustice, and the retraining of workforces in this century. "Societal leadership," concluded the Edelman survey, "is now a core function of business."[24]

It is something many companies have realized. Businesses have woken up and said, "Hold on a second. We are enterprises with values. We believe in treating all our employees fairly. We have an opportunity today to put a stake in the ground around where the future is going—and not keep focusing on the rearview mirror. We need to take a stand and take our responsibilities seriously."

In a world where poverty is a worsening issue in both Western and developing countries, missing today are metrics that quantify not just profits and ESG factors but *societal* factors. Missing, too, are any potential short circuits that could give most of the world's citizens access to improved education, health care, and employment. This means the captains of industry and government must come together to create a new collective bargain that considers all the stakeholders in our society. The words *equality*, *accountability*, and *responsibility* need to be embedded in every company and boardroom, not as narratives or forgettable words but as practical measurement tools. Our tax system also needs to be recalibrated so that access to capital is funneled back into society to ensure that everyone has access to equal opportunities. Inclusive Capitalism, in other words, needs to become the norm.

This implies new models of government and business ecosystems that distribute power closer to the source—and therefore the solution—of the problem at hand. (The power vacuum created by the failure of today's federal governments makes localization and regionalization more important than ever.) If Inclusive Capitalism takes hold, by 2050 the color of people's skin, their gender, the places where they grew up, the schools and colleges they went to, and the jobs on their résumés won't matter. The individual will still matter—they always will—but no one will be frustrated or held back based on their skin color, race, gender, or socioeconomic status.

This doesn't mean that profits, or shareholders, will cease mattering, because nothing could be further from the truth. Business must take up the cause of fairness and equality, though not at the expense of the shareholder or the many millions of people who have emerged out of poverty in the past century thanks to capitalism. It bears repeating: Inclusive Capitalism should not reward stakeholders at the *expense* of shareholders. Every stakeholder in a company's value chain exists to ensure its right to operate as a business. Those stakeholders benefit because the business benefits, the difference being that in the last century, companies distributed capital that affected society in positive ways via tax revenue or philanthropy. That model, which worked well for a long time, is no longer enough.

So what are some of the factors that could get in the way of creating a more Inclusive Capitalism in this century? First, we need to restore trust. Trust in institutions. Trust in government. Our global trust deficit risks derailing the momentum around forming new institutions that could advance a more Inclusive Capitalism. The youthful protestors on the sidewalks outside COP26 in Glasgow were clear in their message that they have lost all belief in global institutions, or even in the possibility of change. The good news is that some very smart, dedicated people are busy focusing on this issue.

Boards today have a responsibility to manage risk, which means that systems have to be developed by management to *define* those risks. I advise adopting the Enterprise Risk Management system, or ERM, a matrix used in many of the enterprises I work with today. At the bottom is Likelihood of Occurrence and on the Y axis is Severity of Impact. Dividing it by three highlights areas that represent risks to your enterprise that you should prepare for and handle, from geopolitical concerns to global factory safety. ERM is also a good template for Inclusive Capitalism. Businesses should adopt the same degree of vigilance that ERM offers to the multiple enablers and disablers of Inclusive Capitalism. ERM allows leaders, management teams, and boards to begin discussing every issue, negative or positive, that could affect your enterprise, which in turn allows your board's audit committee and the board itself to engage in robust and ongoing conversations. Bottom line: operationalize your own risk enterprise system, address all the good and bad potentialities, and present the findings as a living document to your board on a regular basis.

Not least, for Inclusive Capitalism to deliver on its promise, the shareholder and the stakeholder must become one. I dislike the phrase "First among Equals," but that is the nuance of Inclusive Capitalism. Decouple the shareholder from the stakeholder and you risk upsetting shareholders—and encouraging outside investors.

Becoming More Inclusive

Although it is a nascent model, Inclusive Capitalism is predicated on the notion that companies must earn the right to inhabit and operate on our planet. That right of operation should be based on rules that go beyond the benefit of one person, or a narrow group of shareholders, and that instead benefits the collective. Financial owners must earn the right to have a return on invested capital whereby that capital is invested in *all* aspects of society, which will ultimately elevate *everybody*. Along the way, Inclusive

Capitalism involves repairing education, taxation, and regulatory systems to allow people unfettered access to education and jobs, thereby excluding no one.

I'm often asked: Why not begin with the obvious, namely, raising the federal minimum wage for US workers, which is currently $7.25 an hour? Some businesspeople would claim that raising the minimum wage would reward people who, from their perspectives, don't work as hard as they do. I disagree. Unless we can all agree that wage equality is a metric critical to social advancement, Inclusive Capitalism will be elusive. No, an entry-level assistant in a big box store or a counter person in a fast-food restaurant may have a lower-quality job than that of a technician operating state-of-the-art robots on a factory floor. But at some point in their lives, those same factory technicians may have needed to work in retail or fast food on their way up the economic ladder. We need to invest in people, no matter where they might be on their professional trajectories. Bottom line: a quality economy has quality jobs whose compensation should match the quality of those jobs, versus one that is based simply on wage-rate arbitrage.

Creating a more Inclusive Capitalism is a broad mandate. It encompasses governments, corporate tax rates, regulations, the education system, and our own communities. I'll take them one by one.

BRINGING BUSINESS HOME: SOLVING OFFSHORING

For decades now, the US has watched as entire industries—solar panel technologies, advanced computer circuitry, wind turbines, and smart phones—vanish, well, that is, until they resurface in China, Ireland, Germany, or Singapore. High levels of offshoring for US companies are typically explained away using two words: *labor costs*. Overseas employees are known to work longer hours for lower pay, and can anyone blame an enterprise for wanting to reduce its overhead? Unfortunately, businesses that relocate overseas also export opportunity, jobs, and future economic growth—just not to the US.

It's true that lower wages often play a role when companies decide to relocate overseas. But what most people don't realize is that the lower wages paid to employees in developing countries are in the main offset by the much higher productivity rates in the US. American workers may expect and receive higher wages, but they typically get things done faster and more efficiently.

Here's an example: a dozen employees in a developing nation might spend a dozen hours apiece manufacturing a product. Each employee is paid three dollars an hour, meaning that the labor costs for the product end up being $432. In the US that same product is likely to be assembled in two hours by three skilled workers earning thirty dollars an hour. That *still* comes out to less than what a business pays its overseas workforce. The high levels of US productivity (*no one* works harder than Americans do) narrow and sometimes eliminate differences in labor costs.

Rarely brought up in the discussion about offshoring are the underlying causes, one of which is the US's unwillingness to match the incentives offered by other countries. Low-interest loans. Ten-year-long tax holidays. Free or discounted property on which to build plants, factories, and head-quarters. Capital grants for materials and equipment. Fixed prices on inputs that allow businesses to control for economic volatility, along with other inducements that make it possible for businesses to incur high R&D costs without damaging profitability. Companies seeking similar incentives in the US are generally met with apathy. It seems the US isn't all that interested in competing for business. In contrast to countries and nation-states like Ireland, Singapore, and Israel that enthusiastically underwrite US businesses to generate local jobs and growth, the response from the US is more often than not a polite brush-off.

This is why establishing a more hospitable business environment in the US would yield enormous dividends in promoting a more Inclusive Capitalism. The US has been slow to realize that countries these days are acting like *companies*. They are assertive, agile, imaginative, and dogged about seeding and growing their economies. They know that boosting business and investment are critical ingredients in creating local ecosystems that spur innovation and generate long-lasting jobs. Whether it's Singapore, whose business environment minimizes risk and opens markets; Thailand, which offers companies smart incentives and creates partnerships between public and private sectors, leading to investment, job creation, and prosperity; or Germany, a premier investor in modern infra-structure, superior education, and better worker training, it's no wonder countless American multinationals continue to train their gazes elsewhere.

More than serving as supporting players, other countries also want to dominate and win. Whenever I used to travel in Germany for Dow, Chancellor Merkel would always ask me what her government could do to attract more Dow investment. She knew Dow's growing presence in Germany would create sustainable jobs and long-term economic benefits. Did anyone ever ask me that question in the US? Not that I recall.

Matching the incentives that overseas nations offer US businesses would be a strong positive step toward creating more jobs and opportunity *here*. Meanwhile, by refusing to compete for business, the US continues to be at a competitive disadvantage. We would be smart to offer robust incentives to companies in growth sectors, as well as to businesses that can create sustainable jobs and long-lasting growth.

A TAXING PROBLEM

In 1986, President Ronald Reagan signed into law the Tax Reform Act, decreasing the corporate tax rate from 46 percent to 34 percent. Reagan's new tax rate made the US a more attractive destination for business—but almost every other country immediately followed suit by passing corporate tax laws lower than ours. Ireland, at 12.5 percent, came out the winner. This meant that if a technology company rolled out a new factory in Cork, or Dublin today, it would be on the hook for half the tax rate elsewhere in the EU, and roughly 70 percent less than it would pay in the US. Who ends up paying the price for our higher corporate tax rates? American families and workers.

Next up is the R&D tax credit. As everyone knows, innovation has been a longstanding and significant US export. In 1981, the US government established the R&D tax credit, allowing companies to deduct the costs of experimental ideas and innovations. This was a big boon to business, especially younger companies. Not surprisingly, other countries immediately sought to match and even increase the terms offered by the US. Despite

Congress's 2005 expansion of the US R&D tax credit, today more than a dozen countries offer higher innovation tax credits than we do.

Another issue? By law, Congress must renew the R&D tax credit every year. This means American businesses can't predict year by year whether the R&D tax credit will be extended or allowed to lapse. Imagine you are Dow. You're considering expanding your operations—an expensive, five-year project. Once you commit, you can't turn back. Your projects are typically designed using a thirty-year time horizon, with your investments based on expected returns over that time. But year after year, you can't predict that Congress will see fit to renew the R&D tax credit. In many other nations, the R&D tax credit is set for many years. It's another reason why companies can be forgiven for eyeing other countries that offer longevity, continuity, and dramatically less risk.

Bottom line: corporate tax codes must be competitive across the world. If a business chooses to domicile in the US and invest in jobs, and growth, it shouldn't be disincentivized by a disproportionately high tax rate. No one expects a major market like the US to match the low corporate tax rates of Ireland, Singapore, or Hong Kong. The US is a major consumer, and it makes sense for companies to establish headquarters here. American businesses don't need to be at the lowest end of global corporate tax rates, but the higher ends are also excessive, and often lead to inversion, wherein companies establish corporate headquarters in countries with lower tax rates and are no longer domiciled in the US.

As of this writing, the US corporate tax rate is 21.5 percent. Even if it crept upward to 25 or 26 percent, that is still a number that would be acceptable to most businesses—so long as it remained consistent.

MORE THAN A DECADE AGO, Warren Buffett admitted to the *New York Times* that his tax rate was lower than his secretary's. Why? He explained that he was able to take legal advantage of a range of loopholes and deductions that benefited him and his privately owned investment peers. Wrote Buffett, "Some of us are investment managers who earn billions from our daily labors but are allowed to classify our income as 'carried interest,' thereby getting a bargain 15 percent tax rate. . . . Others own stock index futures for 10 minutes, and have 60 percent of their gain taxed at 15 percent, as if they'd been long-term investors."[25] Corporations, of course, can get away with even more. According to a 2021 study by the Institute of Taxation and Economic Policy, "At least 55 of the largest corporations in America paid no federal corporate income taxes in their most recent fiscal year, despite enjoying substantial pretax profits in the United States."[26]

We live in a time when the top 1 percent of Americans own more wealth (31.1 percent) than the entire bottom 90 percent of the US population (2 percent),[27] which, in the case of the latter demographic, means that less well-off American citizens have half as much wealth as their own parents had a quarter century ago.

Opponents of higher taxes on the rich argue that the wealthy are taxed enough already and that raising their taxes would hinder competitiveness, quash innovation, impede job creation, and reduce incentives for future entrepreneurs. Also, why should the rich be penalized for their economic success? Having exhausted these arguments, they add that raising taxes on the wealthy would simply spur the rich to hire lawyers to find and exploit even more creative tax loopholes.

To my mind, the US would benefit from a more progressive tax code than the one that exists today. (Progressive, as it's defined here, simply means that individuals' tax rates go up in proportion to their wages and income.) Contrary to conservative received wisdom, raising taxes on the rich and on companies would accelerate our economy, give the US more resources to continue battling climate change, and fund programs to benefit lower-income Americans.

We should also consider eliminating carried interest. The phrase itself dates to earlier centuries, when Mediterranean ship captains claimed a percentage of financial interest in the profits from the sale of what was in their holds. Today, "carried interest" refers to a tax loophole that treats the earnings of private equity and hedge fund managers not as income (that is, taxable upwards of 37 percent) but as capital gains (subject, at most, to a 20 percent tax rate). Originally designed to spur investment and create, in the case of private equity, a new model of investor, the template has matured.

The *New York Times* estimates that eliminating carried interest would generate $180 billion in a decade. Instead of allowing private equity people to make disproportionate amounts of money while paying low effective tax rates, we should subsidize things society needs, from clean energy to broadband access.

Finally, to anyone who asks, I have always said that as a person who grew up poor but who ended up doing well, I would willingly pay higher taxes if the government established a fixed tax code that requires everyone else in my tax bracket to pay the same amount. It's not a pivot to socialism. It's about redistributing wealth from people like me, who started at the bottom of the ladder and worked their way up, as I did, to those who are just beginning their professional ascent. From my perspective, the wealthy owe that much to a country that allows them to operate in a free entrepreneurial system.

This perspective is influenced by my upbringing in Australia. I worked hard my whole life, but I also benefited from the Australian government providing an educational and health care infrastructure that helped foster my success. Education in Australia was free in most places, and health care is universal. (A cardiologist appointment costs one-tenth of what it does in the US.) Most Australians don't need huge amounts of money to enjoy a high quality of life. Until now, the American model for redistributing wealth has been philanthropy, or the very wealthy making sizable donations or establishing huge foundations. In Australia, the government is the philanthropist. It's unlikely the Australian model will ever migrate to the US, which is why companies like Salesforce, whose 1-1-1 model of giving 1 percent of the company's equity, 1 percent of its product, and 1 percent of employees' time back to the community, are picking up the slack.

SMART PARTNERSHIPS: FIXING REGULATIONS

Generous incentives. Lower corporate tax rates. Still another factor adding to the burden on many US companies and impeding a more Inclusive Capitalism in the future includes regulations so patchy and inconsistent they are nearly impossible for businesses to keep straight. In some cases, no one can even agree on what words even mean.

There are three different definitions of "oil," for example, depending on whether you ask the Coast Guard, the EPA, or the Department of Transportation. How would you define "rural"? Ask the US Census Bureau, the Office of Management and Budget, and the Department of Agriculture, and you will hear three different answers. If our own agencies can't agree on what a word means, how can companies, and how might that confusion affect compliance, especially given that regulations vary from state to state? Many companies and industries are obliged to operate differently in Florida than they would, say, in Missouri. Should an enterprise be asked to deal with dozens of different state regulations around gasoline or oil?

Established decades ago, the regulatory world is made up of autonomous agencies like the EPA and the FDA that create regulations around the sale and distribution of products and services. These regulations are set up based on input from industry experts and third-party studies and are then applied to the sector in question, whether it's chemicals, agribusiness, or finance.

But as time passed, and our society came up against issues like pollution, financial corruption, and shoddy governance, it became clear that these regulations needed ongoing modification. Regulators and regulat*ees* needed to work closely together and exchange input. By doing so, they could collaborate on regulations that ensured a high quality of life, access to modern technology, and safe products and services that eliminated risks from illness, contamination, toxicity, or pollution. Inclusive Capitalism can't hope to thrive unless regulators and regulatees come together and establish a strong partnership model—but it hasn't worked out that way.

Most of the time, in fact, regulations are established in isolation. The sector is not consulted. If an industry doesn't comply with those regulations, it gets fined. Thanks to their in-house experts, regulatory agencies want to believe that their rules are best in class and cutting edge, but they seldom are. The *real* experts, the ones who understand the intricacies of supply chains or financial systems, typically work not for the regulatory agencies but for the sectors themselves. A new "trust and verify" partnership model needs to be established, one focused on creating the best regulations that can ensure profit while considering *all* stakeholders, the growth and protection of jobs, and the health and well-being of *all* citizens.

Ultimately, it's the difference between a government doing something *to* business and a government working *with* business.

FIXING EDUCATION

If global competitiveness has a single motif, it is that the US does something exemplary, or trailblazing, and soon every other country has rushed in to emulate and improve on that thing. To this list we can also add education.

I grew up in the 1950s and 1960s. Back then, America was renowned for many things, one of which was its educational system. But by the early aughts, the US had fallen from first in the world in graduation rates to fourteenth. Credit should go to other countries that did everything possible to match and exceed US educational standards. Longer school days. Longer school years. Summer homework. But nowhere is education more important than as it relates to businesses helping students develop and refine the skills and capabilities for this century's jobs.

Right now, unfortunately, our educational system is at a disadvantage. We are graduating more and more students who are ill equipped for this century's digital economy. A research study conducted by RAND Europe found that the growing skills gap "will be measured in trillions of dollars, and it will fall most heavily on places that don't have reliable digital infrastructure such as internet access, or widespread fluency in digital skills."[28] Like the regulations that addle American businesses, the quality of our educational system varies from state to state, district to district, school to school, and sometimes classroom by classroom. As President Obama warned in 2009, "We are being outpaced by other nations," adding, "It's not that their kids are any smarter than ours—it's that they are being smarter about how to educate their children."[29]

More than a decade ago, the Obama administration passed new education standards designed to help minimize the risk of students falling behind academically. A reform of George W. Bush's 2002 No Child Left Behind Act, the Obama program was known as the Common Core State Standards

Initiative, or Common Core for short. Forty US states participated. But a decade later, political conflict and culture wars had intervened. Parents were opting out. Conservatives cited the Common Core as an example of federal overreach, "with more than twenty American states ultimately curtailing the initiative."[30]

Companies today need high-end engineers and employees able to manage big projects across multiple borders. The problem is finding them, a shortage forecast to get worse before it gets better. Baby Boomers are retiring left and right. Younger workers with the skills to enter advanced manufacturing are in short supply. As I note elsewhere in this book, this scenario sets up a race for qualified workers over the next few years and decades in which the US is unprepared to compete.

The American education system is a pipeline to good, high-paying jobs and a flourishing economy. We take out of it what we put in. Unless we can create higher standards of education that lead to more jobs that ultimately manage to redistribute a greater percentage of wealth to more people, Inclusive Capitalism as a concept and a reality will falter and stall.

First, we need to be more aggressive in finding and training quality teachers. We need to develop better methods to evaluate teachers in the classroom. We need to have uniform national standards of education instead of a patchwork one that varies state by state. In our own Midland high schools, Dow found a way to improve the quality of education by embedding smaller STEM-based ecosystems designed around our own needs. We're hardly alone. Numerous private sector enterprises and publicly listed companies are creating their own education systems—or adding on to preexisting ones—to ensure that they get the workers they need for this century. A good example is IBM's P-TECH system. It's a public education model that offers high school students from disadvantaged or underserved backgrounds the right skills and credentials they need to get jobs in today's economy. In P-TECH schools, students earn both a high school diploma *and* an associate degree focused in STEM fields. It's a collaboration—an *and*, not an *either/or*. Again, this century requires digitally savvy workers—and to date our current public education system and government aren't stepping up. Businesses have no choice but to lead the way.

STRENGTHENING COMMUNITIES

Inclusive Capitalism begins at home. If the goal is to distribute benefits to as many people as possible, companies need to begin with their own towns and cities. They need to invest in their own communities to attract and retain the highest-quality employees. When I became CEO, near the top of my list was collaborating with local businesses and downtown organizations to revitalize Dow's home base of Midland, Michigan.

Originally a fur-trading post in the early nineteenth century, Midland was, and is, a small Midwestern town, population forty thousand. The three nearest big cities, Detroit, Milwaukee, and Cleveland, are a hundred to two hundred miles away. At first the hard winters came as a shock to an Australian boy raised in a tropical climate. But I could also appreciate Midland's neighborliness, friendliness, collegiality, and sense of belonging. Midland may lack the dynamism and urbanity of Silicon Valley, New York, or Boston, but its small-town values more than make up for its Midwestern location. So how could Dow collaborate with local business owners to help turn Midland into a destination for the best possible talent?

Attraction and retention begin with education. Dow regularly hired employees from overseas with school-age children, many of whom eventually returned home to their own countries. Under my watch, Dow introduced an international baccalaureate standard within Midland High School's curricula to ensure that the children of Dow employees would be academically up to par no matter where they finished up their high school educations. We also introduced a new STEM-based curriculum to the local public high school system. That was just the beginning of Midland's ongoing resurrection.

Next we set our sights on Midland's downtown. With support from local business associations, we helped develop condos, restaurants, bars, and shops, and also built the H Hotel, featuring the new Dow Learning Academy, a gathering place for employees and visiting executives. We rebuilt the local country club to attract families and younger people, brought in a Class A minor league baseball team (the Great Lakes Loons!), and constructed a state-of-the-art sports stadium that doubled as a concert arena. We also built a skating rink and an arboretum. Dow supported local hospitals by giving them business and access to finance to upgrade their equipment, which would benefit both our employees and our communities. We expanded some of these amenities as well to the nearby regions of Saginaw and Bay City.

As well as locally, Dow increased investment across the US, including along the Gulf Coast and in Georgia and Illinois. (Dow has more than three dozen different communities throughout the US.) Though half of all Dow employees work abroad, our goal has always been to create strong, vibrant, creative, local communities. This also meant revitalizing our own manufacturing base, transforming our Michigan operations with more than $240 million in new investments and adding more than 160 full-time jobs— proving we *can* keep jobs in Michigan.

No enterprise of any size can risk ignoring what society is asking of business today. Without investing in your own community, you can't attract and retain top talent. That means creating amenities and services for all races, ethnicities, and genders. (An ex-Dow colleague of mine reminds me that when he arrived in Midland as a single man in 1985, there were no barbers or salons specific to African Americans.) That same colleague reminded me that younger generations are reverse mentoring the belief systems of their elders. Is the company and community where they work and live diverse, inclusive, and welcoming? Does it provide genuine purpose to them, other employees, the community, and the world itself?

Last I checked, Midland was still 725 miles west of New York, and 2,401 miles east of Silicon Valley. Today, though, it offers a rich, varied, amenity-filled quality of life to all our residents, while giving them access to sports, culture, museums, restaurants, and nature. As for traffic jams, there aren't any!

The Future of Inclusive Capitalism

Inclusive Capitalism is in its early stages. The new institutions that can carry it forward haven't yet materialized, but they will. We are already seeing some significant progress in the business world. Among the leaders driving purpose-based companies as a means of illustrating and quantifying what Inclusive Capitalism might look like someday are Marc Benioff at Salesforce; Jesper Brodin at IKEA; Emmanuel Faber, the former CEO of Danone; and Paul Polman, formerly of Unilever, and his present-day successor, Alan Jope.

Enormous credit should also go to my own successor at Dow, Jim Fitterling. In 2022, Dow was named for the third year in a row to Just Capital's "Just 100 List," earning first place in the overall chemicals sector and in the workers, stakeholders, and governance categories relative to our industry peers.[31] *Fortune* also named Dow to its 2022 "World's Most Admired Companies List."[32] It is a tribute to Jim's dedication to diversity, inclusiveness, and doing as much as possible for employees, the environment, society, and the rest of the world.

Finally, while Inclusive Capitalism sounds like a concept befitting this century, ironically it has its roots in the multinational, the first of which was the British East India Trading Company, founded in 1600. The multinational as we define it today didn't surface until the nineteenth century. Its very definition was to extend itself across multiple borders. By the twentieth century, the multinational was known among other things for offering jobs and limitless advancement to employees regardless of their race, ethnicity, religion, background, and social or economic status. Long before Inclusive Capitalism surfaced among the table stakes for today's businesses, the multinational was a bellwether.

I grew up in a largely class-based Australian society. In my teens and early twenties, I understood that people like me with an ethnic surname and Mediterranean features would be able to advance only so far in the country's business circles. Observing that the men and women who ran Australia's banks and businesses were mostly the products of our secondary schools and brand-name colleges, I concluded, rightly or wrongly, that I would never be in the running for those positions, no matter how hard I worked. (Since then, Australia has become a far more inclusive society.) Enter the multinational that, needless to say, changed my life.

When I was interviewing for jobs after university, Dow and the other global companies I spoke with made it clear that they would be glad to welcome a lower-middle class but academically gifted Greek boy into their ranks. (The Dow recruiter, a lanky, genial Texan named Lee McMaster, said the magic words: "Join our company and we'll show you the world," and he and Dow were good to their word.) I may have been the grandson of an immigrant from a far-off island, but nothing was standing in my way other than my own self-imposed limitations (and I tried not to have any). This was, and still is, an unusual and pathbreaking model. Multinationals wanted to know only one thing: *Can this employee get the job done?*

Everything old is new again, and once again, business has a lot to teach society. I recently stumbled across a statistic listing off the thirty colleges and universities that had graduated the highest number of current CEOs of Fortune 500 companies. Not surprisingly, Harvard, Princeton, Stanford, and U Penn made the list, but the school that had produced the most CEOs was the University of Wisconsin in Madison.[33] One could go so far as to argue that today, society has caught up with the model historically championed by the multinational, which gives employees from diverse races and backgrounds the same opportunities afforded to those privileged enough to attend private colleges, universities, and business schools.

Takeaways and Tools

- For a long time, business and capitalism have focused on profits and shareholder enrichment to the detriment of everyone else. In an era of widening inequality, exacerbated by COVID, Inclusive Capitalism is focused on creating long-term value for *all* corners of society.

- Inclusive Capitalism doesn't mean that shareholders and profits cease to matter. Championing the causes of fairness and equality shouldn't come at the expense of shareholders or the countless millions of people that capitalism has helped escape poverty.

- Regulatory changes can begin to create a more Inclusive Capitalism. They include raising the minimum wage; increasing business incentives to solve offshoring; making US corporate income taxes more competitive; fixing and streamlining regulations; improving the American education system; and strengthening and investing in local communities.

- The Enterprise Risk Management system is widely used in the enterprises I work with today. ERM is an essential tool for boards and committees to define and prioritize risk. If, for example, a risk is "high likelihood" and "high impact," it is discussed not only at the board level and across audit and safety committees, but with management. Low-priority risks can be touched on annually. Higher-priority risks, and how quickly they are evolving, should be a regular source of discussion.

- ERM is a useful tool and model for Inclusive Capitalism, allowing leaders, managers, and boards to address any issue, pro or con, that might affect your business. Boards should consider operationalizing it as an ongoing document.

3

Leadership Lesson 1

The Leader You Think You Are Going to Be
Is Different from the Leader You Have to Be

omeone asked me once why the business world is preoccupied with leaders and leadership. Every year a cannonade of articles, books, conferences, and symposia appears on the subject. Nor does leadership ever appear to be conclusively defined or solved, as a year later another torrent of papers with *leadership* stamped on the top fills our inboxes and calendars.

The point is well taken, but my answer is always the same: there are eight billion people on the planet. By 2050, that number will have risen to ten billion. That means there are seven billion leaders in the world today, men and women busy implementing seven billion varieties of leadership experience. They may not work in business or adjacent to it. Maybe they are students or parents or people who are serving on a school board or spearheading a local or community initiative. They might not think of themselves as leaders. But they are.

No matter who we are, or what we do for a living, most of us lead *something*.

Leadership in this century matters more than it ever has, mostly because of the array of challenges I've already laid out in this book. Central to the skill set of any twenty-first-century leader is doing well *and* doing good, combining practical financial concerns *with* equally robust values. Those values, by the way, shouldn't be confused with philanthropy or charity. They should be seen instead as a new set of ethics that ideally results in increased social and economic benefits for everyone on this planet.

Still, whether we're talking about this century or the previous one, being a leader has always been a difficult, lonely job. This became clear to me in 2004, a week or so after I was named Dow CEO. I had moved into the C-suite at our company headquarters in Midland, Michigan, and the board and I had just finished up a meeting in one of Dow's conference rooms. After a short (and incredibly dry) presentation, an extended (and surprisingly animated) discussion, and a series of (hurriedly dispensed with) formalities, the room emptied out. Two minutes earlier it had been packed with directors, corporate officers, advisors, and staffers. I was now alone. As I sat there at one end of the conference table, I realized that from now on, *alone* was how I would be spending most of my time.

Not literally alone, of course. Every business leader I know of is perennially sought after, double- and triple-booked, and pushed and pulled in fifty directions at once. But existentially speaking, I was now flying solo. All CEOs do. We live in a bubble. We are surrounded by people who tell us what we want to hear. Most of our colleagues are reluctant to express hard truths or conflicting perspectives. Nor can the burdens of the office be shared or delegated. They belong to you, the CEO. That's the job you signed up for.

Some leadership lessons from last century will never grow old. Others relating specifically to this one fall short or need to be updated to mirror the challenges of today. It's a given that people who arrive at a leadership position—whether they're CEO or prime minister—got there thanks to the same foundational skills they end up using in those jobs. Those skills and capabilities may be content rich, but they haven't been tested yet in unfamiliar and unpredictable contexts. Now, suddenly, leaders are being asked to adapt to this century's 360-degree bandwidth model. To use an analogy, in the last century leaders drove their cars while looking out the windshield, the rearview mirror, and the two side mirrors. Passing and changing lanes required not much more than a blinker. That's not enough today.

For starters, the highway you are driving on today has grown to a dozen lanes. The speed limit is 100 miles per hour. Your chances of getting into an accident are off the scale. You are literally traveling at the speed of *live*. This means that your scanning mechanisms are whirring as you seek to understand every angle from every perspective. What policy changes are coming out of Washington? What are the Europeans thinking? What is the latest technology coming out of Korea? What should you do about the intellectual property loss that results from losing an employee to the Chinese and potentially sacrificing data relating to one of your core businesses? These things occurred in an earlier era, of course, but today they are happening and invading your desk and demanding your full attention, all at once.

That is why the leadership lessons in this book are intended to create calm, purpose, vision, and direction. They are both a North Star and a safe harbor. Though the stories in them reach back into my own life and career, they are also applicable to how best to handle the velocity of *this* century.

BE THE LEADER YOU WANT TO BE

Until I was a few steps away from being named CEO (this was before I put together my manifesto), I didn't know I was in the running, much less that I stood any chance of getting the job. That's not to say I hadn't imagined what leading Dow would be like, because I had. In my favor were the two decades I had spent working for Dow in Asia, especially since the company was seeking to expand its operations there in the early aughts. Another plus was my reputation as a person with good social skills and a willingness to take managed risks. But otherwise, none of the four CEO contenders, including me, were ever told officially they were among the preferred candidates for the top job. I didn't know the identity of the three others or, as I said, that I was in the running until well into the process, and neither did they.

I *did* know that a CEO change was forthcoming. The retirement age for Dow executives in those days was sixty. (This is no longer true.) Dow had never hired a CEO from outside the company. This made the math straightforward. If you were in your late fifties, the chances of you being chosen were close to zero. If you were in your forties, it wasn't impossible, but the pipeline of contenders in front of you was likely stronger. If you were in your late forties—I was forty-eight at the time—well, that was an optimal age. Around that time, management made it subtly clear I should begin taking meetings with the members of the board (the three other candidates were urged to do the same thing, which I didn't know at the time).

Looking back on our younger selves, we tend to pick out only those things we would do differently today. I'm no exception. During my first two years as CEO, I was too polite, too accommodating, too reverent toward the company and its 125-year-old legacy and to my predecessor, who, in classic Dow tradition, had graduated onto the board of directors. I hewed too closely to the script of how a CEO *should* be and what a CEO *should* do, instead of pushing ahead with my plans to remake the company.

Nor had I counted on the element of surprise—unpredictability. I was like an athletic coach whose playbook is overflowing with plays he has seen over the years. He has every trick and maneuver down cold, or thinks he does, and doubts that anything can fluster or floor him—except when it does.

History tells us that strong leaders transform themselves into the leaders they must be when the moment requires it. They do this by narrowing their focus on the fight before them. It's not about the war itself or about any future battles. If they don't win the fight they are currently fighting, there might not be another.

Twice I was floored by unexpected events that happened during my time at Dow. The first was in 2006, when I survived a boardroom coup involving two Dow executives and colleagues. The second came in 2008 and 2009, when I was an inch or two away from bankrupting Dow before managing to save it at (literally) the last second. Both times, I became a different leader than the one I was before, the leader I *had* to be.

The boardroom coup took place two years into my tenure as CEO. As sheer drama, it had everything: treachery, skullduggery, cloak-and-dagger maneuverings, flagrant corruption, and even a Middle Eastern wealth fund. The coup attempt was and still is a cautionary tale with implications for other companies and their leaders. It left me feeling betrayed and embarrassed. It was also a wake-up call, triggering weeks and months of self-analysis on my part that bordered on self-flagellation. The traits that had always served me well—my brain, my people skills, my embrace of inclusiveness, the ability I had to inspire others—were all called into question. So was my judgment, since it was only later I found out that two high-ranking colleagues at Dow had been attempting to sabotage my plans for the company since day one.

The drama got under way when an article appeared in the *Daily Express*. It reported on a rumor making the rounds that one or more private equity groups was contemplating a leveraged buyout of Dow. This came as news to me.

At the time, both executives who were implicated in the buyout were spending a lot of time overseas, representing Dow in a joint venture with the Oman Oil Company. Around that same time, a second private holding company, Access Industries, hired one of these men to serve as a company adviser. That part was above-board. Everyone knew about it. The executive may have been a director at Dow, but his operational duties were winding down, and the board had agreed he could advise Access so long as his work didn't infringe on Dow's interests.

Then things started getting strange. A few months after the article in the *Daily Express* was published, a letter arrived at my office. It was from Access Industries. It proposed that Access acquire Dow's commodities division. I basically ignored the letter. Dow was regularly courted by investment banks submitting similar deals, on the assumption our share price would increase if we divested our commodities business and focused instead on our performance and specialty chemicals division: paints, lubricants, adhesives, polymers, agrichemicals, and cosmetic and food additives. I believed that Dow's commodities and performance chemicals businesses were mutually integrated and that it wasn't the right time to make any radical changes, and I told the board as much. Only one director disagreed—and that director happened to be one of the two executives quietly plotting my overthrow.

When the rumors about Dow being in play persisted, I called on Dow's two long-standing investment banks, Citigroup and Merrill Lynch, to conduct leveraged buyout (LBO) analyses in the unlikely event we were targeted by a hostile bid. I had no reason to suspect that thousands of miles away, in Oman, one of the two Dow executives was working with an Omani sovereign wealth fund to conduct their own breakup analysis of Dow. Weeks later (as I eventually found out), the deal instigated by the two rogue executives began to unravel. On the same day, another article reported that a collective of Middle Eastern investors and US buyout firms was close to finalizing a bid for Dow under the auspices of a J.P. Morgan joint venture in London. I made two phone calls. The first was to Henry Kravis at Kohlberg Kravis Roberts & Co., the LBO firm, and the second was to Jamie Dimon, then and now the CEO of J.P. Morgan.

Henry Kravis confirmed that KKR had been approached by the Omani delegation, but when he learned the proposed bid was hostile, he took a pass. (Before hanging up, Henry told me the Omani delegation seemed to be working alongside people who had insider information about Dow's operations.)

Jamie Dimon agreed to fly to Midland the next day. Over the course of our extremely amicable dinner, Jamie came across as a CEO who had only just discovered his company was party to a deal he knew nothing about, one that he would in no way support. Like Kravis, Jamie believed the Omani-led delegation included one or more individuals with insider knowledge of Dow's businesses. The next morning, the phone rang. Jamie Dimon was on the other end. He gave me two names.

Twenty-four hours later, with the board's approval, the two Dow executives were dismissed. First, though, the board gave them the opportunity to defend themselves. They denied any wrongdoing, and a few weeks later, both had filed defamation lawsuits against Dow. (These lawsuits were settled out of court a year later, as Dow wanted to take the high ground and move on.) Though the financial terms remain confidential, both men admitted in the court settlement to participating in an unauthorized LBO discussion, and Dow, in turn, issued statements that recognized the contributions each man had made to the company.

I was blindsided. Whether it's a weakness or a strength, I have never been capable of sticking a knife in the back of a friend—and the few times it has happened to me have come as a shock. Still, I had a company to run while also managing my injury and outrage. When it was revealed that two of my colleagues had been scheming against Dow and me ever since I became CEO, I had one response: *how the hell did I miss this?*

Whenever I mentor young CEOs today, I counsel them to avoid making the same mistakes I did during my first two years at Dow. First, I assumed that the team I inherited from the CEO before me would align automatically with my vision and strategy. Hadn't I devoted time ensuring that my team and board came together on purpose, strategy, and direction? Any dissent, it was agreed, would be handled in the boardroom or one-on-one—and there *was* no dissent, at least not on the surface. Basically, I waited too long to make management changes. I trusted the team I was given, instead of handpicking my own people. If nothing else, the experience taught me that it's all fine and good for a new CEO to inherit people from a previous administration—but that CEO now needs to make sure those people are on *his or her* team.

Ultimately, I did what I had to do. I installed a few people in my surroundings to act as additional pairs of eyes and ears. (This was plain old Management 101.) Most leaders need three or four lieutenants who are willing to tell them the truth. It seemed I was no different. Lesson learned, and a fairly basic one too.

But the biggest changes I made were internal. I knew I had a strong intellect and personality, which was both an advantage and a potential drawback. Was I guilty of overpowering other people or using sheer force of will to push things through? Too often the answer was probably yes. I resolved to check myself from then on. Working for Dow in Asia, I had become familiar with the Confucian axiom "two ears and one mouth." Put simply, this means, Don't talk so much. Listen. (Put even more simply and personally, it meant, Stop talking, Andrew. Let others talk even if you think you know better.) I grew into a consciously better listener, which I still am today.

The good news was that the feedback I got from colleagues and board members during this period was uniformly positive. My world and identity may have taken a hit, but I still somehow managed to appear confident and in charge, at least on the outside. (My three children have always told me that I'm at my best in a crisis. The stormier the weather, and the higher the surf, the steadier I get. It might have something to do with facing down one challenge after the next my whole life, beginning at age fifteen, when my father died and I became the man of the house.)

Finally, remembering how alone I felt during this experience, I made another promise to myself. From then on, I would do everything in my power to keep other leaders from feeling as cut-off and isolated as I had during that time. To this day, if a fellow CEO gets into trouble, I'm the first to place a phone call. Not to show them what a great guy I am but because I remember how hard it was to navigate a tough situation by myself.

As a leader, I had adjusted to the moment required of me. A second, more challenging one was right around the corner and took place during the global financial crisis of 2008 and 2009.

MERGER TROUBLES AROUND THE BEND

Beyond any feelings of personal injury or betrayal, the biggest by-product of the boardroom coup was that it scuttled my strategy to grow Dow over the next decade.

Since I became CEO, my mission had been to transform Dow from a manufacturer of low-value, cyclical commodities chemicals into a manufacturer of high-value specialty chemicals and advanced materials. To put all that into English, Dow was at the mercy of supply and demand. The marketplace, and not Dow, was responsible for setting the prices. This wasn't tenable, obviously. Hadn't I been hired as a disruptor, an entrepreneur in CEO clothing? Since I arrived, hadn't I had been pushing one risk envelope after the next?

But in the wake of the boardroom coup attempt, Dow and the board looked and felt different for the very sound reason that they *were* different. I could no longer do things piece by piece. I needed to be bold, test the edges, and steer Dow sharply toward a different future. To reignite momentum, we refreshed our tactics and developed a shortlist of companies Dow could acquire and began pursuing them relentlessly. By the summer of 2006, Dow was in full pursuit of DuPont and chasing two other medium-sized companies—Rohm and Haas, a Philadelphia-based specialty chemical company, and Syngenta, a global agricultural business headquartered in Basel, Switzerland. In short, I had not one but three companies in my sights. The board began conducting probes for all three companies to assess their level of interest in a merger. At this point we were thwarted by the first of what would be one unforeseeable event after the next.

George W. Bush was in office at the time. In his 2006 State of the Union address, Bush asked Congress to approve a huge increase in the production of renewable and alternative fuels. Overnight, the coast-to-coast demand for ethanol went through the roof. Where does ethanol come from? Corn. What products help corn grow faster and more efficiently? Genomic seed technology, the kind created by Syngenta and DuPont. If ethanol demand shot up, so did the stock prices of Syngenta and DuPont. For the time being, both companies were too expensive to consider acquiring.

It was a lost opportunity—*two* lost opportunities, in fact. A marriage with DuPont would have to wait until 2017, and a merger with Syngenta would unfortunately never happen. I reset my sights instead on Rohm and Haas, a boutique company, it should be noted, that had never been for sale.

Since 2005, I had been on the board of directors at Citigroup. Maybe I wasn't as attuned as I should have been to the rumblings in the air, including Citibank's exposure to troubled mortgages in the form of collateralized debt obligations and the likelihood of the bank having future issues with regulators. But brushing aside any economic warning signs, I continued my pursuit of Rohm and Haas, a company that had now let it be known it was looking at being acquired.

In July 2008, Rohm and Haas held a silent auction—a mergers and acquisitions procedure in which interested parties submit their bids in sealed envelopes and the winner is announced on the spot. I didn't know who the other bidders were but assumed they were the usual suspects: DuPont and BASF, the huge German multinational chemical manufacturer. Confident of Dow's chances and determined to prevail, Dow submitted a fully priced bid and won the auction. The deal, including direct payments and preexisting debts, came in at $18.8 billion. Rohm and Haas would become a subsidiary, which perfectly complemented my own strategy for Dow.

By then, the financial markets had been unsettled for a while. Knowing this, was submitting a full bid to purchase Rohm and Haas for almost $19 billion the best business decision I could have made? Of course not. But no one, me included, could have predicted the collapse of Lehman Brothers two months later, or the temblors about to roil the global economy.

Helping Dow finance the Rohm and Haas deal were equity commitment letters from Berkshire Hathaway, Warren Buffett's company, and the Kuwait Petroleum Corporation, or PIC, the daughter company of Kuwait Petroleum, which is 100 percent owned by the Kuwaiti government. Dow had a long history of collaboration with PIC, and in return for them agreeing to help fund the merger, I agreed to sell PIC half of our plastics unit. I also arranged for a $13 billion one-year bridge loan from a consortium of nineteen banks including Citigroup, Merrill Lynch, and Morgan Stanley. The Kuwaitis signed off on the deal, but when it became clear what was happening in the markets—the implosion of Lehman Brothers, followed by Bank of America buying Merrill Lynch in a fire sale—and concerned about their own exposure, the Kuwaitis announced they were pulling out of the deal. I immediately flew to Kuwait and spent the next two weeks trying to salvage the agreement. Only by taking a significant haircut was I able to renegotiate the terms and keep both sides happy. "Crisis averted," I thought, not knowing that what was around the corner was much worse.

By November, the share prices of banks globally were down dramatically, with the S&P 500 having fallen by 40 percent since the end of the summer. Among the worst-hit industries were chemical manufacturers like Dow. The demand just wasn't there. In the twenty-three trading days from September 19, 2008, to October 22, 2008, Dow's stock price dropped from $37.56 to $22.11 (that's 41 percent, for anyone doing the math). Dow ended 2008 with a share price of $20.08, a decrease of more than 50 percent from that year's high. Our stock price would bottom out at $6.33 on March 9, 2009—but I'm getting ahead of myself.

Capping a stressful year with a vacation, I flew with my wife and children to an island in the Caribbean. On December 27, I was lying in a hammock when my cell phone rang. It was the CEO of PIC, the Kuwait Petroleum Corporation, with some bad news. The Kuwaiti government was pulling out of the deal again. In addition to the ongoing global market volatility, he said, oil prices had fallen to dangerously low levels. "You can't pull out of the deal," I said. "Yes, we can," he said. When I told him this left Dow no option but to get the lawyers to find a way to sue a sovereign state , he told me to go right ahead. I hung up, my vacation over. I flew home that day to Midland in time to watch Dow's stock price drop another few points.

For most people, the first few days of a new year are marked by optimism and resolve. For me, it was the opposite. Dow's deal with the Kuwaitis was defunct, but on January 1, our legal team informed me I had to appear anyway in our law offices for the official receipt of the Kuwaiti money and the signing of papers. It was just a formality. No money was wired, of course, and no papers were signed. Three weeks later, Dow reported a fourth-quarter loss of $1.6 billion, further reducing our liquidity. Dow's credit rating was reduced to BBB—a little above junk status. People were defaulting on us left and right.

I convened an emergency meeting of the Dow board. I told the directors that though I wasn't personally responsible for the global financial meltdown, I was responsible for everything that took place under my watch. "I got us here," I said, "and if you give me three months, I promise I am the best person to get us out of this mess." In the end, the board asked me to stay on. The burden of rescue was now on me, which was only right.

I now had to raise a lot of money, ASAP, while simultaneously mobilizing our lawyers to go after the Kuwaitis for monetary damages. Yes, I could have sold off a few of Dow's crown asset jewels and made all our problems go away in a minute, but Dow would have ended up debilitated as a company. I needed to find other solutions.

Fortune intervened briefly when the FTC, the government agency responsible for approving all mergers and acquisitions, agreed to extend the January 26 closing for Dow and Rohm and Haas. That created a short-term stopgap. But the future clouded over again when Rohm and Haas announced they were suing us to force us to close on the deal, thereby placing Dow, and me, in shareholder litigation. Our legal team responded by pointing out the very obvious fact that we couldn't close the deal without destroying both Dow and Rohm and Haas. Nonetheless, a court date was set—March 9 in Wilmington, Delaware.

Legal challenges aside, the delay had the effect of buying me an additional two months' time. Nonetheless, if I couldn't raise billions of dollars before March 9, Dow would be legally obliged to finalize the Rohm and Haas deal. Twenty-four hours later, Dow would be technically bankrupt.

The next sixty days were a march through hell. By then, Dow was trading at around eleven dollars a share. (Ironically, during February and March 2009, Rohm and Haas had a bigger market cap than we did.) I was still confident I could get us out of this mess, but I would be lying if I said I wasn't apprehensive. Had I been too overconfident, too brash? Should I have played things safer? Had I gotten caught up in a deal frenzy? Had the boardroom coup fed my desire to show the board and Dow's stakeholders that I couldn't be defeated? I had always thought of myself as measured and practical, but was I really? Was I instead thirsty for accolades and recognition as the CEO who transformed Dow but who now found himself at risk of being remembered as the leader who bankrupted a great American institution?

February and early March, as I said, were brutal. I spent those days and weeks scrambling to find as many sources of funding as I could. There were eighteen banks in my consortium. Four of them by that point had bowed out. I had to find new banks to take their places, while ensuring that the other fourteen banks would re-up their commitments to Dow. (This wasn't a done deal by any means and required a lot of badgering and monitoring on my part.) By mid-February, four new banks had come aboard. The heavy lifting continued. I flew to Omaha to meet with Warren Buffett, who agreed to chip in $3 billion, albeit with onerous repayment terms. Still, it was cash and liquidity. Ironically, the Kuwait Investment Authority (which is separate from PIC) threw in another billion dollars, in exchange for the same stiff terms I agreed to with Buffett.

Two weeks before the March 9 court date, there came another hitch. The Haas Trust, which owned a third of Rohm and Haas, was persuaded to allow part payment using a "preferred equity currency," as opposed to all cash. I spent the next ten days going back and forth on speed dial with Janet Haas, a physician, who was leading the negotiations on behalf of forty-five members of the Haas family.

March 9 finally came. Dow's lawyers were due in court at 9:00 a.m. in Wilmington, Delaware. At 4:00 a.m. that same morning, I was still busy negotiating down to the last penny from my offices in Midland. I had worked through the night for seven days in a row, sneaking in two hours of sleep for every twenty-two hours I spent working the phones. Still, I was hopeful. I had secured bridge financing at reasonable terms, and the only thing left to do was finalize things with the Haas Trust. At 5:30 a.m., I remember sitting at my desk, fiddling with a ring of keys, and looking out the window. Midland is the kind of place that comes to mind when you think "small-town America," but the winters can be savage and last until the early spring. That morning, the lake-effect snow was coming down steadily in the darkness. It accumulated on the sills and blanketed the stripes in the empty parking lots.

One of the keys I held in my hand unlocked the local Dow Museum. I thought, *What would H. H. Dow do if he were in my shoes?* Dow's founder was known to Midland locals as "Crazy Dow," an eccentric inventor who rode around on a broken-down bike. Nothing kept him down for long, including two bankruptcies. When Crazy Dow died in 1930, he was still busy building up the company he had founded.

The image of H. H. Dow getting knocked down and rising again and again hardened my resolve. At 8:15 a.m., I called Janet Haas (again), so she could sign off on the preferred equity vehicle. Janet and I had a good relationship, but during the call, she said something slightly chilling: the Haas family insisted that Dow pay the bank fees associated with the deal. "How much are the bank fees?" I asked. Janet had no idea. She would get back to me.

"This is it," I thought. "Dow is about to go bankrupt." Fifteen minutes later, the phone rang. It was Janet. The bank fees were around $5 million. She reiterated that the Haas Family Trust had no intention of paying those costs.

"Janet," I said, trying to hide my incredulity, "let me get this straight. You want to stop an $18 billion deal from going through, and push it onto the courts, and bankrupt two extraordinary American companies, which will cause tens of thousands of people to lose their jobs, all because of *$5 million in bank fees*?" I paused. She was silent.

"Okay," I said at last. "Give me another half hour, and I'll see if I can come up with the funds."

I made a few frantic phone calls to our bankers and lead director. A half hour later, I had secured approval to offer $5 million to cover the banking fees. Relative to the billions of dollars at stake, it wasn't a lot of money to pay. I called Janet Haas again. When she picked up, I said, "I got you your five million. Call off your lawyers."

It was now Janet Haas's turn to wake up groggy family members and call an emergency meeting of the Haas Trust. By 8:30 a.m., both Dow and the Haas Trust had signed contracts in hand. Dow's legal team literally intercepted the Rohm and Haas lawyers as they were making their way up the steps to the Wilmington courthouse. There would be no court case. It was all over. Dow would survive. Rohm and Haas would survive. I would survive.

I'm not sure how, but I had staved off a cataclysm, the bankrupting of a great American enterprise. But there were damages. My wife, Paula, and I had lost friends in Midland. Hate letters appeared in our mailbox. Strangers showed up on our doorstep, accusing me of running Dow into the ground. Later, Warren Buffett told me in private that I had done as good a job as anyone given the circumstances, and though I've never required much validation, I appreciated him saying that. My son Anthony, who was seventeen and away at school at the time, wrote me a letter. "No one has the right to judge you, Dad. No one knows what you have gone through and what you have fought for. Without you, your company would have faded away in time. It is because of your unorthodox technique and willingness to adapt to the environment that you thrive." I keep that letter in my office today.

Dow was now the owner of Rohm and Haas. It was a high-quality acquisition, the business equivalent of buying beachfront property, albeit one we had bought in the middle of a hurricane. The winds and waves had taken a few whacks off its value, and we had overpaid, but when the storm went out to sea, we still had a formidable oceanside location. In the three weeks left before our (new) official closing, I got busy, selling off a Rohm and Haas division, Morton Salt, to a German company, and raising additional capital. Ironically, March 6—three days before the scheduled court case—was when the S&P 500 bottomed out and began reversing course. Dow's stock price soon rose from six dollars to fifteen dollars to thirty dollars and into the high thirties and low forties. In 2021, the stock price reached a historic high. Today Dow is more profitable than it has ever been, a result of all the hard work we did to transform the company for the twenty-first century.

But there was no time for celebration. More than anything, I reflected on what I had to do from then on to run Dow differently. Certainly, I became more fiscally conservative, a person who stuffed cash under his pillow. Now and then I allowed myself a moment or two of pride. Through good and bad times, I kept reinventing myself. I never gave in to the traps of victimhood. I resisted second-guessing myself to death. And though it took a few years, in 2013 the ICC (International Court of Arbitration) awarded Dow a record amount—$2.2 billion—as compensation for the Kuwaitis reneging on the deal they signed to buy one-half of Dow's plastics business. It was a huge win, the biggest compensation package in history ever awarded to a company. From a legal standpoint, the relationship between Dow and the Kuwaitis had been testy, and occasionally antagonistic, but it was over, and Dow continues to do successful joint ventures with the Kuwaitis to this day.

From my perspective, Dow was the biggest winner. When I arrived, I knew the company had to change or it would be changed *for* us, whether via an activist investor or a private equity bid. Dow had to go on offense. At the time our business mix was volatile, and our earnings were inconsistent. Worse, in a growth market, we weren't growing. We had virtually no presence in Washington, D.C., or other world capitals. Added to which, Dow had a public relations problem, and was routinely pasted with labels like "chemical" and "pollution" and "toxic." Unless I did something, the company was headed for the exit door.

One upside was that we had a cash pile on hand that we could use to transform our business mix. I was resolute in what I knew I needed to do, the only variable, as the Rohm and Haas deal reminded me, being timing. Among other things, acquiring Rohm and Haas meant that I had to divest a handful of other business, volatile underperformers that no one liked, including H. H. Dow's original chlorine business. Once that was done, I set my sights on Dow Corning.

Four decades earlier, during the Second World War, Dow was approached by Corning, a business based in Elmira, New York. Corning had recently developed a new technology based on silica, which is used to make glass. Since Corning wasn't a chemical company, it naturally wondered: Shouldn't a chemical company get involved in the manufacture of silica? The two CEOs at the time went ahead and formed Dow Corning, a fifty-fifty joint venture, with Dow Corning constructing its facilities in Midland, literally next door to us. Over time, despite being our next-door neighbor, Dow Corning not only created its own strong culture, it also grew to become the world's preeminent supplier of silicone materials for buildings, adhesives, cosmetics, medicines, and more. As Dow kept track of Dow Corning's growth over the decades, we kept repeating, "What *they* are is where *we* need to be."

Previous Dow CEOs had tried without success to buy the remaining 50 percent of Dow Corning, being rebuffed at every attempt. But one of my aspirations when I became CEO was to transform Dow into a customer-centric, culture-centric, innovation-centric enterprise. I knew that along with being a phenomenal company, Dow Corning was an ideal hand-in-glove fit that would enhance Dow's own innovation-centric culture. Better still, the company was our neighbor, and everyone involved lived in the same town and knew one another.

Still, it took me eleven years working with Corning's CEO, Wendell Weeks, who is still there, and who became a very close friend, to seal the deal. Whenever Wendell and I had dinner, at some point during the evening he would ask, "Okay, when are you going to ask me when I'm going to sell Dow Corning?" "Wendell," I said, "I will *wear you down.*" "No, you won't!" he always said.

Time passed. Corning shifted its focus to becoming the preeminent supplier of glass for phones, tablets, and computers. I kept pushing until one day, finally, they gave in. Over a boozy dinner in the original homestead of Corning's founder in upstate New York, I passed Wendell a napkin. "Write down on this napkin the three things you need for me to buy Dow Corning's shares." Looking down at what he wrote, I saw that it was precisely within the scope of what I planned on offering. "Okay," I said, "I'll come back to you tomorrow," and I did.

In 2015, Dow became the full owner of Dow Corning's silicone business. Many CEOs had tried; after working on it for more than a dozen years, I had cracked the nut. The Dow Corning deal broke the same day headlines for the Dow-DuPont merger were announced. The Dow Corning acquisition didn't drive the Dow-DuPont merger, but it certainly enhanced it. Credit belonged to Dow's strong performance—we kept hitting or surpassing our numbers—the divestment of old, tired franchises, the acquisition of Rohm and Haas, the strong culture transformation I oversaw at Dow that emphasized risk taking, and, of all things, shale gas. In an ironic twist, when the Kuwaitis reneged on their agreement to buy one-half of our plastics business, it turned out to be a huge boon for Dow. We now owned *all* the business, and the role that shale gas played in petrochemicals ultimately benefited Dow enormously. *This* was the Dow that was ready to merge with DuPont, a deal I had been planning even before becoming CEO, and which I go into in more detail in a later chapter.

Takeaways and Tools

- It's tempting for inexperienced CEOs to behave in ways they think leaders *should* act—to play the part, so to speak. This is counterproductive and a time waster. If you can, hit the ground running. Respect your company's past, but don't let corporate tradition slow down or compromise your vision or strategy.

- Even if you think you've seen it all, unexpected and first-time events will invariably materialize, especially nowadays. Expect and plan for a wide range of unpredictable scenarios.

- As a new CEO, don't assume that the team members you've inherited fully support your purpose, vision, strategy, or direction. As soon as possible, make sure the people around you are on *your* team. If they're not, make management changes immediately. Handpick lieutenants to serve as additional pairs of eyes and ears.

- The Confucian adage bears repeating: two ears and one mouth. For leaders, the ratio between listening and talking should be 2:1 (at minimum).

- Don't just look around *one* corner. Always look around *two* corners. Don't discount your own intuition and emotional intelligence. Trust your judgment that you know the business as well as or better than anyone else. Instead of letting consultants lead you, strive to become your own best consultant.

4

The New Role
of Geopolitics

Whenever we look at global events through a rearview mirror, what we didn't know at the time is often conspicuously evident. Hindsight, as they say, is everything.

Examples of this recur throughout history. Consider the collapse of the Berlin Wall in 1989, and what took place afterward—a reunified Germany, the swift, domino-like fall and transformation of other Eastern European regimes, and the 1991 dissolution of the USSR. Or the events that took place fifty years earlier, in 1938, when UK prime minister Neville Chamberlain signed the Munich Agreement, ceding the Czech region of the Sudetenland to Germany. Adolf Hitler wasted no time annexing the neighboring Czech regions of Moravia and Bohemia, and five months later invaded Poland.

What if we could apply the lessons of hindsight to this century's geopolitical stage? In the case of China, and its growing strength and influence, we can.

Beijing's ruling party has made it clear that by 2049, the rejuvenation of the People's Republic of China will be complete. Much can happen in the next few years and decades, but most analysts and experts agree that the twenty-first-century world stage will be dominated by a G2 consisting of two powers, the US and China. Together they represent roughly 42 percent of the world's GDP, and one-half of all global military spending (China spends $293 billion compared to the US's $801 billion).[1]

Of all the tectonic shifts highlighted in these pages, one of the most pressing is the geopolitical evolution—and revolution—likely to play out in the next few decades. Less obvious than two global powers staring each other down is the formation of a new shadow map of regional alliances and trading blocs that forms a labyrinth that today's leaders and businesses must understand and navigate. Some of these alliances have been in place for decades. Others have formed more recently. Still others haven't been born yet. All are critically important for this century's leaders and enterprises.

We are, in short, in the early stages of a new world order that will define the world going forward. Unlike the world of the previous century, this one is defined not by big continents but by relationships based on shared value systems. Yet most businesses and CEOs don't know how to make sense of these existing and inchoate alliances. Many present-day institutions were built in the twentieth century *for* the twentieth century. More recently formed companies have been slow to consider what the effects of a transformed geopolitical chessboard will have on their enterprises. Nor are governments able to offer guidance or a way forward. All companies and leaders are on their own.

Some of the questions CEOs should be asking themselves nowadays are: Who are our partners? Where will we keep our technology? How do shifting regional alliances and trading blocs affect our workforce as it relates to immigration? With whom should we ally, economically, politically, militarily, and even within our own country and communities? Against a backdrop of political and cultural division, should we as CEOs remain agnostic, or should we take a stand?

As the Russian invasion of Ukraine in 2022 taught us, these are some of the conversations businesses and leaders need to be having *now*.

China's Role in Twenty-First-Century Geopolitics

The port city of Darwin, Australia, where I was born, and lived until the age of sixteen, is a polyglot society. Darwin's proximity to Southeast Asia makes it a key link to nations and regions like Indonesia, East Timor, Micronesia, the Philippines, and Singapore. Over the years many immigrants have chosen to call Darwin home, including my own Greek grandfather. Having been raised in a multicultural city alive with Asian cultures, religions, traditions, rituals, and gastronomy, I learned to appreciate and respect Far Eastern heritages early on.

This background served me well during my first two decades at Dow, where my career took me to fifteen countries in Asia, including the five years I spent as president of Dow's entire Asia-Pacific operations. Living and working in Asia for two decades gave me a front row seat to the changes taking place in the area during the late 1980s and 1990s.

In 1997, my predecessor as CEO, William Stavropoulos, paid a visit to the region. The two of us traveled from Hong Kong to Beijing to meet with one of China's vice premiers, an extremely senior Chinese official. Before the meeting, I told our CEO that the handover of Hong Kong to the Chinese was imminent but that he shouldn't talk about it—it was a sore subject.

For whatever reason, he ignored my advice and brought up Hong Kong during our Western-style dinner with the vice premier. Seated across from him, I didn't know what to say. Neither did our translator. But I won't ever forget what the vice premier did next. Reaching over, he picked up the saltshaker and shook out a line of salt. "I want you to understand something about China," he said. "This line of salt"—he pointed at the crystals on the table—"represents the history of China." He grasped a grain of salt and rolled it between two fingers. "*This* represents the British occupation of Hong Kong." A gravid pause. "So don't talk to me again about Hong Kong being anything other than Chinese."

Those words stayed with me. So did the notion relayed to me that China woke up every day determined never to return to the humiliation it experienced during the Opium Wars, when the Chinese people were made to feel like second-class citizens. Western multinationals that wanted to do business with Beijing would have to agree to play by China's rules and respect China's long-term ambitions. China was intent on lifting its people out of poverty. China's approach to governing its numerous ethnicities was top down. China would protect the sanctity of its borders, including disputed territories. China would take back Macao, Hong Kong, and eventually Taiwan. China would never allow itself to be pinned to the mat again.

This message underscored the conviction I felt at the time that Dow's ongoing presence and strategy in China was at risk if we didn't acknowledge and commit fully to Beijing's ownership of Hong Kong. Under my watch, we shrank the Hong Kong offices that had been Dow's regional headquarters since the 1960s and invested $300 million in what was then one of the largest multinational headquarters and R&D complexes in Shanghai. The new building was concrete evidence that Dow would be operating in mainland China for the long term, and the long term mattered to the Chinese. Relationships did too.

In the mid-1990s, I was struggling to close a deal when the Chinese businessman seated across the table from me gave me some advice I've never forgotten. "Andrew," he said, "please understand that there are three tenets to society as those of us in the Far East see them." He paused. "There is the tenet of law, the tenet of logic, and the tenet of trustworthy relationships. But you in the West confuse the order of these three things. In fact, you have things *backward*. In the West, everything is contractual. For you the law drives logic. The law drives relationships." In Asia, he went on, the opposite was true. The tenet of *relationship* drove the tenet of *logic*, which drove the tenet of *law*. In the East, he added, written contracts meant almost nothing. A contract in Asia was sealed when two businesspeople looked each other in the eye. "You have only one opportunity to make a mistake on what we agreed on, and if and when you make that mistake, that's the last time you'll do business with us." He smiled. "We consider a business relationship to be a *life* experience, not a *term* experience."

Over the course of my career at Dow, I visited China every decade (I can remember driving through Shenzhen, today a city of almost thirteen million people, back when it was all duck farms and rice paddies). As Dow

CEO I went to China up to five times a year, most recently in 2014 as part of a delegation under President Obama that traveled to Beijing on behalf of the Asia-Pacific Economic Cooperation (APEC). As chairman of the US-China Business Council, I also regularly played host to Chinese delegations visiting the US, where I often found myself seated beside then vice premier Xi. I also played lead roles in an assortment of US-and-China-related economic forums, one where I was the voice of one hundred CEOs addressing Chinese leadership, and another as a member of Secretary of the Treasury Hank Paulson's team looking to find ways Chinese and American companies could collaborate on environmental issues. I still serve today on the sustainability board at Tsinghua University, a leading research institution in Beijing.

All this is to say that as a former longtime resident of Hong Kong (one of my three children was born there), an active participant in America-China relations for nearly four decades, and a businessman who has done his fair share of deals there, China considers me a "friend," a word I define as someone who supports the idea of China engaging in a positive, constructive relationship with the rest of the world.

These and other experiences gave me the opportunity to observe a series of small but significant changes taking place in China over the past few decades. Until 1990, for example, it was unimaginable to be in a meeting with Chinese speakers without a translator present. But in the past two decades, there has been no need for translators since everyone in the room speaks English. (There are more English-speaking people in China today than there are Chinese-speaking people in the US.) The changes accelerate from there.

As recently as ten years ago, I could have flown to Beijing, stayed in a hotel, gone to a state dinner, ridden in a car, and walked down the street without feeling I had to watch my step. Those days are over, and that China is gone. I haven't been to Beijing in several years, but if I did go there, at a minimum the contents of my cell phone might be downloaded. If party officials decided I was a person of interest, my hotel room might be monitored. If I even hinted at criticizing the Chinese Communist Party, I might be detained or accused of espionage, which is what happened to a

Canadian businessman, Michael Spavor, and a former Canadian diplomat, Michael Kovrig, who were both apprehended in 2018 by Chinese authorities in a move widely perceived as retaliation for the Canadian government's detention of Meng Wanzhou, the CFO of the Chinese technology firm Huawei Technologies and the daughter of Huawei's founder and CEO, Ren Zhengfei. All three parties were released in late 2020, an exchange some referred to as "hostage diplomacy."[2]

It was a vivid example of the blurring between Beijing and private industry in China, a phenomenon some have dubbed CCP Inc., short for Communist Chinese Party Incorporated. Today, even globally renowned Chinese companies and their CEOs are vulnerable to criticism and punishment if they don't carry out the bidding of party leaders. In 2020, two highly anticipated IPOs—the Ant Group, the world's largest fintech group, founded by Jack Ma; and Didi, the global ride-sharing app that owns Uber China and has half a billion users—were canceled at the last minute by party leaders.[3] Beijing accused Didi of violating the private data of its customers and banned its app from Chinese stores.[4] Jack Ma was hit with antitrust penalties and stripped of the presidency of Hupan University, the business school in Hangzhou he founded and endowed in 2015. Some surmise that by becoming too powerful and overlooking the fact that private capital exists to serve the many versus the few, private capital risks increasing societal inequality and subverting communist party control.

When Xi was named president in 2013, almost immediately he launched what some have called China's "third revolution," proclaiming himself the natural successor to Mao Zedong and Deng Xiaoping. Determined to amplify China's profile on the world stage, Xi set to work fortifying the military and arresting and jailing critics, dissidents, and human rights lawyers, while continuing to prohibit China's 1.4 billion natives from the internet or from any outside information calling into question party tenets. In 2018, Xi was named president for life. Given his relative youth—he was born in 1953—it's safe to say President Xi will be leading China for the foreseeable future.

While China and America face some of the same issues—the climate emergency and worsening social inequality, among them—the similarities end there. China today is a nation determined to extend its reach by any means possible and is taking on leadership roles in more and more areas. Since 2009, for example, China has been the world's largest energy consumer[5] and is responsible today for nearly one-quarter of the world's overall coal consumption.[6] China is also the world's largest producer of steel, aluminum, and computers.[7] Until 1980, the US led the world in the production of rare earth materials, seventeen metals that are widely used to create electrical and electronic components, glass, and assorted industrial processes. Thanks mostly to reduced labor costs and weaker environmental regulations, China has now taken the lead.[8] China has also begun making incursions across the globe, via its Belt and Road Initiative.

The BRI was launched by Beijing in 2013. The centerpiece of Xi's foreign policy, the Belt and Road Initiative is a staggeringly ambitious infrastructure project stretching from eastern Asia across Europe. Its goal is to construct building ports, highways, skyscrapers, airports, railroad tunnels, and whatever else it can in seventy countries across the world, using Chinese financing and Chinese labor. The BRI is the most expensive infrastructure project ever carried out by any nation—over the next three decades, Morgan Stanley estimates it could cost China north of $1 trillion.[9]

The BRI is lots of things at once: an outsized vision, a trade network, a footprint, and in many people's opinion, a predatory trespass. Few believe the BRI is simply a way to link China with the rest of the world. Instead, they say, China's motives are both economic and geopolitical. Many think the sole purpose of the BRI is to advance China's strategic interests by burdening poorer nations with debt, balking when it comes time to renegotiate the terms, and then taking ownership of the bridge, highway, or airport in question.

This happened in 2020, when the small nation of Montenegro, a NATO member since 2017, negotiated with China to build a state-of-the-art highway designed to serve as a transport hub for the Balkan region. At a cost of close to $1 billion, it was, noted the *New York Times*, "one of the world's most expensive roads."[10] Today the amount of money that Montenegro owes China exceeds a third of the Montenegrin annual budget. How, then, can Montenegro be expected to maintain its alliance with the West when it's financially beholden at the same time to China? An arguably even bigger issue is that if Montenegro defaults on its loan, China could seize the highway, as it did in 2017 when it took ownership of the Hambantota Port Development Project in Sri Lanka when the Sri Lankan government couldn't honor its loans.[11] It's no surprise that some countries, including the US, Australia, and India (which would prefer that China *not* forge an alliance with its longtime foe Pakistan), are suspicious of China's motives.

Adding to their distrust is China's ongoing drive for technological dominance. Historically, China has brought in foreign companies with a mandate that they create joint ventures with Chinese firms. Even big tech companies had to transfer their technology to navigate Chinese security laws, or as simply the price cost of doing business there. For a long time, intellectual property and copyright infringement have meant nothing in China. In 2020, the FBI publicly accused Beijing of stealing US technology across every industry sector "by any means necessary,"[12] with a premium placed on technology linked to aviation and electric vehicles. (China is also the world's largest car market.)[13] Many believe that Huawei's push to install its 5G technology globally is no more than a stealth operation of surveillance and manipulation engineered by Beijing's ruling party. Even those with more charitable views about Huawei concede that China has created a state-of-the-art surveillance state (to which China typically responds by accusing Western democracies of playing power politics).

Technology, stolen or homemade, also plays a part in China's 2015 "Made in China" initiative. The MIC hopes to transition China beyond its "workshop of the world" reputation, defined by low labor costs and advantageous supply chains, into a global technological powerhouse and a leader in twenty-first-century robotics, artificial intelligence, aviation, and electric vehicles. Today China not only continues to invest heavily in its own technology and military but is also investing heavily in space travel and even hopes to establish a permanent space station in the next five years.

Technology, in fact, is a sticking point between China and one of its closest neighbors, Australia, which is also America's most critical Asian ally. Along with Japan and India, the US and Australia are members of the Quadrilateral Security Dialogue, known informally as the Quad. Launched in 2007, the Quad is perceived as a firewall against growing Chinese military and economic power in the region. But even without the Quad, the decades-long, mostly harmonious trading relationship between China and Australia is fraying.

Things started going downhill a few years ago when Australia's then prime minister Malcolm Turnbull publicly criticized Chinese encroachments in the South China Sea, including China's decision to construct artificial islands in neighboring archipelagos, islands that were clearly created and designed to buttress Chinese claims that the South China Sea belonged to them. In 2018, citing national security concerns, Turnbull's government barred Huawei and ZTE, another big Chinese telecom, from creating the next generation of high-speed mobile internet in Australia. Things worsened in 2020 when Marise Payne, the Australian foreign minister, asked for an independent investigation into the origins of the COVID-19 pandemic. Angered, China responded by placing trade sanctions on Australia, targeting a dozen or so goods including wine, beef, lobster, and coal. Australia announced it would simply find new markets for its goods and materials. In summer 2021, China announced it was suspending all trade with Australia indefinitely.

But beyond highways, bridges, technology, artificial islands, and space travel is the probable likelihood of future war between China and the US. In his 2014 APEC speech in Beijing, President Obama remarked that he had twice hosted President Xi in the US. "The last time we met," the president went on, "[Xi] pointed out that the Pacific Ocean is big enough for both of our nations."[14] It may be—but the South China Sea apparently isn't. Crisscrossed with as many frictions as there are vessels, it remains a geopolitical pivot point, as does Taiwan, one hundred miles off the Chinese mainland coast.

Does the South China Sea belong to China, or is it a neutral waterway open to all nations? Who owns the archipelagos and island groups in the South China Sea known as the Spratly and Paracel Islands, on whose reefs and shoals China has built its new military bases? Vessels from all over the world pass through China's territorial waters every day. But China believes they damage and threaten national security interests, which is why many believe those newly built military air bases are a forerunner of future conflict.

Amplifying the beat of war between the US and China was China's 2021 crackdown on Hong Kong, where prodemocracy activists were jailed, a prodemocracy newspaper was shut down, art and films were censored, and the election system was overhauled, with a new law introduced stating that from now on only "patriots" could run for office.[15] Many analysts believe that having brought Hong Kong back into the fold (with, I might add, minimal response from the US), Beijing will soon invade Taiwan and reclaim it as part of mainland China. China has also been clear that if the US chooses to defend Taiwan, it wouldn't hesitate to deploy its military or even go to war. To most experts, this is less a question of *if* than *when*. If the US retaliated, and most likely it would, along with potential loss of life, the world order as it stands today would become further disrupted.

This brings us, circuitously but pointedly, back to the world of business.

Today, the US and China are at odds. Neither trusts the other. China believes the US wants to hem them in. The US suspects that China wants to continue expanding until the world is in their pocket. If the US continues its new Cold War with China, how should global institutions and their leaders respond to a new world order that is effectively divided up on one side by China and on the other by the US? Where is the line in China and elsewhere between conducting business as usual versus *not* doing business in countries where gender and human rights abuses, child labor, and slavery are the norm? In a world increasingly defined by new, shifting, and sometimes contradictory alliances, who are your friends and allies? Whom do you trust economically, politically, and militarily? Finally, what happens if your business is at odds with the value system of your own government?

A Shift in Globalization

A few months before I retired from Dow, I gave an address to the Business Council, which I chaired at the time. The crux of it was that in a dynamic world order, US-based multinationals like Dow were now finding themselves asking a question that would have been unthinkable in a previous century: "Are we an American company that operates globally but has our headquarters in the US, or are we a global company that just happens to be headquartered in the US?"

It may seem like a simple question of framing, but the answer has consequences for your business, its identity, and its values. To explain, let's look at the great American multinational (of which I am a proud beneficiary) over the decades.

When the US multinational appeared, it achieved something that no other country-based company in Europe had done before. By prioritizing freedom, talent, and inclusivity, the American model served up democracy *inside* an organization. Instead of colonizing, it recruited. Whenever a company like Dow or IBM expanded internationally, it attracted top talent from those countries' best colleges and universities. Where employees came from or went to school didn't matter. They could go as far as their talents, skills, and ambitions took them.

This model also operated on the assumption that the world's borders would keep opening, trade would become more widespread, and human and financial capital, goods and services would continue to move freely around the world. In essence, this was Globalization 1.0. It allowed an entire generation of American companies to globalize since they could scale easily based on people, money, and goods. Then things hit a wall.

Globalization, it turned out, meant that all the spoils went to the top 20 percent of the population, or even the top 1 percent, leaving everyone else behind. Household incomes went down, and so did education and employment opportunities for succeeding generations. American workers became incensed about offshoring—how was it even allowed? Globalization was ultimately seen as just another means for the rich to benefit off the backs of the less rich and for the top echelons of society to accumulate even more benefits. Business as usual, in other words.

That said, Globalization 1.0 can be credited with bringing the subject of corporate identity and allegiance to everyone's attention. What does it mean to be an American company with headquarters or multiple operations all around the world? For one thing, it means that leaders must address questions like: What is my priority market? What is my priority workforce? What are my values? If I am an American company that operates overseas, should I be thinking about those overseas markets differently, and should I create a different set of metrics for those markets?

On the opposite end are institutions that identify as *global* companies but have their roots in the US. Their American customers are important, but not more or less than their overseas consumers. This means that all those relationships—and lots of different governments—need to be factored in when making decisions.

In a century that will continue to be dominated by the US and China, determining which one of these two categories your company falls into is a decision you should make sooner rather than later. With the likelihood of future conflict between the US and China (some are saying by the end of this decade), businesses will have to pivot quickly. Can they afford to *not* do business in a major market like China? Right now, every boardroom in America should be doing a supply chain risk analysis on this topic and analyzing their dependency on China. If a small or large war broke out, will their company be forced to make a choice? What will that choice look like? In the event of war, companies will have to make the decision of where they are domiciled and where their culture and values most line up.

But why should they even bother with this question? Won't their governments make the decision for them?

When I was at Dow, no one thought twice about this question. Governments led and businesses followed. The US government prohibited any companies registered in the US from transacting with enemy governments, such as Libya, North Korea, and Yemen. The relationship between business and government had clear, well-defined roles and protocols. Governments were responsible for addressing the issues you cared about as a company, and companies in turn dovetailed behind those decisions. Ideally, businesses could influence governments to pass laws or regulations that benefited their businesses *and* their industries. You could also approach the Business Roundtable, or the Business Council, or the National Association of Manufacturers and articulate your policy ideas and let those groups take the lead on advancing your views, whether they had to do with policy or finding purpose beyond profits. Like so many other twentieth-century templates, all that is a thing of the past.

Nowadays, whether you're a CEO, chairman of the board, or a board director, your responsibilities go beyond your fiduciary responsibility to your shareholders. You are accountable to every one of your *stakeholders*. Dow's headquarters may be in Midland, Michigan, but we have a significant presence throughout the US, with two of our biggest plants located in Texas and Louisiana. Dow operates manufacturing plants in forty-eight countries, has sales offices in 162 countries, and employs tens of thousands of people worldwide. These people and those communities make up our stakeholders.

The emphasis on *stakeholder engagement* means that, at a minimum, leaders of today must engage fully in strategic and economic dialogues with governmental officials and organizations. The question, though, is where to find them! Under the presidential administrations of George W. Bush and Barack Obama, a close connection existed between the government and business. Businesspeople served in cabinet positions or as industry czars. There was no reason to believe the relationship between business and government wouldn't continue to grow and flourish.

But business and government diverged under the Trump administration, and they haven't recovered under the Biden administration. For the first time in decades, substantive decisions affecting the business community are being made without any input from the business community. The business world is mostly excluded from policy decisions. That means that no obvious pathways exist for businesses to participate in a solution set that helps create a world in which these two ecosystems can coexist. It also means that if the US and China go to war, most businesses and leaders won't know what to do or how to respond.

Most governments and businesses today are running around like chickens with their heads cut off. If you as a business are on the sharp end of the spear around tariffs, supply chains, cyber issues, or the ability to manufacture or sell your products simultaneously in the US and China, you will be dealing with these issues without a template or blueprint. This is a seminal shift that today's leaders need to understand.

An Intricate Chessboard

There is a well-known *New Yorker* cartoon that exaggerates how the typical New Yorker sees the world. It shows the cars and pedestrians of Ninth Avenue and across the Hudson River, the banks of New Jersey. From there the world gets smaller and blurrier. Texas, Chicago, and Kansas City lie side by side. Farther off is the Pacific Ocean. Beyond that, as unserious and low priority as everything else that isn't Manhattan, are faraway chunks of Earth labeled China, Japan, and Russia.

When I was coming of age at Dow, our thinking was similar in its way. There was North America. There was Europe. And there was a third "thing" known informally as ROW—the "rest of the world." Dow had its headquarters in Midland, Michigan, but ROW was managed out of Houston or Miami. At some point, the business world awoke to the notion that ROW was, well, huge. This meant that Dow and other multinationals now needed to build headquarters in countries around the world. A half century later, the model of defining the world via geographic location has become redundant. Instead, companies and countries are using regional alliances and trading blocs to organize themselves before deciding how to mobilize company resources *within* those alliances, whether it's the Pacific Rim, MERCOSUR in South America, or the European Common Market.

In case it's not clear yet, the new world order is less about countries, and the traditional relationships among them, than it is about trading alliances and blocs. These new partnerships can appear abruptly and unexpectedly. To appreciate their complexity, cast your mind back to 2021, when the member nations of the G7 met for their annual meeting in Cornwall, UK.

On the surface, little had changed. It was generally agreed that Russia would never be readmitted to the G7. China was on everybody's radar, but then again, it had been for decades. The Western democracies—the US, the United Kingdom, Canada, France, Germany, Italy, and Japan—made up another alliance. So where did that leave relations between Germany, a NATO ally, and Russia, a NATO outcast?

Since the USSR folded, Germany and Russia have had a transactional partnership based on energy supply. Russia needs German investment to help build its energy infrastructure, and Germany depends on Russia to supply natural gas. Many Western analysts believe this non-NATO-approved alliance gives Russia leverage over other EU nations—but at the same time, no NATO country wants to alienate Germany. In 2020, the Biden administration signed off on an agreement allowing the completion of the Nord Stream 2 pipeline that exports gas from Russia to Germany. In return, Germany agreed to invest in Ukraine, with both Germany and Ukraine consenting to do everything in their power to try to limit Russian influence in the EU. After Russia invaded Ukraine in early 2022, and both pipelines were partially damaged in September due to explosions, the Nord Stream 2 pipeline is expected to continue operating.

Turkey, a member of NATO since 1962, is in a similar dilemma. By purchasing missiles from Russia, Turkey is showing disloyalty to the other NATO members. Or what about O-RAN, a telecom industry consortium of three hundred or so mobile carriers led by AT&T that was launched in 2018 with the goal of making cellular equipment interoperable and affordable? In 2021, Finland's Nokia recused itself from the alliance over concerns that two Chinese companies also belonging to O-RAN had shown up on a US Commerce Department blacklist,[16] meaning that O-RAN represented a potential national security risk. It seems that Kindroid and Phytium Technology Company are semiconductor manufacturers that produce technology that could benefit China's military.

More surprising was the sudden announcement in late 2020 of a new trilateral defense pact among Australia, the United Kingdom, and the US. AUKUS, as it's called, is an agreement that helps Australia acquire a fleet of nuclear-propelled submarines and share cybersecurity and artificial intelligence. AUKUS was a canny geopolitical chess move that fortified both the Quad and the Five Eyes, or FVEY, the older alliance made up of Australia, Canada, New Zealand, the UK, and the US. A few days after the announcement, the *Washington Post* called AUKUS "an Anglo-Saxon military alliance fitted to a multicultural and globalized world,"[17] and "nothing less than the Atlantic Charter to finally extended to the Pacific, eight decades later."[18] When the announcement was made, no one brought up China. No one had to.

Equally jarring was the abrupt sidelining of France, a longstanding US ally. Until AUKUS was announced, France thought it was contracted to build $66 billion worth of submarines for Australia. Surely a French company could assume it was allied with the US via NATO. Surely, too, the other NATO nations could be expected to play a role in any new Asian-Pacific defense pact. Wrong on both counts. This ever-shifting network of regional cooperations and storylines has superseded the old twentieth-century model and thrown into question what the notion of alliance even means anymore.

The Quad. AUKUS. ASEAN. The East Asia Alliance. The TPP. These trade- and technology-based institutions are based less on value systems than they are on having a single enemy—China—in common. Today, countries and companies must obey the rules of the pacts to which they belong. A company's strategies need to align with regional alliances, as opposed to the geographical location of their headquarters or the legacy relationship between two countries. The problem is that boardrooms have been slow to adapt to this new model. It's as if they wish it didn't exist. But they can't ignore it away. The good news is that these new alliances also offer opportunities.

By embedding themselves in these infrastructures, businesses can enter new, collaborative ecosystems to *supply* these alliances. These new pacts have also created new consultancies and practices devoted to helping companies become, say, the suppliers of choice to AUKUS nations. By necessity, those countries will be either British or American. As businesses in this century become more likely to have to take sides—are you with China or are you with the US?—they will find additional subecosystems focused on creating preferential agreements. This century's leaders need to have all this knowledge at hand, along with knowing what relationships in what nations will allow their companies to evolve and grow.

From Business as Usual to Transparency as Usual

Last year at Liveris Academy, a visiting speaker—a CEO a few years younger than I—was asked by students about what role "purpose" played in her life when she was beginning her career. She laughed, surprised, and I did too. When she was in her twenties, she said, life was pretty straightforward. She applied for a job and crossed her fingers she would get it. The ethics of a company's supply chain weren't an issue for her—she wasn't even aware of them. She kept her head down, put one foot in front of the other, and didn't spend too much time thinking about where her career might take her.

Her experience was familiar. Like her, I came of age inside a company where I was taught how to make money. If I learned to become a good citizen along the way, it was always within the context of creating profits. (I *was* a good citizen, it turns out, but in those days no company was in the business of teaching its employees how to become good citizens.) If the company *did* make money, the businesspeople of my generation reasoned, we couldn't help but become better citizens.

Dow may be domiciled in the US, but we have operations in more than 160 countries. Whenever we entered a new region of the world, our strategy was simple. We prided ourselves on having the highest standards in the industry. If we were doing business in developing nations, we tried to import our standards to those countries, ideally elevating them along the way. We also made it a point to benchmark the local competition. In most cases we found out that the salaries other companies were paying their workers were less than what we offered. Their factories were often in poor shape. No attention was paid to the environmental factors or to pollution. Yes, in the short term, it cost Dow more to build top-flight facilities and create better working conditions, but those things mattered to us. We also knew that if our competitors couldn't match our standards, they would go out of business. Finally, we believed that any improvements to the local quality of life would benefit the US, specifically, and the world in general (though *benefit* was a hard word to quantify).

Contrast this to other industries, from fashion to footwear to textiles, where the prevalent overseas strategy was closer to *see no evil*. If, say, the conditions in a Malaysian or Indonesian clothing factory were subpar, no one knew about them. Yes, occasionally a company might hire an inspector whose job it was to guarantee that the goods produced in that country were in good condition, but usually it went no further than that. No one studied a company's books in detail or took the time to figure out how much a factory was paying its workers.

In hindsight, was the business world that myopic? Probably *yes*.

Things have changed since then, of course. Over the last two decades, and especially the past decade, the business world has seen a dramatic transformation, namely, the rise of the "for purpose" business. Profits are as important as ever, but today profits share a mandate with *doing good,* and *doing good* is now built into how many companies operate and in what they measure.

This probably explains why Liveris Academy students greeted what the visiting CEO said with respectful confusion. For a younger generation, taking a 100 percent capitalist approach to your job or your business is unimaginable. Our students are digital natives who grew up with 9/11; a global financial crisis; a gig economy; and a nearly three-year-long pandemic and quarantine. For them, a mission and a purpose need to underpin the businesses where they work and every decision those businesses make. Credit or blame goes to the internet, which has illuminated supply chain issues that were once in shadow and that can elevate or destroy a company's reputation overnight. The internet has transformed what it means to do business today in overseas markets. It turned out some companies and countries with spotless reputations weren't as pure as everyone thought, and workplace abuses were just as likely to take place in Eastern Europe as they were in Southeast Asia. The internet, among other things, gave rise to new standards of transparency in business.

Practically speaking, this meant companies had to understand what was *really* going on in their overseas markets. Once, a company might have sourced a product from China without knowing that China sourced a component of that product from Vietnam or Malaysia or Africa under suboptimal conditions. Once, a company's level of purview and self-auditing was limited. Plus, to be fair, how could companies afford to audit every link in their supply chains? Today, nothing is hidden. Issues or frictions concealed by inattention or apathy, or camouflaged under layers of bureaucracy—slavery, child labor, prison labor, gender and racial inequality, appalling working conditions—today stand exposed. Countries and companies that overlooked these issues, brushed them aside, covered them up, or weren't aware of them are no longer welcome at the table.

It's a net positive whenever any company holds itself to account—and this century's purpose-based businesses have no choice but to pry open their cupboards before someone else does. From what part of the world do you source your products? Do you use child labor, even indirectly? Do you manufacture your products directly or indirectly in parts of the world where human rights or gender violations and abuses exist? If your supply chain relies on countries that don't do business using values that match those of your company, those disconnects are bound to come to light. It's your responsibility to find another supplier and stop doing business with the country until it improves its labor, equality, or gender practices. These new levels of transparency are barriers companies must consider. Opaqueness no longer works. It's not your responsibility to transform the child labor laws of another country—until the owners of your company tell you it is.

With watchdogs today *inside* organizations, businesses are now free to raise objections to countries where they see fit. In 2021, Ben & Jerry's, which is owned by Unilever but maintains its own board, made headlines for its corporate owner by announcing that selling its ice cream in the Israeli-occupied West Bank and contested areas of East Jerusalem was "inconsistent with our values."[19] By doing so, Ben & Jerry's joined Airbnb, who in 2018 decided to eliminate its listings in Israeli settlements before reversing its decision after the Israeli government exerted pressure.[20]

Other companies have taken an opposite tack and shown leadership that governments haven't. Under CEO Paul Polman, Unilever announced its intention to minimize its global environmental footprint and create the most positive social impact worldwide possible. Along with acquiring more and more ecofriendly brands like Seventh Generation and Tazo Tea,

Unilever launched new policies, including 100 percent sustainable sourcing, improved health and hygiene for over a billion people, and making the transition to zero waste.[21, 22] More recently, as I mentioned earlier, Marc Benioff at Salesforce has pledged that 1 percent of Salesforce's equity, time, or products are donated to tens of thousands of nonprofits and educational institutions globally every year.[23]

But what happens if the geopolitical issues take place in your own country? Cultural conflicts and new alliances are also redefining what it means to be the leader of an organization.

The Left, the Right, and the Middle

In 2017, former president Donald Trump formed the American Manufacturing Council, an advisory board set up to advise his administration about domestic manufacturing initiatives. It was made up of over two dozen prominent CEOs, including the CEOs of Dell, Merck, Under Armour, General Electric, Intel, Lockheed Martin, 3M, Campbell Soup Company, Boeing, and others. I was asked to chair the group.

Elon Musk was the first CEO to withdraw from the council when the Trump administration pulled out of the Paris Climate Change Accords. Then, less than two months later, everything fell apart. In August 2017, a white supremacist rally was held in Charlottesville, Virginia, ostensibly to protest the removal of a statue of Confederate Civil War general Robert E. Lee from a local park. More protestors than were expected showed up. They roamed the streets carrying tiki torches and Nazi flags and chanting racist and antisemitic slogans. Fights broke out between civil rights groups and white nationalist factions. A neo-Nazi drove his car into a crowd of protestors, killing one person and injuring thirty-five others.

In his first public remarks, Trump said he condemned hatred, bigotry, and violence "on many sides." Later he added there were "very fine people on both sides."[24] After conferring with his own board, Merck CEO Ken Frazier, an African American leader whose grandfather was born a slave, announced on Twitter that he was resigning from the council, saying, "Our country's strength stems from its diversity and the contributions made by men and women of different faiths, races, sexual orientations, and political beliefs." Frazier later clarified his stance to the *New York Times*: "It was my view that to not take a stand on this would be viewed as a tacit endorsement of what had happened and what was said." He added, "I think words have consequences, and I think actions have consequences."[25] Two days later, Brian Krzanich, the CEO of Intel, and Kevin Planck, the CEO of Under Armour, also resigned.

Frazier's and Planck's positions were understandable. Ken's decision was personal, and Kevin, who operates a consumer business, and who as a CEO is inseparable from the company he runs, couldn't afford to have his company be seen as noninclusive. None of us could. (Two years later, Kevin also came to the defense of Baltimore, where Under Armour has its headquarters, when Trump disparaged the city and Elijah Cummings, its Democratic congressman.)

Then and now, the US was politically divided, with both sides screaming at each other across social media. I had no interest in inflaming matters more by engaging with the media. The best solutions in my experience are found by working the middle. Which is why I didn't attack the president in public, a decision that some people later criticized me for. Instead, I made it clear to Jared Kushner that his father-in-law's remarks had made it untenable for the leaders of inclusive enterprises to continue serving as council members. Kushner could frame it to the president as a choice. Trump could either disband the council or the remaining members would walk out en masse. An hour later, we were all dismissed. I had nothing more to do with the Trump administration.

Both Frazier's and Planck's positions make it obvious that this century's leaders are more and more being asked to take stances around divisive and polarizing political and cultural issues. Should leaders speak as civilians or on behalf of their companies? CEOs may oversee large enterprises, but enterprises are also political. Problem is, if CEOs take sides, or throw their hat in with one or another political party, their boards would be right to fire them.

Last year I found myself speaking regularly with a handful of leading CEOs as we sought to create consensus around President Biden's infrastructure plan and determine what the US needed to spend to bring its physical and nonphysical infrastructure up to speed for this century. As I listened to my colleagues speak, between the lines I intuited the broadening of their own agency, as well as a newfound responsiveness. As their companies evolve into business *and* political enterprises, today's leaders need to find a new language to express their own definitions of social responsibility.

Online critics generally attack from the far sides. Most are invested in fringe conversations and seem uninterested in coming up with solutions. The middle has become an opportunity zone. CEOs today should lead, and attempt to build, from the middle. Deal with the hand you have been dealt by making things better. You may disagree with the leadership running the country, but you also need to find ways to collaborate. You won't achieve that by turning your back on that leadership, or on your own company's values. Speaking personally, over the years I've tried to help governments get better not by raising my voice but by being more inclusive, whether it's around social justice issues, the environment, or plastics recycling. In short, *always focus on the solution.*

Here's an example. It's all well and good for a government official to say "I hate plastics." But when you ask if the government has a recycling plan in place, the answer is no. There is no price point with recyclables. Why not? Because no government policy is in place. How can we fix that? Well, we can create a mandate, and a price point, around returning cans and bottles to recycling depots that *pays* for that recycling. Now, that is a *policy* answer *and* a solution.

I bring up plastics because the language of the middle shows up acutely around sustainability. The CEOs of any enterprise that lacks a net-zero 2050 climate change goal, and who hasn't convinced the board and shareholders to put their full weight behind that metric, will not last long in his job. More forward-looking CEOs say 2030. The *most* forward-looking CEOs make it clear there needs to be a price on carbon. These are all *layers* of language. CEOs who gravitate to the middle will continue to make their presence known in decades ahead. Instead of opining behind the safety and cowardice of social media, they realize it's better to work with the company or political leadership in charge and collaborate to bring about better outcomes.

The biggest advantage of the middle is that it showcases a CEO's allegiance to the enterprise and its values. "My value system as an enterprise is the reason why we can't do business with you anymore. Therefore, we are severing ties." It's never personal. I'm speaking as the CEO of Dow, not as Andrew Liveris, and I have drawn a red line that our company will not cross. This issue came to the fore when in May 2022 a stacked Supreme Court voted to overturn abortion rights in the US. Then and now, CEOs and companies need to step up and make a statement about this or any other social paradigm that affects their workforce, half of which are women, allowing employees to travel to safe jurisdictions if they wish to have an abortion. Period, end of story.

That a collective new line had been drawn was obvious in the days and weeks after Russia invaded Ukraine in early 2022. Almost immediately, Exxon Mobil suspended operations of a multibillion-dollar oil and gas project in Russia's Far East that it co-owned with Rosneft, the state-owned oil giant. Exxon was joined by British Petroleum, which announced it was divesting its 20 percent stake in Rosneft. Other enterprises including Apple, Starbucks, McDonald's, H&M, IKEA, Ericsson, Canada Goose, Toyota, Honda, General Motors, American Express, Visa, Mastercard, Harley Davidson, Nike, and Adidas quickly made their own objections clear, whether via sanctions, refusing to sell goods and products to Russia, or suspending Russian operations altogether. DirecTV removed the Russian-controlled TV station from its channels. Disney, Sony, and Warner Brothers suspended the release of any new films across Russia. Boeing shuttered its offices in Kyiv. FedEx and UPS both suspended delivery service. Meta, the parent owner of Facebook, prohibited Russian state media from advertising on Facebook. Netflix, PayPal, and YouTube bowed out. Delta Airlines suspended its alliance with Aeroflot, Russia's largest government-majority-owned airline, and so did Sabre, the Texas-based global distribution system used by a billion consumers globally to browse, book, and service flight reservations. Not least, the world's largest container ship operators, AP Moller-Maersk A/S and Mediterranean Shipping Company, both suspended shipping to Russian ports.

What caused this line to be drawn? After all, in 2021 numerous reports surfaced about the Chinese government's mistreatment of the Uyghurs, a Turkish-speaking, Muslim minority group, including detaining more than a million Uyghurs inside "indoctrination camps" and sentencing others to prison.[26] You might wonder: Isn't it hypocritical for an enterprise to suspend business with Russia but continue operating in mainland China? What about the countless other examples of dictators and despots committing crimes against their own people, within their own borders?

There is a difference—and it is the violation of the respect we offer our neighbors when they are different from us and have different views and beliefs. Russia's invasion of Ukraine crossed a line, one that, if I were still the CEO of Dow, I wouldn't hesitate to support, as I do today in my various board positions. Not only did Vladimir Putin invade and attempt to obliterate a sovereign neighboring country, he also massacred women and children. The closest parallel is what Germany did to Poland during the Second World War. China, by contrast, even with their Belt and Road Initiative, is not a geographically expansionist nation. Its goal is to someday reclaim regions and territories it believes belong to it. (Arguably, Russia does too, but Ukraine belongs to Ukraine and not to greater Russia.)

In the days following the invasion, purpose-based businesses acknowledged that a new line had been crossed. Are the Russia-based employees who work for these companies suffering too? Yes, but that has more to do with bad national leadership and does not compare with the obliteration of a Ukrainian maternity ward. The response of the business world, in fact, recalls the disinvestment campaign that happened in the 1980s in South Africa when businesses en masse withdrew from the country in protest of apartheid.

The Russian invasion of Ukraine had one unintended consequence. It will force China to think twice about invading Taiwan. The economic sanctions levied against Russia, and the unity displayed by Western nations, were muscular and swift. If it hasn't already, China will likely realize that as a force in the global economic order, it has far more to lose economically by invading Taiwan than Russia ever could. China, after all, is tied into *everything*, and to date at least, Beijing has done nothing to trigger a fraction of the response that Western countries and companies have shown in Russia.

At Dow, we had an enterprise risk management system that included bringing in outside experts to help us analyze geopolitical risk. A decade ago, Dow opted *not* to invest in Russia or to place our first-generation technology in China. We invested in Saudi Arabia instead. In other words, geopolitical risk played, and still plays, an integral role in our company's decision making. This speaks to every company whose leaders and boards need to manage an enterprise's risk around ESG factors, digital concerns— and geopolitical conflicts. Today we are in a new era of decision making around geopolitical risk—and that conversation needs to be front and center.

Should there be a strategy in place today for Western alliance companies to withdraw from China? Boardrooms should seriously consider this question. China's value system is different from the West's. Non-Chinese companies are almost guaranteed to lose their intellectual property. Sooner rather than later, China will invade Taiwan. Businesses should ask themselves, as they did in the wake of the Russian invasion of Ukraine, will we keep doing business here, or pull out? The response, as we saw in Russia, depends on the business, with numerous US and European companies withdrawing, and many Asian companies staying put. But if you're not having this conversation, you're not paying attention.

Embracing Reality

In a world of newfound alliances and relationships, what can businesses do to prepare for a readjusted world stage?

The first phase of leadership comes down to two words: *embrace reality*. *Reality* in this case means that leaders recognize the qualities and characteristics of this moment in time. The next step, it bears repeating, is to begin to uncover solutions.

If last century was about lobbying, advocacy, and communications, this century is about *strategic insight*. Topics like cyber issues require a different kind of government department, or even a group of people inside your company who are dedicated to working with governments to influence and maybe even set policy. Among other things, this department must consider all the various correlations and overlaps that exist among government, business, and society, from supply chains to technology to environmental and digital and technology issues.

The ever-shifting ground of geopolitics brings up another issue I emphasize to the students at Liveris Academy: get started early in understanding the triune of business, government, and society, while bearing in mind that ESG factors permeate the axes between business and government, government and society, and business and society. If business and government are in dialogue to the exclusion of society, it is at their own peril—because today society's voice is ascendant. The dialogue between society and government is seen in the protestors outside Glasgow's Scottish Event Campus and in citizens who vote for political candidates. The dialogue between business and society, though, is a new one, and to my mind, by far the most important one given the conspicuous absence of governmental leadership worldwide. This road map will help you begin to navigate these questions. My advice is to focus on two lenses, the first local, the second global.

Local comes first. Get involved. Join a school board. Run for office. Become a leader in your church or community. How are taxes raised in your town, state, or locality? How are resources and revenues allocated to your community? By understanding the dynamic between the state and the federal government, you will gain a stronger feel for the intersections that exist in business, government, and civil society.

Another step involves doing what you can to attract businesses and industries to your community. When I arrived in Midland in 2004, the city was atrophying, making it harder for Dow to attract top talent. Our mission was to help create a municipality that would attract cutting-edge jobs and talent. Dow's strategy was to go outside in, rather than inside out. This is what I mean by focusing on the local lens.

If the local is outside in, the global lens is inside out. For example, leaders can join forces with institutions that operate in multiple places, for example, universities. (At Liveris Academy we can do this by recruiting talent from other Australian states and the world.) You can join a company like Dow that is already global, or you can join a company that has global ambitions and help them get there.

If you're a businessperson, you also need to figure out how to deal with government officials. Go in with a targeted mission. Introduce yourself. You're with X or Y company, and you're interested in investing in their country. Who should you talk to? If that sounds too bold, or forward, believe me when I say it's how people do business in this century.

This also means that the bandwidth of this century's leaders needs to expand to take in a more global perspective. The best leaders of today and tomorrow—rather, the ones who will survive—must go simultaneously wide and deep. If your company identifies as an American enterprise, ask yourself: What is my country doing in the world? What is its reputation? What irregularities or inequities should I be aware of? If your business identifies as global, the question is more complicated. These same questions should be asked of all the countries you operate in, and you should make the right decisions accordingly.

The good news is that boards are becoming aware of these risks. They are pushing forward with CEOs and finding directors who are better able to manage the dichotomies of purpose that characterize this century. The best companies know they can no longer depend on their government—or any government—for help and that business needs to step up and take on the leadership role that government has vacated. By aggregating the voices of like-minded companies into a coalition of leaders seeking to find solutions to the biggest challenges of the twenty-first century, they will come closer to finding a solution space that adheres closely to the middle and benefits *all* society.

For example, an American company that has operations in China may disagree (strongly) on issues around the military, or cyberspace, but are there areas where the two sides can find accord? What are China's priorities? If they're having water supply or agricultural problems, can your company be part of the solution without compromising its values? Can you create what great businesses have always created, a win-win for everybody? Using society's input, can the world's wealthiest people come together with the world's wealthiest institutions to find solutions?

I've always been drawn to the expression, and framework, of forming, storming, norming, and performing. Most often used to describe the stages of development in a team, the term was coined in the mid-1960s by American psychologist Bruce Tuckman. In the forming phase, the members of a team assemble for the first time. They have high expectations. Maybe they're slightly anxious. They have come together to define the problem that they want to solve as a team.

From a geopolitical standpoint, right now we are in the forming phase. We know that what *was* is *over*. What *is* isn't working. Today we are in a period where the lack of leadership in the UN and elsewhere has created the need for new alliance structures to form. These won't be top down. They won't involve governments or institutions saying, "*This* is how we get China back into the fold," or "*This* is how we tame Russia." It won't happen, and the reasons why are on public display. China refuses to adapt to the vision of someone else's world order and is focused instead on its own China-centric perspectives and decision making. Russia has made it clear it seeks to reclaim its Russian-speaking territories. This battle of value systems means that geopolitics is in urgent need of a new model, one built from the ground up. What would this look like? While I don't see it happening anytime soon, countries with similar value systems need to come together and over time begin the critical-mass creation and formation of new global alliances. This is the storming phase of creating the future structures of the world that *will* be. Until that happens, the world will be asked to pass through period after period of threat and provocation among the world's superpowers.

Takeaways and Tools

- We are in the early stages of a new world order that will define the world going forward.

- Geopolitics in this century is dominated by a "G2," the US and China.

- A secondary geopolitical map also exists and includes an ever-shifting array of smaller regional alliances and trading blocs, like the Quad, AUKUS, ASEAN, and the TPP.

- By the end of this decade, most experts expect China to reclaim Taiwan. With the probability of the US being pulled into a global conflict, is your enterprise prepared to respond to a world order and business environment divided by China and the US?

- Go to where the hockey puck is going—not where it was. Businesses of all sizes should be asking themselves *today*: Who are our partners? Where do we place our assets? Where do we keep our technology? Do we identify as a US company or a global enterprise? If it's the latter, that means that multiple relationships and governments must be factored in when you make decisions.

- Businesses should be having the China discussion *today*. Will they withdraw or remain if and when China invades Taiwan?

- Internet transparency and pressure from younger generations are among the factors why today's businesses must *do well* and *do good*. Is there integrity in your supply chain? Do you operate in countries where slavery exists, or child or prison labor, or gender or racial inequalities? Find out *now* and root out those problems before someone else finds out for you.

- CEOs are being asked more and more to take political and moral stances in public, both in the US and overseas. CEOs of inclusive organizations—that means everyone—need to realize that this is a new facet, and description, of contemporary leadership.

- Learn and master the new language of speaking out. My advice, always, is for CEOs to gravitate toward the middle, while always focusing on the solution.

- As early as possible, younger leaders should try to understand the triune of business, government, and society—while never forgetting that ESG factors bridge the axes between business and government, government and society, and business and society.

- My advice to CEOs? *Turn up.* Go to Washington. Travel to Beijing. Go to wherever the issues, opportunities, or trouble spots are emergent. Understand them and figure out your position on them.

- Leadership gives CEOs a podium, and not just for their own opinions or perspectives. That podium also gives leaders access to the places where problems and opportunities exist. Enterprises and boards should appoint CEOs who have the energy and optimism to be *present*—and who also have the *podium presence* to handle all present and future geopolitical realities and concerns.

- Contemporary leadership requires an expanded bandwidth that considers both the local and global perspective. In this century, CEOs need to go simultaneously wide and deep.

5

The New
Long-Termism

When I began leading Dow in 2004, my primary mission was to transform our portfolio and bring us forward into the twenty-first century. I *had* to innovate, and over the next fourteen years, I did, over and over.

A common refrain I heard back then was, "We need people on the commercial side of things who can tell us when market opportunities present themselves."

"You're right about that," I would answer, "but the biggest issue for us now is to fire up our labs, ignite our discovery engines, look for breakthroughs, hire the right people, and start changing the makeup of our R&D portfolio from an *expense* item to an *invest* item."

I didn't have to do any of this. I could have avoided all risks and kept the company as it was. But playing it safe is both a fallacy and a fantasy. It presumes that CEOs are in control of a hundred different variables, and they're not. At a time when financial owners, global institutions, governments, and corporate measurement systems are failing us, who can afford to play it safe? As CEO, I was also aware of the traps and downsides of success and incumbency, among them that when you stick to your own lane you tend to overlook the other lanes. A good analogy is the German Autobahn. The recommended speed limit is 80 miles per hour, but in some sections, drivers can drive whatever speed they want. Slow is fast; faster whizzes by; and the fastest lane of all nears Formula One speeds. Ambling along isn't an option. You'll get clipped or rammed or run over.

Since I retired from Dow, people have often asked what I learned from the transformation I led—the creation of a new Dow, a new DuPont, and a new crop-science technology company in Corteva. The acquisitions of Rohm and Haas and Corning. The doubling of our footprint in Texas and Louisiana. The launch of a massive new operation in Saudi Arabia. Working alongside four US presidents and publishing an influential book about manufacturing. "What would you have done differently?"

My response is always the same: "I wouldn't have tried it. It's too hard to change culture. Another thing? It's lucky human beings don't know how hard things are in life—because isn't that why we do what we do and keep pushing forward?" I bring this up because Dow is also where I learned firsthand about the epidemic of short-termism.

At Dow, our project return decisions were always fifteen years minimum. Mergers and acquisitions in a normal non-high-growth sector won't return the capital allocated to them in a time frame shorter than eight to fifteen years. This means that whenever we allocated a single dollar on a project or acquisition, it could take anywhere from eight to fifteen years before we began yielding the financial outcome of the original investment hypothesis. Eight to fifteen years, you say? Isn't that a long time? (In today's private equity model, after all, five years is considered an eternity.) But let me clarify what I mean when I say I would never have tried it.

The transformation I strategized for Dow would take at least ten years to execute. (Nothing I did at Dow fell short of a twenty-year horizon.) Dow was on a roll at the time and exceedingly profitable. When I tried to explain my strategy to the markets, I ran headfirst into the realities and limitations of short-termism. I also found out that most of the owners of Dow's stock weren't "owners" at all, not in the way I defined the word. They were *renters* of Dow's stock. They were *value investors*, accustomed to a fixed, traditional profile and an unvarying formula. Dow, for them, was predictably, comfortingly cyclical. The company made money for a while. Then the stock dipped. Maybe we lost money, ideally not for long. Then the stock rose again, and investors took their profits. The only concern that value investors had was around the volume and dependability of Dow's dividend.

Someone once said that just as countries get the leaders they deserve, companies attract the investors they deserve. Absent among many of Dow's shareholders were investors who believed in our long-term growth. Whenever I explained the forward-looking strategies I had in mind to our investor base, the response was typically, "That sounds interesting, Andrew—but for our purposes, how much money do you plan on making this year? Wait, you say you want to focus on R&D? But you guys are terrible at R&D! What makes you think you can develop new products in higher margins in less than five years? Wait—you plan on acquiring a company? But you guys are bad at acquiring things! In fact, you're known for making the worst capital decisions at the worst possible time by buying high and selling low!"

The message, or warning, I kept brushing aside was that investors didn't care about my long-term ambitions or visions for Dow. They wanted short-term profits, full stop. Our investor class found Dow's cyclical share price reassuring. What made me different from any of our other CEOs who came in thinking they could transform Dow and restore it to its past glory?

Again, it would have been easier to tell the board that our investors weren't interested in a "new Dow." I could have sold off an asset or two (like agriculture) and sat back as Dow was inevitably privatized. The variability of our income streams would be treated more benignly in a private equity setting than it would in a public company. Wasn't this the fate of Nova, Lyondell, and Huntsman, competitors of Dow that private equity firms had swallowed up, carved up, and repurposed? But in the end, I told our investors that we were under no obligation to follow suit. Ours was and still is a growth story.

The fact is, unless you're a new company in an apparently limitless growth sector that triggers "fear of missing out" (or FOMO) in investors, there is virtually no incentive to give up short-term results in favor of longer-term visions and strategies.

Neuroscientists often remind us that this is an adaptive function of the human brain. If someone offers us ten dollars today, or twenty dollars next year, most of us choose the ten. (After all, the world might not even exist a year from now.) Companies, executives, investors, and boards say the same thing: the long view matters. Seldom, though, do they follow through. The prospect of weaker quarterly performance persuades most companies, leaders, and investors to put aside longer future growth in favor of shorter-term gains.

What about considering the ten-versus-twenty-dollar question through another lens? Reframe this choice in the context of climate change or social justice or any other parameter that improves humanity or the Earth. Money is nothing more than an output of an activity that has been assigned a value—and the values we place on those activities are transforming as we speak. Focusing on the short term and the long term at the same time doesn't mean tearing up the ten-dollar bill and waiting for the twenty to appear a year from now. In fact, by creating institutions *today* for *tomorrow*, we are effectively transforming the ten-dollar bill *into* a twenty. The changes we make today will only gain in size and value until the day comes when the ten and the twenty are indistinguishable.

Now reverse the thought. Accepting the ten-dollar bill and forgoing the twenty means that you miss out on the potential, and the right, to receive that twenty (or thirty or forty) a year from now. There might not even *be* a twenty in twelve months, or the twenties in circulation might be so degraded in value as to be worthless. I don't know about you, but I would much prefer to work with the ten *and* the twenty.

The Importance of the Long Term

In 2013, Dominic Barton, the former managing director of McKinsey, published an article, "Capitalism for the Long Term," in the *Harvard Business Review*. Barton noted that the public blamed businesses and other private sector institutions for the global financial crisis. He argued that to address a growing demand for large organizations to deliver improved societal outcomes, instead of focusing exclusively on their shareholders, capitalism "needed to undergo a reckoning."[1]

Three years later, then US vice president Joe Biden published an article in the *Wall Street Journal*, arguing that short-termism weakened the American economy.[2] The trend of denying, or delaying, long-run investment for the sake of increasing near-term stock price, Biden wrote, threatened long-lasting prosperity in the US. With private investment arguably the leading stimulator of economic growth in America, businesses needed to build for the long term—but were seldom asked to. Biden blamed a variety of factors. Executive compensation linked to short-term success that typically leads to increases in companies' share prices. Poor regulations that permit unlimited share buyback. Tax laws that define "long term" as a year or longer. A financial ecosystem that emphasizes quarterly earnings. Lastly, "a subset of activist investors determined to steer companies away from further investment."[3]

Today, business leaders are operating their businesses in a world that requires more from those enterprises than the mere enrichment of shareholders. They are being asked to deliver better outcomes for *everybody*. Many of the points Barton raised nearly a decade ago—that business and finance need to jettison their focus on the short term in favor of the long term; that leaders have a responsibility, even a mandate, to serve the interests of *all* stakeholders; that corporate boards should be allowed to govern like owners—are even truer today than they were back then. Yet not much has changed.

As I said in the introduction, as humans we seem to have lost our innate capacity to carry out long-term planning. It's hard to see beyond ourselves and our moment in time. This myopia shows up conspicuously in the face of climate emergency. Every day we are reminded of extreme weather as we look out the window, browse online, or watch the nightly news. But how can we figure out where we are today as a human race, much less in ten, twenty, or fifty years, if the only thing our political and business industries care about is realizing profits in the next ninety days or cobbling together stances and beliefs that ensure their reelection four years from now?

Whether you are a company or a country, it's not a question of choosing between short-term metrics and long-term strategies. It's not *either/or*, it's *and*. Put another way, companies and leaders need to build for the long term while executing on their short-term objectives. To many companies, this probably sounds like a stretch. But it *must* be done.

The Origins of Short-Termism

When did short-termism begin? Hard to say. But it was surely accelerated by two phenomena that prioritized immediate profits to the detriment of longer-term growth, namely, desktop software and the rise of the activist investor class.

It wasn't until the 1990s that the corporate world was introduced to software that allowed analysts and traders to do financial engineering on their desktop computers. MBA graduates—for example, Ivy League graduates in their early thirties who had never run anything, much less a company—began to study and dissect spreadsheets, the result being sum-of-the-parts analysis, or SOTP. Traders could now assess the individual businesses in a company's portfolio and compare their individual performances to the company's overall value. If the rating of an individual business was lower than that of the company itself, it was a sign that activist hedge funds should take notice.

In the 1980s and 1990s, activist hedge funds went by other names. They were greenmailers. Or corporate raiders. Regardless of what they called themselves, their playbook seldom varied. Their strategy was to target a company with one or more underperforming businesses in its portfolio. Usually their argument was that the only reason an underperforming business hadn't been sold off was that the CEO and the board didn't want to divest a legacy institution to which they were sentimentally attached. Do things *our* way, the hedge funds said, and the results will exceed shareholder expectations.

Then and now, most activist hedge funds will tell you they are doing God's work. The business world *needs* them. Their mandate, as they see it, is to protect David-like small investors from Goliath-like bad management, pampered CEOs, and sleepy boards. Do what they say, and they will create long-term value by forcing companies to shape up and do the right thing. That's what they say at least.

Others see activist hedge funds differently. The term *pump and dump* comes to mind, referring to the artificial inflation of a stock in order to sell it later at a higher price. So does the difference between "owners"— investors who hold company stock for the long term—and "renters," investors who focus exclusively on short-term profits. In exchange for buying a small percentage of a large enterprise—sometimes no more than 1 or 2 percent—activist hedge funds accrue a share of voice disproportionate to their investment. The quickest, easiest way they have found to make money is by robbing from the future to pay for the present, otherwise known as "bringing earnings forward." They focus on selling *now*. After all, most activist investors will have moved on in three years' time.

Once an underperforming business is sold off, or a company split up, the activist hedge fund loses interest. Theirs was a onetime gain. The longer-term fate of the portfolio business doesn't matter. They sell their stock, pocket the profits, and scope out their next target. The profits they earn accrue to their huge institutional clients, like TIAA-CREF, the Teachers Insurance and Annuity Association, and CalPERS, the California Public Employees' Retirement System. These firms manage the pensions and 401(k)s of teachers, police officers, and firefighters. Ironically, as hedge funds accumulate sizable capital from blue-collar and white-collar people while agitating for change in large companies, they are directly responsible for substantial job losses among that same blue- and white-collar employee base.

The Specter of Activist Hedge Funds

It's impossible to tell when an activist hedge fund is on the move. At least not while it's happening. Only three months into the new year does a CEO realize that last December an activist hedge fund began buying shares in the company. If CEOs needed reminding, they can turn on cable news or go online.

The rise of activist hedge funds wouldn't be possible without a voracious finance media ecosystem. Preinternet, agitating a company took time and careful planning. But in a twenty-four-hour news cycle, hedge funds can plant a rumor with a media contact or publish a letter on their websites addressed to a company CEO and board. Many activist hedge funds are skilled at media relations. They position themselves as radicals and reformers battling against a lazy, swampy status quo. Cable TV and social media find these stories irresistible. Soon, with the media's help, activist hedge funds have succeeded in infiltrating the top tiers of a company, at which point CEOs find themselves under pressure from shareholders, board members, and local communities to respond.

More problematic are the campaigns that activist hedge funds wage against these stakeholders. Buttressing their mandate for change are reams of misleading, skillfully massaged financial data. An activist hedge fund might hire an external company to publish a benchmark study of how a single portfolio business performs relative to its peers that concludes that during one recent ninety-day period, the portfolio business was in the bottom quartile. The study finds its way to the company's portfolio manager, who sees that the hedge fund has a good track record of buying into companies whose share prices eventually pop. Why not encourage the board to go along with these changes, especially given that the portfolio manager's bonus is linked to that year's performance?

Having now joined forces with the portfolio manager, an activist hedge fund proceeds to launch a campaign against the CEO. It's personal too. Nothing is taboo, including the CEO's family and children. Personal attacks generate more headlines, and headlines beget more headlines. Creating scandal also gets an activist hedge fund a meeting with top leadership sooner rather than later. This meeting can be used to headhunt other investors eager to exert pressure on the company or, more cynically, to raise capital to finance future attacks on other companies. Ultimately, activist hedge funds are hoping the board will cave in and fire the CEO. With the top spot free, the activist fund fills it with a candidate of its own choosing. The next step is demanding board representation. Very soon the business is focused almost exclusively on short-term profits.

Ironically, the success of activist hedge funds is attributable to moves companies were planning to make anyway (which is what happened at Dow). The hedge fund simply acted as an accelerant. But Wall Street doesn't care about backstories or scenarios that may have played out behind the scenes. It celebrates success and profits. No matter how things *actually* happened, Wall Street frames the arrival of a new CEO and new board representation as a triumph for the activist investor.

If it sounds like I speak from experience, I do. The scenario I just described happened to Dow when an activist investor targeted Dow in the years leading up to Dow's 2017 merger with DuPont. In the end, the attack on Dow turned into an opportunity with a second activist investor, allowing both parties to enhance a merger the board and I had been planning for a dozen years. Today, both activists would claim ownership of the Dow-DuPont union. Neither one knew that my own strategy was to ensure that the merger became a win-win for all sides, since the idea of Dow merging with DuPont was hardly a new one.

Two years into my CEO tenure, DuPont was one of three companies (Rohm and Haas and Syngenta were the other two) I was pursuing. In late 2006, or early 2007, DuPont's then CEO gave me the hardest possible no. DuPont, I was told, would *never* do a deal with Dow. We, Dow, were nothing more than Midwestern barbarians who traded in commodities. Dow could never understand a high-tech company like DuPont. The Dow board and I considered making a hostile bid but ultimately decided against it, instead redoubling our pursuit of Rohm and Haas. In 2013 and 2014, I approached DuPont again, telling Ellen Kullman, the company's then CEO, that it was time Dow and DuPont did a deal. The idea was to create two companies, with DuPont being the agricultural entity (at the time DuPont was betting big on agriculture and biotech) and Dow the chemical and special materials business. It would be less a merger than an asset swap. Ellen entertained the prospect seriously, but she and I couldn't agree how to divide the assets. Sensing she was dragging things out, for the second time I again considered making a hostile run at DuPont. It was then (timing is everything) I found out Dow was being targeted by an activist investor.

The activist investor came into my life in the fourth quarter of 2013. Like most activist hedge funds, his fund had a time-tested strategy. Buy shares in companies they deemed to be underperforming. Fire existing management and replace them with new team members or favored outsiders. Break up the company. Maximize profitability in the short term. Then sell the stock. Move on to the next company. This activist fund had an impressive track record, too, having mounted attacks at several other high-profile companies. Adept at media relations, the activist was known for his public skirmishes and for publishing letters to CEOs and boards on the fund's website, accusing them of mismanagement and shareholder negligence. Knowing an activist fund was on the march against Dow, my team naturally worried I was in their sights.

That year, the activist and I both attended the World Economic Forum meeting in Davos. Knowing he was there, my team did everything possible to keep us from crossing paths. If we had, it would have been impossible for us not to discuss his plans for Dow. Confrontation was averted in the Swiss Alps, for a few days at least. Then, just as Davos was wrapping up, I arranged to appear on CNBC's *Squawk Box*, where I announced publicly that Dow would do a share buyback, thus preempting the arrival of the activist. Being short-circuited on cable TV couldn't have brightened the activist's day.

CEOs under attack are under no obligation to meet with an activist investor. They generally respond either by fighting, capitulating, running and hiding, or engaging. We decided to engage. When the activist requested a meeting, we agreed to one, during which I provided as much information as I could, though our discussions were limited to what was already in the public domain. Mostly, though, I listened: "Here is what's wrong with Dow, Andrew, and here's what I want you to do to fix it."

By way of context, at the time Dow had three divisions—agricultural, commodities, and downstream specialty (chemicals used in polymers, resins, adhesives, automotive, and acrylic derivatives, to name just a few). Our own long-term strategy, engineered to rebuild Dow for the new century, involved selling off the commodities division, doubling down on the agricultural side, and increasing our investment in downstream specialty. By contrast, the strategy proposed by the activist was to sell off two of Dow's three divisions. Ideally, in his view, we would become more like one of our commodity competitors, Lyondell, a company with no R&D costs, low capital output, and high returns. But the activist wasn't interested in the long term. His timeline was five years at most (some investors operate nowadays on a three-year timeline). This was the impasse he and I faced when we first met.

Mindful of his fund's reputation, I was wary. Making me more cautious was their impressive nine-out-of-ten hit rate of ousting boards and firing incumbent CEOs. This they accomplished in part by targeting company CEOs and sometimes their boards in public. The idea was that publicly disgraced CEOs would generate such negative PR for their companies that their performance risked being compromised. And with the activist fund circling Dow, the attempt to undercut my reputation got underway fast. It began with travel before branching out to include my family.

Like most large companies, Dow had strict policies around CEO travel. For security purposes, I used the company plane any time I flew anywhere, for business or pleasure. (If, say, I went on vacation with my family, I reimbursed Dow for the transportation costs.) To show I was using the Dow jet for frivolous purposes and putting one over on Dow, the activist employed a team whose job it was to track the tail number of the Dow plane. Around this time, Paula, my wife, was helping renovate a hotel in downtown Midland. Out of the blue came a bogus Reuters story alleging that Paula was bullying staffers and deserved the blame for any cost overruns. None of it was true, but it didn't matter.

When the story was published, it was hard not to detect the activist investor playbook at work. Several videos mocking me had already appeared on the activist fund's website. Along with tracking my air travel, they also hired people to track me. I was always looking over my shoulder, whether I was having dinner with my wife at the country club or walking the sidewalks of New York on the way to see a weekend show. The goal was to create the narrative that Dow's CEO was spoiled, indolent, and out of touch, and that if the board was paying attention, they would fire him and bring in someone new.

I was never a CEO ivory-tower type. I visited factories, knew the names of many of the factory workers and security guards, drove my own car versus having a driver, and went grocery shopping in the local supermarket. People who knew me even glancingly knew I wasn't the kind of CEO I was being painted out to be. That was probably the hardest part of all this—defending myself, my wife, and my children from a torrent of personal attacks while continuing to take meetings with the activist and doing all this without betraying any emotion. I also had my hands full assuring Dow's customers that the company wasn't being affected by the attack and that we would continue being value-add innovators as well as the best chemistry company on the planet. Nothing would change. The company wouldn't be broken up. Neither our physical plants nor our employee bases in Michigan and Texas would suffer. Looking back, I'm proud of how I stood up to all that pressure.

But I was up against a tough adversary, and some of his arguments couldn't help but land. "They have some very good points to make," a Dow owner would tell me. "Maybe you should listen to them." Reminding the owner that the activist and I spoke very regularly, I would explain point by point why the activist fund's strategy made no sense for Dow. Nonetheless, I assembled a special team that included Dow's then CFO, my corporate strategy leader, my general counsel, corporate secretary, vice president of public affairs, and a few key outside advisers with experience defending against activist attacks. My playbook and the activist's, we agreed, would differ in all ways. I would keep calm. I wouldn't get flustered. I wouldn't raise my voice. I wouldn't engage in media firefights. I would continue ignoring the personal attacks against me and my family.

In the meantime, we were putting together our own strategy.

As we did, I remained in ongoing communication and engagement with my lead director and board. We repeatedly confirmed that strategy. We understood the short-term gains inherent in the strategy proposed by the activist fund versus the long-term gains inherent in our lengthily deliberated and thoroughly researched long-term strategy. We also agreed to ignore the noise and commotion and to change our investors' mindset and not be swayed by the activist fund, which after all used selective information and owned only 2 percent of the company. The only way to do this was to make sure there was a win in sight for all parties. Among other things, my end goal involved convincing the activist fund that our plan aligned with *theirs*. I was positive we could do so—and create that win-win. Activist investors focus on only one thing—victory. They repurpose the publicity they garner from their latest attack to attract more media attention and investors, and raise more money to underwrite the *next* attack. My goal, as I said, was to make the activist hedge fund feel like victors. At the same time, as CEO, my responsibility was to Dow and its stakeholders. If the activist *did* end up winning, Dow would be cut up into pieces that wouldn't last more than a few years. The short-term owners would make a lot of money, whereas the real owners and stakeholders would be robbed of the opportunity to make more money over the long term. I was determined not to let that happen.

As I saw it, it was a question of survival, and survival was in my blood. After emigrating to Darwin, Australia, my grandfather spent the next few years working in a slaughterhouse. My mother barely spoke any English. My ancestors were people who somehow figured out how to eke out a living on a dry, rocky, barren, distant Greek island. They were unskilled workers who traveled to the northern tip of Australia hoping for a better life for their children and grandchildren. I had more than enough survival genes in my DNA. They would come in use.

I was up against someone who believed I was trashing Dow's stock and deserved to be fired. I would counter by showing him that ours was the right strategy and business model all along. To get there, first I had to figure out how to create an environment where we were talking to the other side and they were processing the facts logically and unemotionally. The attacks on my family and me were difficult to tolerate. The activist had made me out to look like a person and a leader I wasn't. But my personal injury was irrelevant. What mattered was winning on behalf of Dow, our employees, and *all* our stakeholders.

These instincts informed the strategy I came up with that played out beneath the public face of diplomacy.

As I mentioned, in addition to trying to get the CEO of the company under attack fired, the activist had a history of demanding board representation.

Soon, not surprisingly, he asked that Dow appoint three new members to our board. As part of our due diligence, my team and I studied other boards the activist had coerced into doing his bidding. We soon realized that engaging in a proxy battle was untenable. It was too risky. Even if we won, we would lose. The fund was liable to sway enough of Dow's institutional investors to vote against us. How could we settle with the activist so it didn't look like we were surrendering our vision and strategy while giving him just enough of a win so he could assure his own investors he had succeeded in making all the changes he was after?

At this point, a *second* activist investor began inching his way toward the center of the gameboard. At the same time Dow was being targeted, this second activist was using a similar playbook at DuPont. This second activist believed DuPont was being mismanaged. He had already installed two activist-approved directors to the DuPont board, one of whom, Ed Breen, would eventually be named DuPont's CEO.

Under the influence of the second activist, DuPont was pivoting away from its strategy, in the works for more than a decade, of transforming itself into a biotech company. But this second activist had an advantage at DuPont that Dow's activist lacked at our company. DuPont was performing poorly at the time and was vulnerable to attack, whereas Dow was performing strongly and delivering results. I had been advocating for a Dow-DuPont merger since before being named CEO, having made my intentions clear in the manifesto I wrote back when I was in the running. In fact, the wisdom of a Dow-DuPont merger was one of the few points on which Dow's activist and I agreed. But there was little value in going around saying that.

A few weeks later, I met with the DuPont activist. "What do you want to do with the company?" I asked. He replied that he thought DuPont should merge with Dow. "Huh," I said, "you're probably right." Soon the DuPont activist was telling Ed Breen, DuPont's new interim CEO, that Breen should do a deal with Dow.

Soon after Ed was named DuPont's interim CEO, I called his office, and Ed and I agreed to meet a few days later in a coffee shop at a Ramada Inn on the outskirts of Philadelphia, where he lived. We were the only customers there. Together, on the back of a napkin, we sketched out the contours of a merger. The two companies couldn't have been more complementary and value creating or more of a natural fit. Many of our businesses were in similar markets but in different areas of the value chain or in different applications.

Instead of Dow and DuPont exchanging assets, my idea was that the two companies merge and split, a strategy known as a reverse Morris trust. It's one of the most complex financial engineering transactions there is, one that had literally never been done with two companies of Dow and DuPont's scale. Before going ahead, Breen said he had to talk to the DuPont activist, and a few days later, I found myself walking the activist through the details.

Success has many fathers and mothers. Soon this concept became DuPont's idea, driven by the second activist's firm and Ed Breen. We at Dow stayed low and kept quiet, doubling down on the idea that a Dow-DuPont merger was an idea whose time had come and that the DuPont activist's firm had inspired it. Throughout this period, I continued having regular conversations with Ed and the two activists, Dow's and DuPont's. The strategy of making everyone feel like a winner was working. Our activist settled for a fifteen-month time frame to back off and agreed not to engage in a proxy battle if Dow was willing to accept certain conditions. Dow would also take on two new board members nominated by the activist's fund. It was then that we insisted on a condition of our own. In exchange for nominating the activist's two board members, Dow would get to nominate two new board members of our own.

The board voted in two of the activist fund's three candidates. During the interviewing process, I made it clear to both men that despite the activist's sponsorship—and him giving them additional shares from his own portfolio, which increased their compensation beyond that of the other directors—they now had a fiduciary duty to Dow and its stakeholders. They no longer represented the activist or the activist's firm. One other thing: for the sake of transparency and trustworthiness, every time they were in touch with their boss, they had to keep me and Dow's lead director in the loop. Left unsaid was that by keeping us apprised, I could be assured that neither man was leaking insider information back to the activist fund.

It was time for part two of my strategy. During the onboarding process, I made sure both new board members received a thoroughgoing education in everything Dow. Under strict NDAs, we gave them real data and numbers. I sent in teams of Dow people to give them both a crash seminar on all aspects of Dow's business. Implicit in the activist's insistence on appointing two board members was the hope that he was installing obstructionists and interventionists. We were sure that if we showed the two new board members that we had a better strategy for long-term value creation, they would align with the rest of the board. The plan worked.

Both men quickly understood—and supported—Dow's strategy. The data we gave them detailing my plans for the company turned them both into Dow-strategy converts. They may have come aboard as nominees of the activist fund. But now they were aligned and doing what every director had a responsibility to do—represent *all* shareholders. What's more, when we were in full discussions with our board about DuPont's interest in a merger, and how Dow had a methodology in place to make it happen, it was obvious they saw the value and the returns. During the meeting, I gave both activist funds, Dow's and DuPont's, full credit for the strategy.

In the end, the Dow activist believed he had forced Dow and our leadership team to capitulate. In fact, Dow had been on that same path for more than a dozen years. The path twisted and turned, and there is no question both activists were responsible for accelerating and enhancing where the company ended up, but it had nothing to do with their individual strategies, both of which would have resulted in different outcomes. Dow's board and management team stayed the course. The way I saw it, everyone won.

From then on, I was vigilant in all my public communications. "We have listened to a wide variety of viewpoints," I told Dow's investors. "A marriage with DuPont makes perfect sense. In fact, we have always supported the idea of merging Dow's and DuPont's agricultural businesses. What we have now is an extraordinary confluence of circumstances and people and businesses that allows us to transform Dow and DuPont for the next few decades." This message was consistent with what both activists wanted—and it resulted in Dow not only surviving but thriving.

A series of articles later published in the *Wall Street Journal* confirmed that I had been pursuing a merger between Dow and DuPont for a long time. Other accounts gave credit for the merger to one or the other activist. Today both activists might claim they forced the deal to happen, but regardless, their contributions certainly enhanced the deal. It doesn't matter. As I said, everybody won.

When the merger was announced, Dow's stock rose into the seventies, at which point, inevitably, the two activists began selling off their positions in Dow and DuPont. Soon both were gone. As for the two board members approved by the activist's firm, one retired, and the second eventually joined the board of directors at DuPont.

Again, to my mind, the biggest victor was Dow. DuPont had always been the top prize due to its agricultural portfolio, and the best marriage possible was between Dow's agricultural and chemical businesses and DuPont's bioscience division. With the merger in place, we created a successful runway for both Dow and DuPont for the next two decades, while giving birth to a new company, Corteva. Any other option would have been destructive; if we did it any other way, there would never have been a Corteva. In all modesty, I was instrumental in making the merger happen and injecting new life into two great American companies. Armed with new portfolios, Dow and DuPont had new relevance for this century. But what came next wasn't always smooth going, and I didn't get 100 percent of what I wanted.

Ed Breen arrived at DuPont from Tyco International, a company made famous by its high-living CEO, Dennis Kozlowski. Ed had broken Tyco up into half a dozen businesses, delivering huge value to the company. Unfortunately for me, Ed—and the hedge funds that had his back—still had the idea of taking our new Dow and DuPont units and reconfiguring them one more time before the deal was solidified. Ed and I battled constantly over this, and we both ended up having to compromise, with me telling my board: "If we don't do some of what they want, the owners and the hedge fund crowd will keep fighting us. We need to eliminate the noise." In the end, I achieved 80 percent of the position I was after, versus 100 percent.

(That said, the learning point that came out of this is that if you insist on 100 percent, you risk ending up with zero—and 80 percent is a lot better than nothing.)

This meant that the new Dow was created minus some key businesses that were moved over to the new DuPont. In an era of the disappearing conglomerate, where many owners prefer valuing the pieces of a business rather than the whole, Ed set to work selling off various DuPont units, satisfying the hedge funds by providing them with immediate profits. After the merger, Ed was named CEO, and I was named executive chairman. Ed was directly responsible for the new DuPont and the agriculture business, and I was directly responsible for Dow and our materials business. We didn't have to work together closely except when there was overlap—but those overlaps triggered some fierce debates, as Ed and I fundamentally disagreed about what belonged to Dow and what belonged to DuPont.

By then, it was clear that DuPont under Ed planned to follow the Tyco playbook, splitting the new DuPont, which then consisted of four divisions, further. The value creation this generated surely pleased the DuPont activist's fund, but a minimized DuPont also foreclosed on a future long-term value creation story. Among the dangers of short-termism, after all, is that companies stop investing in R&D because the payback is too far off. They are left with the choice of scaling back or splitting up. Meanwhile, they can win in their current market, at least until their products and technologies no longer work or are lapped and replaced.

The DuPont I knew once is slowly vanishing, but its fate is beyond Dow's control. By contrast, Dow and Corteva keep going from strength to strength, with higher and higher values. The new Dow features a stable portfolio with growth vectors and platforms worldwide. But overall, a merger primed by the acquisitions of Rohm and Haas and Dow Corning, along with the divestment of a handful of legacy businesses, and Dow's own continually strong earnings, means the marriage between Dow and DuPont merger can be counted as a big success.

During this time, I also introduced a new playbook that is widely used in other companies today.

If an activist hedge fund targets your company, the advice I give CEOs is to pivot, defer—and engage. Is there a path to give activists what they want in the short term without surrendering your long-term strategies? Take a bow to whatever they are proposing. Execute a few of their points. Give them time and a runway. But don't ever acknowledge the extent to which their strategy duplicates yours. When activists propose adding new board members, select them in—but select your own board members at the same time. Not only were we able to convert the two activist-approved board members to Dow's strategy, but the two additional directors we appointed turned out to be sensational. One had extensive experience running a bank, and the other was the former second-in-command at IBM. Both understood the necessary trade-offs between strategy and money and that money doesn't appear magically once a company has been broken up. (A broken-up company simply brings up new questions, such as "What's next?" and "Now what?")

I struggle to find a lot of positive comments to say about activist investors. Unlike private equity firms, many of whom deserve credit for cleaning up businesses that have lost their way or that are careless with their resources or that deserve a wake-up call, activist investors generally target solid, high-performing, high-profile enterprises. That isn't to say some companies don't deserve to be attacked or streamlined or even taken over and dismantled. But not when an attack is predicated on the hypothesis that the shareholder comes first when it's really about increasing a hedge fund's profitability at the expense of companies' future R&D development, not to mention at the expense of their communities and stakeholders.

The rate and pace of activist hedge funds targeting good-performing companies has decreased in recent years. These attacks are also less publicized, less inflammatory, and more collaborative, a likely consequence of earlier battles, including the one we waged at Dow. When activist funds targeted Procter & Gamble and Occidental Petroleum, both companies were quick to accommodate them. "Show me what you think I should be doing differently," these businesses said, "and we will explain our strategy to you in turn. If some of what you say makes sense, we will consider incorporating it." The new playbook, then, is more synergistic than confrontational. I like to think that the deal we struck with Dow's and DuPont's activist investors was a harbinger of a more enlightened way of coming to terms with differing opinions, perspectives, and strategies.

Another positive is that the activist investor playbook has shifted in direct proportion to the growing savviness of companies. Activist hedge funds have obliged companies to adopt new lines of defense. Many businesses have acquired board members who understand activism and are also skilled capital allocators. Companies have had to become their *own* activist investors and are now asking themselves the hard questions, like Are we challenging ourselves? Are we stress-testing our own strategy?

Nor do I wish to imply that activist investors are solely responsible for the epidemic of short-termism in the business world. Still, if someone asked me the best way to reduce short-termism, I would begin with the underlying causes, starting with big institutional investors and encompassing portfolio managers.

Institutional clients like the Capital Group, CalPERS, and TIAA-CREF that invest with hedge funds are as complicit as the hedge funds themselves. Institutional clients talk at length about long-term value add, the environment, society, social justice, and the license to operate. They then proceed to align themselves with activist hedge funds that, in turn, impel companies to focus exclusively on their upcoming quarterly earnings and stock buybacks. By investing with those funds, institutional clients can keep their hands clean while allowing the middlemen to do all the dirty work. Letting activist hedge funds enrich themselves while institutional clients do nothing to hold businesses to account over the long term is another failure of capitalism and a dynamic that contributes to companies operating using only short-term metrics. In the end the shareholders of the company under attack are the ones most negatively affected by the long-term consequences of a diminished, hacked-apart institution.

Nor are many portfolio managers immune from criticism. Imagine that as CEO I announced that my company is making a substantial investment in a Saudi Arabian plant. It will take us anywhere from five to ten years for us to realize any returns. That's too long for most portfolio managers, whose year-end bonuses rely on what their company is doing right now. In the future, bonuses need to connect to metrics including a company's long-term performance, innovation, and efficiency.

Also overdue are regulatory changes. Present-day regulations make it impossible for companies to steel themselves against outside attacks. Companies have no idea a hedge fund is on the march until three months after they buy into those companies. Beyond a certain financial threshold, company stock ledgers are hidden, giving activists a ninety-day head start to approach investors and get them aboard while poisoning the well against the CEO, the board, and the company's long-term strategies. That threshold needs to be lowered. No wonder the number of publicly owned companies continues to decline.

Finally, if an activist appears in your company with the goal of eliminating an incumbent CEO, or replacing the board, a rule should be in place requiring that activist to stick around for at least five years. If the activist seeks to transform the strategy and the portfolio, he should remain in place twice as long. There is no other way to ensure that all parties align on long-term strategy.

Strategies for the New Long Term

From 1985 to 2005, the funding and flow of capital increased by a thousandfold. That meant a thousand times more money began making its way across the globe. It also meant the world's political and financial orders had consensually agreed to funnel money toward addressing short-term crises, as opposed to coming together to create longer-term win-win fiscal policies and solutions. That ethos still exists today in a few oversized hedge funds that, as present-day fiscal overlords, take it upon themselves to redefine the meaning of "horizon."

The measured decline in the number of listed companies worldwide, and especially on Wall Street indices, is the direct result of the ninety-day march through the next quarter required by companies. The reality is that many businesses are long-cycle industries. While remaking Dow during my own tenure, I committed to building chemical plants that would take two decades to become profitable. Today, five years is too long. Three years is too long. What do "short term" and "long term" even mean for companies in this century?

In the 1980s, when the phrase (and bestselling book) *Barbarians at the Gate* appeared, the ownership model was five years. The investor community back then considered a five-year time period to be risibly short. Nowadays, a five-year ownership plan is practically the definition of "stable." This is one of the reasons why more and more public sector companies are casting longing glances over at the private equity side and murmuring, "I wish I had the kind of owner who allowed me to make investments that are necessary to grow this company." Privately held US companies like Cargill, Koch, and Berkshire Hathaway, to name just a few, have been enormously successful in their acquisitions of public companies unbeloved by the investment community but that have grown exponentially under private ownership.

But in general, the public ownership model of corporate America is incongruous with the innovation and ESG model that society is demanding in this century. Unless companies and CEOs can simultaneously produce short-term results within the context of longer-term investment, and inside a high-growth space and time frame, it is almost impossible to pull off.

Imagine, for example, that a pharmaceutical company is willing to invest a billion dollars or more to develop a blockbuster drug that cures diabetes or Alzheimer's disease. The pharmaceutical industry is high risk, high liability, and high margin. The market, and investors, understand that the process of getting a potentially revolutionary drug to market will take anywhere from five to eight years. They also know that if everything goes according to plan, they will eventually see big returns.

But most other industries and companies lack similar regulatory controls and margins. Most of today's businesses are busy creating product lines or transitioning their model from yesterday's products to tomorrow's innovations. To do that, naturally, they need to invest in long-term R&D. Add to this the need to convert the way they manufacture products to zero emissions, meaning they now need to invest in new factories that remove CO_2 from smokestacks and eliminate emissions from landfills as they transition toward a recycle economy. Few investors are willing to tolerate a time span so long and indeterminate. Most would prefer to invest in funds that in turn invest in new green technologies, allowing them greater control. In sum, investors are both unwilling to support industries and enterprises as they seek to invest in innovation and R&D and *demanding* that those enterprises align with today's (and tomorrow's) ESG metrics. It's a conundrum.

One solution? The scorecards and metrics that determine whether an organization is successful must change. For decades they have stayed the same: What is the ROI on invested capital? What is the ROI on tangible capital? Equally static are the margins that are developed and reported on every ninety days. Today, if you are a leader contemplating the long-term capacity of your enterprise to create a sustainable business via your investments, you need to understand that the new costs of doing business in this century include a company-wide path to zero emissions and safe, efficacious, and 100 percent recyclable products that don't harm humanity or the environment along your entire value chain. None of these costs show up on a balance sheet. In fact, they represent two trains on the same track, traveling in opposite directions, and always on the verge of collision.

To date, society hasn't yet come up with any institution that could remake this scenario or alter, through their owners, the behavior of boards or CEOs. It must. Putting aside private ownership, the metrics needed today to convince a public owner to adapt to the public will redress the negative impact humanity has had on our planet await future development. Boards need to ask themselves three questions. First, are environmental, societal, and governmental metrics embedded in our enterprise scorecard and are the CEO and management reporting those metrics to the board at every meeting?

Second, are our company's environmental, societal, and governance metrics expressed as *financial* outcomes, including all long-term costs and investments associated with those outcomes?

And third, does our board include one or more directors who bring long-term thinking, strategic planning, and strategic direction to our organization?

The final questions are for CEOs. Have you shifted earnings reports to twice a year versus every quarter? Are you educating your asset owners and asset managers without being told to? Is your enterprise committed to a zero-impact-on-the-planet strategy, and will you hold it accountable via the appropriate allocation of capital?

You must inspect what you expect, according to the old axiom. This means that without rigorous monitoring during all points of a corporate journey, goals and initiative can go astray. Fortunately, this can be solved.

For more than a century, publicly owned corporations have had a single stakeholder, shareholder, and owner making all the decisions about the best ways to allocate capital. Business schools have taught these owners to become financial wizards and to limit their input exclusively to a company's financial dimensions. That means that the owner whose job it is to allocate capital is ignorant about all the ways those capital allocations affect the behavior of the *operators* of those assets. Asset operators in turn don't understand capital allocation well enough to converse with the financial owner about why capital allocation in the medium to long term matters to *their* short term. In short, there is no convergence. In an ideal universe, governments would create regulations to force the two together. You can't have a conversation about environment, society, and governance without first understanding a company's financials—and the conversation about those financials won't happen without first considering a company's ESG factors. These two need to be brought together in the next decade, and the only way to do that is by developing the right metrics and processes that result in *lasting* behavioral changes.

Some progress has been made—but not enough. Quarterly guidance is an outdated practice that promotes short-termism since it attracts short-term shareholders. Some organizations have shifted their focus away from the short term in their earnings guidance practices, but roughly one in five companies in the S&P 500 today still provide quarterly guidance. This also needs to change.

Another area where change is overdue is CEO tenure. The length of time most CEOs stay in the job (historically a way of measuring the length of an organization's outlook) also suffers from chronic short-termism. In

2016, the average tenure of a CEO was 8 years. Today it is 6.9 years. On the other side of things, investors continue to have disconcertingly short-term perspectives. High-frequency traders, and payment for order flow, are both contributing to a shrinking average holding period for stocks.

In "Capitalism for the Long Term," Dominic Barton pointed out that executives "must infuse their organizations with the perspective that serving the interests of all major stakeholders—employees, suppliers, customers, creditors, communities, the environment—is not at odds with the goal of maximizing corporate value; on the contrary, it's essential to achieving that goal."[4]

I wrote about ESG metrics in chapter 1—but as everyone knows, they are widespread in corporate strategy and a growing factor in the investment process for both asset owners and asset managers. According to Morningstar, ESG funds secured $51.1 billion of net new money from investors in 2020, more than double the amount of 2019.[5] A BNP Paribas survey also showed that the percentage of both retail and institutional investors that apply ESG principles to at least a quarter of their portfolios increased from 48 percent in 2017 to 75 percent globally in 2019. These trends indicate that corporations, asset managers, and asset owners alike have begun to recognize the convergence of values and value—the idea that combining strong values with serving the interests of all major stakeholders maximizes financial value in the long term.

Nor is this a trend likely to fade as businesses and investors prioritize other business strategies and principles. Longer-term ESG principles need to permeate a company's strategy. It's like the early days when financial institutions allowed digitization to infuse their corporate strategy, not only in the form of online banking statements for customers but throughout the entire organization. ESG factors should and must be no different.

In addition to CEO tenure, another important task of governance has to do with executive compensation. Present-day compensation still doesn't incentivize executives to act like company owners. Instead of linking executive compensation to share price, why not link it instead to longer-term metrics like innovation and efficiency? This would extend the time frame for executive evaluation, while also creating downside risk for executives.

Society today is demanding that institutions of all kinds reinvent themselves in this century and focus more on long-term societal well-being. CEOs and companies need to move faster, and with more conviction, to focus both capital and capitalism on long-term visions and strategies. We must repurpose the regulations in *all* parameters around how we measure the success of an enterprise—and do it today *for* tomorrow.

Takeaways and Tools

- Short-termism is widespread across all enterprises today. Long-termism and short-termism aren't *either/or*, they're *and*. Leaders need to build for the long term while executing simultaneously on shorter-term objectives.

- A counterintuitive approach to operationalizing the long-term approach in your management team and board—one I did repeatedly in my time—is to engage in offense by neutralizing any attacks. Make it clear you can realize short-term profits and that short-term profits can be realized in any number of ways— but that any approach that disables long-term profits is *not* the way forward.

- To wit, cutting R&D and business-development budgets, while failing to invest in scope 3 emissions reductions, all of which are future based, will likely lead to short-term profits while foreclosing on potentially greater long-term profits.

- Implant in your management team and boardroom a portfolio optimization process that illustrates your thinking around capital allocation. Sometimes CEOs must get *out* of preexisting things to get *into* new things. You may have to divest activities that realize profits today or tomorrow but that aren't as robust or promising as investing in future R&D or business development.

- A good example is IBM, which recently divested its infrastructure business—computer farms that conduct baseload work for other companies—and is doubling down instead on AI. IBM's infrastructure business was profitable, but by divesting it, the company has freed up capital to invest elsewhere in the future.

- Prioritizing long-termism requires an intensive degree of engagement and capability at the board level. CEOs need to be better portfolio managers than owners. Let investors know you can do both. By giving investors what they want, you defeat short-termism without sacrificing what investors will *eventually* want.

ACTIVIST INVESTORS

- If an outside activist fund targets your business, meet with them. Pivot, defer, and engage. Figure out a way to give activists what they want in the short term without surrendering your enterprise's long-term strategy or vision. If the activist's strategy mirrors your own, don't let on.

- When an activist fund proposes adding new board members, select them in—but insist on adding the same number of your own board members at the same time.

- Incentives for portfolio managers must be reimagined, as must current regulations that make it impossible for businesses to foresee and steel themselves against future activist attacks.

- If an activist wants to eliminate the company CEO, the activist should be mandated to remain in the company for a minimum of five years. This number goes up to ten if the person seeks to transform the company's strategy or portfolio.

6

The New Role
of Boards

I t was 2007, and Dow was making its third attempt to do a significant deal in Saudi Arabia. But after a pair of earlier attempts hadn't worked out, why should this one be different?

Three years into my role as CEO, Dow was busy investing money extracting value from its existing assets. This strategy was running thin, and we were at risk of lagging the marketplace, shrinking, or, worse, becoming irrelevant. We needed to keep pace with the market and with customer growth.

At the time, the Middle East had the lowest-cost inputs on hydrocarbons (it still does), which is why I had proposed a deal, a joint venture between Dow and Saudi Aramco, Saudi Arabia's public petroleum and natural gas company. Dow and the Saudis would split the $25 billion cost down the middle. The only thing left was to convince our board to go along with it. If that sounds easy, it wasn't.

Some board members were hesitant, others outright negative. Few welcomed the idea of Dow doing an expensive deal in a part of the world most of them knew nothing about and had no reason to trust. Dow's two previous attempts to do a deal with Saudi Arabia had become part of corporate lore. The first was in 1981, when Dow's then CEO, who was

Jewish, canceled the deal when the Saudis denied him a travel visa for religious reasons. He was understandably furious—the entire company was—and that was that. The second attempt happened in the late 1990s. Dow's then CFO was sponsoring two deals, one in Oman, another in Saudi Arabia. By coincidence, both deals came before the board during my first-ever board meeting as the incoming CEO. Asked my opinion, I explained that the products the Saudi deal would bring Dow were the same products we were trying to divest. Was I missing something? I voted no. (Looking back, that might have been the moment the CFO decided to back-stab me, though the coup he tried to mount behind my back wouldn't be exposed for two more years.) The bigger point was that the Saudis were told for a second time that the Dow board wouldn't support an alliance. No wonder they were fed up with us.

To resurrect what was left of our relationship, I spent the first three years as CEO establishing my credentials and the basis of what I hoped could be a new relationship with the Saudis. Our CFO's deal may have been wrong, but it was with the right partner. By rebuilding what was good about it, I could create a new venture with a new product mix, eliminating risk via a series of new incentives. By 2006, the Saudis agreed to proceed with a deal if, again, I could get the support of the Dow board.

Marriage is one long conversation, Robert Louis Stevenson said—and so was winning over the board. The conversation between the board and me lasted six years. It was complex and now and then volatile. I stood firm. Dow would be taking a risk, but the bigger risk in my opinion was in *not* doing the deal. The Saudis were going to only expand their dominance in the hydrocarbon industry in the years ahead, as I saw it. To help convince board members to trust the Saudis (and the Middle East), I flew the entire board to Dhahran and, later, members of the Saudi team to Midland for follow-up discussions. I brought in knowledgeable former US and Saudi Arabian ambassadors and former UK prime minister Tony Blair to address members' apprehensions. I gave numerous presentations and risk analyses. I met repeatedly with the board, and with the four or five board members who were heading up our committees, and fully engaged Dow's lead independent director.

Later I calculated that I made eight round trips to Saudi Arabia overall. The last meeting I had with Saudi Aramco's then CEO lasted seven hours. He was as wary of Dow as our board was of the Saudis. How could Saudi Aramco be certain Dow wouldn't pull out of the deal? "You *can't* be certain," I said, "but all I can say is that I have flown here eight times in the past twelve months, more than I've visited any other country." I was a new CEO, I went on, who fully expected to have some tenure. If I could bring the board along with me, I knew the deal would be a huge success. (I was right, and today, ironically, having outlasted most of the players in place back then, I serve on Saudi Aramco's board of directors.)

I bring up the Dow-Saudi deal as an illustration of the twenty-first-century Activist Board (the term is mine). This template came into being in the early aughts in the wake of two earlier iterations, the Engaged Board and the Country Club Board. Establishing an Activist Board is minimum table stakes for any enterprise doing business in this century—and sets the stage for an even more advanced, effective model that I call the Enlightened Board.

Today's business leaders find themselves operating in a society that requires more from its institutions than the baseline enrichment of shareholders. Boards today have no choice but to be diverse and inclusive, made up of individuals who reflect a diverse society, including minorities, women, and members of the LGBTQIA+ community. The businesses that will survive and thrive in the next few decades are ones that serve the interests of *all* their stakeholders and that allow board members to govern as *owners*.

Before I sketch a portrait of tomorrow's Enlightened Board, it's worth tracing the evolution of corporate boards from their earliest beginnings to today.

Corporate Boards, Then and Now

Herbert Henry Dow, or "Crazy Dow," as he was better known, had the first rumblings to form his new company in 1897. Dow was a kid from Ohio, a twenty-one-year-old Ontario immigrant who had a patent for a new process of extracting bromine—an element used in products from frame retardants to gasoline—from the brine lakes and rivers in and around the old logging town of Midland, Michigan.

The first company H. H. Dow founded went bankrupt, but he kept plugging away. Twelve months later, with the help of fifty-seven investors and $200,000, and using an invention known as "the Dow Process," a method of extracting bromide using electrolysis, Crazy Dow created what would eventually become the Dow Chemical Company.

Like most turn-of-the-century founders, H. H. Dow convened around him a board made up of family members, friends, and local community leaders. This model was widely replicated by other businesses. The Country Club Board, as I call it, is easily understood when you consider that the earliest sources of funding companies generally have come from the pockets of relatives and close friends. New enterprises require capital, and a board's mission is to shore up CEOs as they take risks and try to transform a private company into a publicly owned enterprise.

The Country Club Board's commonsensical beginnings were responsible for its staying power. In practice, that meant that nearly all publicly listed companies had boards mirroring an alumni reunion at a small, homogenous private school or college. Old-fashioned, chummy, and crony-like, the Country Club Board served as a rubber stamp for whatever the CEO wanted. Belonging to one of those boards required little time, effort, or work. Meetings didn't last long. No one asked tough questions. Everything management said was received as gospel (mostly because the board usually had no understanding of the business, or the sector, which is still true of the boards of some companies today). Any outstanding issues could be resolved on the tennis court or fairway. Board members were there to placate market regulators and do their leaders' bidding, and leaders in turn could advance their own agendas with minimal resistance.

The Country Club Board lasted a long time. Before then, the perspectives and backgrounds eventually supplied by an Activist Board weren't considered socially or fiscally necessary. Throughout the twentieth century, most management teams wouldn't have considered engaging with a disparity of opinions. If accused of patronage, or uniformity, board members would have surely quoted the axiom *Growth forgives all sins.*

Dow was no different, though a few quirks set it apart. The company was run as a troika. Rather than one individual running the company, three people—the CEO, the CFO, and the chairman—were in control. The disposition of the board was also unusual. To explain, when I became CEO, Dow's board included my predecessor, a succession planning device put into place by the founders, one that allowed an exiting CEO to graduate seamlessly into the role of chairman. As you might expect, a retiring CEO had close, long-standing alliances on the board. When the first non-family CEO was appointed to the top job, the runners-up also joined the board. It was a good way to keep a new CEO under watch and prevent him (always male) from drastically changing the strategy. If, say, Dow's new leader wanted to do something radically new or different—"We are no longer a chemical company! From now on, by God, we will sell insurance!"—it could never happen.

One of my early moves as CEO was to explore separating the chairman and CEO roles. My predecessor as CEO was still chairman for twelve months, but with his encouragement, I became Dow's combined CEO and chairman, and we appointed an independent lead director. The Dow board at the time had four insiders on it from my predecessor's tenure, perpetuating a long tradition. That meant that independent directors couldn't change anything at Dow even if they tried. With the encouragement of my predecessor, Bill Stavropoulos, who was always ahead of his time, we made the board independent. We began retiring insider board members, replacing them with independent directors, to the point that five years into my tenure I was the only nonindependent director on Dow's board. As the company's longest-serving CEO (apart from founding family members, four of whom remained in the job longer than me), I stayed on as CEO and chairman until my retirement.

By the late 1990s, the Country Club Board was on its last legs. The internet had introduced transparency around companies and directors, and the financial cable news ecosystem was busy chronicling corporate transgressions and mismanagement at companies like Enron and Tyco. Every day it seemed there was another story about another CEO stepping down from his job with a staggeringly generous golden parachute. Did CEOs *really* deserve all those goodies, investors wanted to know? Yes, that was business as usual in those days, but what shareholders in their right minds wouldn't speculate about the effect these exorbitant payoffs had on a company's performance, and their own returns? Plus, many boards were now realizing that if they woke up one day to find their company was being taken over by Ron Perelman, they would be in trouble. Things had to improve.

These and other factors gave rise to the Sarbanes-Oxley Act of 2002, otherwise known as the Corporate Responsibility Act, which set out new rules and reforms for accountants, auditors, and corporate officers. After Sarbanes-Oxley, many shareholders began to insist that boards represent their interests better. The trend at the time was for CEOs to appoint external, independent directors onto boards—changes that saw the birth of the Engaged Board, a collective that was knowledgeable and experienced, but not *too* knowledgeable or *too* experienced. Nonetheless, the Engaged Board was now here to stay.

If Country Club Board members were known for asking the rote questions that CEOs expected them to ask and brought only a superficial knowledge of the business and the sector to their directorship, Engaged Board members understood the business and the sector in depth and asked their CEOs sophisticated, targeted questions. They also hewed to strict governance practices. Why, an Engaged Board member might ask, should all that money go to *this* project and not *that* project? Why don't we give those funds back to the owners and let the owners allocate them to another sector—or why don't we simply increase the dividend yield?

Around this time, new transparency standards were obliging boards themselves to field new questions. Banks, analysts, and other outside firms were now able to track enterprises on their financial scorecards in real time. Companies were subject to an ongoing series of x-rays. Being under watch promoted short-term focus—"Yes, we appreciate the investment you just made in Saudi Arabia, and a decade from now, you may turn a profit.

But what are you doing for us *now*?"—and brought up additional questions around board representation. If a board included one too many management retirees, the shareholder base couldn't be blamed for wondering if their boards were being exposed to independent perspectives, as opposed to management ones. Everyone could agree that boards needed to become more representative of company shareholders, and again, why believe what management has to say?

Rather than simply serving as a rubber stamp to the whims of the CEO, Engaged Board members took their directorships seriously. They understood the obligation they had to the business and its shareholders. This meant CEOs had to educate Engaged Board members on facts, figures, advantages, downsides, and possible outcomes of all decisions being made in the hope that directors would align with the CEOs' visions and strategies. By the time a proposal reached board level, Engaged Board members knew as much about the decisions under consideration as their CEOs and had also asked the tough questions necessary to protect the company's (and their own) reputation. In turn, CEOs became less all-knowing, cult-like icons (think Jack Welch) and more like traffic cops in the middle of a busy intersection. CEOs now had to play defense *and* offense, mollified by the knowledge that if something befell the organization, and boards now recognized their exposure, directors would end up shouldering the blame.

The Engaged Board ratcheted up the levels of professional responsibility—at least to a degree. Directors would meet, ask (relatively) smart and informed questions, offer their opinions—and call it a day. The plastics expert on a board might ask, "Why aren't you focusing on plastics?" The government person might ask, "Who can help us with this in Washington?" The automobile person might ask, "Why can't we do this in the automotive industry?" The expertise, and interrogation, generally went no further than that.

Investors, by then, were falling even more into firm categories. Value investors sought a predictable dividend check, and growth at a reasonable, measured pace, or else tried to find bargains, stocks that grew at consistently low valuations. Then there were growth investors, who couldn't help but notice the opportunities offered by the newest, hottest tech companies like Amazon or Tesla and who didn't care much about present-day unprofitability given those companies' stratospheric growth potential. It was no surprise that growth investors tended to shun companies like Dow. In contrast to the boundless future profits of tech, Dow was considered an anomaly whose best days were probably in the past. Rumor had it that Andrew Liveris was trying to reinvent the company as an innovation machine, but didn't history show that nine out of ten CEOs and companies that tried something similar had failed? Go ahead, Dow, play things out. Let the value investors invest in Dow while the growth investors plant flags in the intersection of Amazon, Facebook, and Twitter.

The recognition of investor bases was one of the new realities prompting the Engaged Board to evolve into the Activist Board. Fighting the investor allocation model meant that CEOs needed directors on their boards who understood that by allocating capital to X or Y, companies could provide their investors a glide path to long-term returns while simultaneously providing short-term profits. Obviously, this was and is a hard trick for companies to pull off. Few companies can manage to secure a rerating by transforming themselves from a low-growth company with a hoary reputation into a fast-moving, high-valuation enterprise. But in fact, this was the transformation I pulled off at Dow. To bring in board members who understood what I was trying to do, I had to pivot away from people who *understood* the business—the Engaged Board—and surround myself instead with directors who would *challenge* the business. I needed an Activist Board.

An Activist Board—this is my own term, and not to be confused with outside activist investors—would be made up of directors who could impart to Dow their experience and expertise in *other* industries. Ideally, I needed a director from the consumer goods sector who could serve alongside someone from the credit payments industry and the tech sector and the appliance industry and the automotive industry. Dow wasn't a consumer markets business, but having a board director who came from that background would help me understand the trends and consumption patterns that might affect our business someday. More than a board that asked questions, I needed one with which I could be in ongoing discussion. This led to the six-year-long dialogue I had with our board around our alliance with Saudi Aramco.

As a new entity, the Activist Board could be challenging and contentious—and necessary. Some Activist Board members posed questions I wasn't all that eager to think about, pushed back on the answers I supplied, and forced me to expand my thinking and deepen my understanding of a subject before they agreed to sign off on my decision. If the Engaged Board mostly played defense, the Activist Board played defense *and* offense. Unwilling to simply serve as a check on the CEO, Activist Boards sought to create real value by challenging management to pivot the enterprise into unfamiliar directions. By studying the business under a microscope, Activist Board directors preempted the likelihood of external investors targeting the company, selling off chunks of the portfolio, or worse. Activist Board members made it clear they represented the company's capital and weren't shy about telling the CEO and management how to *use* that capital.

Another characteristic of the Activist Board? Members were as diversified as most Country Club directors were homogenous. Challenging management, after all, requires a variety of viewpoints and perspectives. Boards can't play offense unless they include directors with profound industry expertise and experience, which usually means former CEOs.

Prompting the end of the Engaged Board, and the birth of the Activist Board, was the rise of activist hedge funds, new regulatory changes, and investor communities demanding more from the companies in which they invested—as well as a belated recognition that the people making the decisions about how company capital was allocated were at a minimum six degrees of separation distant from the actual owners of the company. The Activist Board was, and is today, an attempt to close that gap.

The Dow board of 2007 was an Activist Board. By the time our deal with Saudi Aramco was approved six years later, no stone was left unturned. I didn't always love the process, but I appreciated why it was necessary. The decision to sign off on the deal couldn't just be mine, or management's. It had to be the best deal for the company. Nor, I might add, did it begin auspiciously. Over the next few years, the Sadara Chemical Company, as the new Dow-Saudi venture was named (*sadara* is an Arabic word meaning "in the lead," or "out in front") experienced overruns and debt issues and missed its profits forecast. But we stayed the course, and by the time I retired in 2018, Dow and my successor as CEO, Jim Fitterling, were still fully committed to Sadara, which has worked out better than anyone predicted.

Sadara still holds the title of the largest chemical complex ever built in the world in a single phase. Encompassing twenty-six different manufacturing plants, and more than three million metric tons of capacity annually, the site is roughly the size of twenty football fields. Confirming my forecast, today the Saudis are a behemoth in the making in a world once occupied by Dow. Yes, the conversation between Dow's Activist Board and me was long and drawn out, and intermittently rocky, but I'm glad it happened. Should what I did to get that deal approved happen with every major commitment made by every publicly owned corporation? In my opinion, *yes*.

The Case for Change in Corporate Boards

One of the biggest reasons I'm writing this book is to do my part in driving change *in* this century *for* this century. Among the factors that will help society converge (as opposed to keep diverging) are new models of leadership, new institutions, new ways of running those institutions, and new individuals entering government and serving on corporate boards. In the twentieth century, changes this big would be made piecemeal, but given that our planet currently shoulders the burden of seven billion people, rising to nine billion by 2050, these changes need to happen before humanity runs out of time.

In the 2013 *Harvard Business Review* article I cited earlier, Dominic Barton, the former CEO of McKinsey, and Mark Wiseman, the founder and former chairman of FCLTGlobal, a firm I cofounded (FCLT is short for Focusing on the Long Term), wrote that public companies needed to "cure the ills stemming from dispersed and disengaged ownership by bolstering boards' ability to govern like owners."[1] As to how they might do this, Barton and Wiseman wrote that CEOs and executives needed to find new ways of thinking centered on the idea that serving the interests of "all major stakeholders—employees, suppliers, customers, creditors, communities, the environment—is not at odds with the goal of maximizing corporate value."[2] The board, Barton and Wiseman continued, must be as adept a portfolio manager as the owners of the business. The days when CEOs could simply check the "good governance" box on boards were gone. In this century, the nexus between management and portfolio needs to be bridged at the board level.

A year later, in a follow-up *HBR* article, Barton and Wiseman put things more succinctly: "Boards aren't working."[3] In a McKinsey survey cited by the authors, only 34 percent of the 772 directors surveyed believed the boards they served on fully understood the strategy of their businesses, with only 22 percent of those same directors reporting that their boards understood how the enterprise created value, and an even scantier 16 percent attesting that their boards had a deep understanding of their companies' industries. Even contemporary Activist Boards mostly failed to deliver on their mission of "providing strong oversight and strategic support for management's efforts to create long-term value," an issue that dovetails with the widespread epidemic of short-termism that I write more about in chapter 5. The issue of short-termism, it appears, has been and continues to be very much a *board* problem, with little positive change in the past decade.

In a 2014 *McKinsey Quarterly* survey, more than a thousand board members and C-suite executives worldwide assessed their own progress in taking a longer-term strategy to running their companies. Four percent of respondents reported that the pressure to deliver strong short-term financial performance came from their own boards. In turn, board directors made it clear they were often channeling the pressure for short-term gains they felt from investors, including their companies' own institutional owners.

Put simply, every enterprise has a value chain. At one end of the chain is the publicly owned company, the CEO, and management. Atop the CEO sits the board, which represents shareholders, who can be found at the far end of this value chain and who are the *owners* of the company's assets and include pension funds like TIAA and CalPERS. Next up on this chain are the asset managers—Fidelity, Vanguard, and so on—that aggregate assets by sector and manage those assets for the asset owners.

In the middle of our chain, between the asset managers and the board, are the sell-side analysts employed by investment banks and brokerages. Their job is to monitor and analyze companies for future earnings growth, information that is then sold to the asset managers, who make recommendations to the asset owners. The data produced by these sell-side analysts allows the asset owners to get up-to-the-minute data and metrics about a company's performance. Where, you might be wondering, is the *citizen* in all this? Well, the citizen provides assets to the pension funds on one end, and on the other end, that same citizen can also potentially be a company employee.

If the value chain is working the way it should, the company's long-term decisions and strategies, represented by the board and the CEO (and therefore the company employees), are consistent with the wishes of the asset owners—who, as I said, might also be the employees by the publicly owned company. But unfortunately, this value chain isn't working. Why is that? Because the asset managers—the Fidelitys and the Vanguards—are typically paid on the basis of yearly bonuses. If the stock of a public company appreciates during a twelve-month time frame, those asset managers are seen as doing a good job and they secure bigger bonuses. To ensure that appreciation happens, asset managers sometimes force companies to do things, quietly or via activists, to create gains in the stock price independent of the underlying fundamentals of the business.

For example, if you are the Dow Chemical Company, and you've just invested in Saudi Arabia and won't see a return for ten or twenty years, what message does that communicate to asset managers? They will decide not to invest in Dow since our stock price won't go up for years. They lack the patience and the metrics to wait things out.

Which is why unless an enterprise stands up and announces it is no longer focused on short-term profits and returns—and that same enterprise is also supported on its long-term journey by the board *and* the owners—CEOs will increasingly be asked to step down, and boards will continue running the risk of getting attacked by outside activists. The failure of the Activist Board is one reason why the corporate value chain model is broken.

Enter a new type of board, one that all companies should consider establishing, that I call the Enlightened Board.

Six Traits of an Enlightened Board

In fairness, some companies, including Mastercard, Yum! Brands, PepsiCo, Disney, Salesforce, and Unilever, have already taken steps toward reconstructing the board of the future. For those that haven't, below are a few characteristics of the Enlightened Board of the twenty-first century.

DEPTH

The Enlightened Board consists of verticals and horizontals. *Verticals* are board members with deep expertise and/or experience in a single subject, for example consumer markets or financial portfolios. *Horizontals* refer to individuals whose expertise is more widespread and encompasses a wide variety of subjects and areas.

The Enlightened Board also features a disproportionate number of former senior executives and CEOs, as well as asset owners or asset managers, who bring with them real-life experience and expertise more aligned with those of owners. (Incidentally, appointing those directors can create its own issues, given that asset owners and managers tend to be pure financial animals who may not understand how to run a company or operate R&D.) Enlightened Board members should have an active understanding, too, of the risk management around the enterprise—and the best ways to manage that risk from a business point of view.

SIZE

Most boards have too many people on them. The Enlightened Board should consist of eight to ten members, though in some cases, a company's desire for inclusiveness can push that number up to ten or twelve. One CEO who was actively trying to expand his board's expertise and ethnic representation told me his board now numbered a dozen people. When I advised him not to exceed ten, he agreed, adding that he had gone big for the sake of going small again in the future. Point well taken.

To reduce the possibility of "over boarding," directors should limit their service on boards. They should also be compensated better than they are now, with their compensation based on longer-term metrics. If nothing else, this will remind them that serving on a board is a *job*.

RIGOR

Anyone who has ever served on a board knows that CEOs and directors are assailed on a quarterly basis. Enlightened Boards should be made up of directors who can take the same heat in the medium to long term as the CEO does. Board members also need to do the work. They should know about the business and the sector or sectors in depth. That way everyone is prepared, and no one wastes time on presentations (a carryover from the Country Club Board era). Basically, Enlightened Board members should be line executives without literally being line executives, while understanding that patient capital most of the time results in medium-term returns.

Directors serving on Enlightened Boards also need to put in their time with the company. Not just with the CEO, either, and not just scanning materials on a computer tablet. Ideally, they should meet as many people employed by the enterprise as possible. They should visit plants. They should understand customers and the regulatory environment. Only then can they challenge management in positive, proactive ways.

Finally, an Enlightened Board should meet on three subjects: strategy, risk, and people. That's the entire sum of its agenda.

INCLUSIVENESS

Unless you are a private owner, or a state-owned, government-operated enterprise, you can't ignore that today, you need to make room for voices that have been ignored, excluded, or sidelined. If you're not comfortable hearing those voices, well, it's not up to you to judge. You need to make room for additional seats, and diverse representation, at the table.

Society has recently woken up to the fact that rich, white guys have been dominating our culture for too long and that it's time boardrooms more accurately resembled the makeup of the world in which they operate. It's more than just pulling up more chairs. Being an enterprise in this century means engaging with a broad chorus of vistas, backgrounds, and perspectives. Diverse boards increase engagement with women, minorities, LGBTQIA+ community members, academics, environmental managers, and anyone else historically excluded from the centers of decision making. CEOs of a certain age may not like a big percentage of what they hear—either it's alien or it feels irrelevant to running their business—but they have no choice but to incorporate that percentage into their thinking, perspective, strategy, and vision. Quite simply, it is what's happening today in society, and incorporating it gives CEOs additional bandwidth on everything their companies need to consider now and in the future.

Nor does inclusive mean *everyone*. An *inclusive* board is made up of a snapshot of contemporary society, along with the CEO's best estimate of what society will resemble in the future. Ironically, there is a lot to be learned from the supervisory boards that sit atop management boards in many European countries. Historically speaking, supervisory boards include representatives from labor unions and academia, as well as government experts and spokespeople from a variety of other industries. American companies tend to dismiss the idea of a supervisory board—too hierarchical—but don't these boards mirror the array of backgrounds, races, identities, and perspectives we now require from Enlightened Board members? Finally, more than diverse opinion being responsible for better *thought*, the goal of diverse opinion is better *outcome*.

In spring 2022, I was honored to be named the president of the Organizing Committee for the Brisbane, Australia, 2032 Olympic and Paralympic Games. The board I lead is made up of people from all walks of life whose job it is to represent stakeholders in what most people would agree is the most global of events. More than good intentions or utopian words and knowing that a board where everyone looks and sounds the same is a relic from twenty years ago, the mission of our board is to bring *substance* to inclusivity. Diversity in this case isn't just an idea whose time has come but a necessity for humanity to give all kinds of athletes, abled and disabled, the honor, dignity, and celebration they deserve. Inputs like these need to be integrated across all boards to create a new synergy that's frankly missing in many of today's balance sheets. Right now, it's undetermined how to do that. It's as if today's boards are being asked to learn a new language instantaneously. In truth, this will take time and will involve stumble. But as the century goes on, I'm confident boards will become fluent on the way to becoming truly enlightened.

BLEND

Equally important as the diversity of an Enlightened Board is composition and balance. Enlightened Boards should be a well-considered blend of the company's stakeholders. Remember, though, that *more* isn't always better. A financial engineer might serve alongside a portfolio manager—but a board doesn't need *six* financial engineers and portfolio managers. If a board is engineered exclusively for the financial community, employees, customers, governments, and members of the community will end up shortchanged.

LONG-TERMISM

Range, experience, diversity, and vertical and horizontal depth are all necessary ingredients of the Enlightened Board. But if board directors can't understand the trade-offs between short-term and long-term visions and profits, then they risk becoming another layer the CEO must manage.

Here's an example. A board member whose background is in academia might wonder what the business is doing in the long term around its R&D spend. As CEO, I might tell him that an R&D strategy alone is insufficient and that I am investing in an R&D strategy that will provide results in five or ten years. That means that right now at least, I can't spend the money on R&D that the academic board member wants me to spend. (Here is an area where businesses and universities differ!) Unlike in academia, as the CEO I am responsible to all our stakeholders. Of course, I would welcome the same board member's input on what field of research to pursue—but it's *my* job as CEO to determine our company's financial priorities.

This same evaluation might take place with another board member with a government background. Why, she might ask, am I favoring one political party over another? Where does the company stand on climate change, and why haven't I prioritized the elimination of all factory emissions? I might reply that if we eliminated all factory emissions overnight, we would risk destroying our business, and we should transition away from emissions more gradually.

None of this would happen with a Country Club Board, an Engaged Board, or even an Activist Board. But today these conversations *have to* happen. CEOs in turn must be agile, adroit, and knowledgeable enough to manage multiple layers of the board that represent all the company's stakeholders—while never forgetting that the board is a hitch point that connects company executives and stakeholders.

Final Thoughts

The poor performance of most corporate boards always reminds me of the increasing number of public companies that have chosen to delist from the New York Stock Exchange in favor of private ownership. Why? Well, one big reason many businesses join stock exchanges in the first place is to get access to capital. Today, with capital ubiquitous, and private investors and family offices exploding on the wealth curve, why would any business voluntarily choose to go public? BlackRock, State Street, Bain, Blackstone, Carlyle, Apollo, KKR, and other private equity firms have today become long-term portfolio holders, "long term" in this case meaning five years or longer (bear in mind that in the late 1980s, "five years" was understood to be the definition of short term). The trend toward private ownership directly implicates boards and the pressure to achieve strong returns every ninety days.

One CEO I know of recently delisted his public company, aware that under private ownership, he would be able to transform the portfolio, a process that could take years in a public setting. The markets, the ninety-day pressure to perform, and the rate and pace of change in the technology sector, simply wouldn't give him the time he needed. Michael Dell, the CEO of Dell Computer, did the same thing in 2013. In the 1990s, Dell Computer's explosive growth helped make it one of the world's largest tech companies before it started getting undercut by competitors like Lenovo, Acer, Samsung, and HP, who flooded the marketplace with cheaper laptops. When Michael Dell realized that the higher company valuation he was after was unattainable, he delisted Dell Computer from NASDAQ and the Hong Kong Stock Exchange, took it private, remade the portfolio, and a few years later relisted the *new* Dell—now a computer company, a storage company, a data analytics company, and an AI company—at a higher valuation. Michael Dell was saved from having to deal with a board and the market's preoccupation with quarterly returns.

But companies don't always *have* to go private. The transformation I undertook at Dow was in public. After becoming CEO, I divested our low-profit, low-valuation businesses—75 percent of the portfolio—while doing everything I could to improve profitability. I *literally* had to bet the entire company (which is why boards in general don't approve of pervasive risk-taking on the part of CEOs). When I arrived at Dow, the company was half the value of DuPont. As time went on, we got smaller *and* higher margins, with our higher margins giving us a higher valuation to the point where Dow was literally the equal of DuPont. I pulled this off in seven or eight years, without going private, while sustaining one hit after the next, most of which I go into in this book.

The Enlightened Board may not yet be ubiquitous, but establishing it will go a long way toward creating what the enterprises of this century have no choice but to become.

Takeaways and Tools

- Twentieth-century corporate history reveals three distinct models of boards: the Country Club Board; the Engaged Board; and the Activist Board (not to be confused with activist investors!). The future requires a fourth model, the Enlightened Board, which is diverse, inclusive, and represents all avenues of society.

- Already established in enterprises including Mastercard, PepsiCo, Disney, Salesforce, and Unilever, the Enlightened Board has several distinguishing characteristics. These include:

- *Vertical and horizontal depth. Vertical* refers to board members who have deep, focused expertise in a particular subject. *Horizontal* refers to board members with broader perspective and wider experience.

- *Size.* Boards should feature no more than eight to ten members. If additional members can expand the board's inclusiveness, that number can go as high as twelve.

- *Rigor.* Board members should be knowledgeable and well prepared and understand that patient capital usually yields medium-sized returns.

- *Inclusiveness.* Enlightened board members should represent all corners of society, including those whose voices have been historically overlooked. *Inclusive* doesn't mean everyone, either. It should be seen as a snapshot of present and future society.

- The Brisbane Olympic and Paralympic Board, which I've recently been named to lead, is a good example of a future Enlightened Board. Every stakeholder is represented and heard. Among other things, all board members provide me with their top three issues and concerns, which are then aggregated from highest to lowest, in addition to their individual comments. Better still, we have ten years to perfect this model!

7

Leadership Lesson 2

Never Let a Good Crisis Go to Waste

When COVID-19 found its way to the US in early 2020, the US government had no pandemic blueprint in place. It wasn't that the Obama administration hadn't left one behind, because they had. The sixty-nine-page National Security Council document laid out the best ways to execute against a dark possible scenario, one that officials had no doubts was going to happen. Among the recommendations was that the government accumulate a surplus of PPE supplies for frontline health care workers and define the role the Strategic National Stockpile might play.

Still, when COVID first appeared, the response from the US government ranged from chaotic to negligible. No one seemed prepared. Nothing was in in place. Not vaccines, not masks, not ventilators. Nor was the US alone. With a few exceptions, most EU countries also found themselves scrambling.

Who would imagine that along with Singapore, New Zealand, and South Korea, Australia would come up with a best-in-class COVID response that would become, at least for a time, the envy of the world?

"Never let a good crisis go to waste." Words reputed to have been said by Winston Churchill after World War II as he worked alongside other member nations to help form what would become the UN. These words also put me in mind of another great twentieth-century leader, Lou Gerstner of IBM.

When Gerstner was named CEO, IBM was in crisis mode and losing billions of dollars a year. The company was bloated and inefficient, a sea of white shirts, dark suits, and too many divisions to count. There was talk of a breakup, especially since IBM was competing in the 1990s against younger, more agile tech companies including Apple, Microsoft, and Oracle.

Gerstner got to work. He immediately recognized that centralization and integration were keys to restoring IBM's fortunes and growth. One of the first things he did was cancel plans to chop up IBM into a series of independent operating units. He also decreed that employee compensation would be linked from then on not to the division in question but to IBM's overall success. By selling off unproductive assets, dissolving fiefdoms, and thinning employee ranks, Gerstner cut billions off IBM's operating expenses. By the time he left in 2002, IBM had made comebacks and inroads in countless markets. Legacy product lines were revamped and reanimated. R&D entered a new age. The workforce had increased by a hundred thousand employees. The stock had split twice. Lastly, the culture was completely transformed.

What sets a winning institution apart in the end is the strength, depth, and integrity of a company culture. As Gerstner found, a company and its leaders must create a culture that allows the business to evolve *away* from its founder or founding family and *toward* the leader who is creating the culture of tomorrow. Not the company or the culture of ten, twenty, or fifty years ago, and not even the ones from today. Dow was in a similar position as IBM in the 1990s and early aughts. We had both incumbency and strength. Yet time and again, we found ourselves literally losing our right to operate as new, unplanned-for, and unforeseeable paradigms— environmental, regulatory, and market based—hit us from all sides.

Gerstner took culture, and the need to take risks, to heart. He later told students at Harvard Business School that the transformation of an enterprise "begins with a sense of crisis or urgency," and that "no institution will go through fundamental change unless it believes it is in deep trouble and needs to do something different to survive."[1]

The reason I bring up Lou Gerstner is that he waded into a crisis and ended up transforming IBM. It was similar to an opportunity I was given when COVID arrived in Australia to help marshal a plan that would have been impossible in the absence of a crisis.

In spring 2020, I was one of a dozen or so people from the private sector invited to advise Australia's newly minted COVID Commission on an industrial manufacturing strategy. For the next six months, the commission set about implementing three phases en route to creating a potent response to COVID, the goal being to transform what everyone agreed was a cataclysm into an opportunity.

From the start, Australia's prime minister, Scott Morrison, perceived the epidemic as a war. He knew he had to create a war footing and a war cabinet, made up of experts in their fields. The cabinet would eventually include the senior leaders of each of Australia's six states, along with their prime ministers and key teams. They set out to address the three key phases of the COVID epidemic.

First, of course, the commission needed to manage the health crisis itself. This involved sourcing the necessary equipment and finding and shipping ventilators to wherever they were needed. I was more involved in the second phase, which focused on the eventual recovery from the pandemic. What was the best way to stabilize and protect the Australian economy in the future, despite none of us knowing how long the pandemic would last? What bridging mechanisms could we put into place so the recovery wouldn't take longer than it should?

As well, the commission was given the opportunity to do something I have been advocating for decades, one that absent a crisis, as I said, would have been impossible to implement: top-down planning. Together, we put into place a series of globally competitive, sustainable twenty-first-century gas, industry, and manufacturing policies, while focusing on measures to grow these sectors over the long term. The challenges were immediately identifiable.

Australia's high levels of innovation, for example, didn't always translate into commercial products. Every year the Australian government invested significant funds into advanced manufacturing, but compared to other countries, which were more aggressive and strategic in their approach to industry and innovation, those investments weren't marshaled for competitive advantage. Nor was Australia's skilled labor system as competitive as it should be, too often failing both industry and students. The curricula and systems of our schools needed to become more dynamic, stringent, and aligned with technology and global standards of execution skills.

We set out what we felt were realistic target outcomes. We would create up to 180,000 new, well-paid, high-value direct jobs in manufacturing, and 3,000 to 5,000 indirect jobs in associated industries—an increase of anywhere from 255,000 to 850,000 jobs overall. The Australian government promised to support the retraining of countless workers affected by the pandemic and provide security for jobs under threat in energy-intensive industries. We would also create an ecosystem to support high-value skills, engage Australia's raw materials and agriculture, and improve the resilience of the Australian economy via diversification. To create a competitive domestic gas market, we would eliminate barriers to supply; build a bridge of supply in the near term; reduce the cost of pipelines; and complete the country's network of gas infrastructure.

Why did it take a debilitating global pandemic to make this happen? The answer requires some context. First, as most people know, Western democracies aren't big fans of top-down anything. Market economies believe markets should drive all the answers and facilitate all productivity, efficiency, and innovation. Yet the tectonic shifts we have witnessed in this century, whether connected to climate, social justice, equality, trade, or energy, and the effects those things have on our water and food supplies, make it painfully clear, as I've said throughout this book, that the playbook from last century no longer applies. For example, even if officials from the incoming administration *had* digested the Obama administration's pandemic playbook, they still would have had to execute against an unimaginable event.

Another problem? Language. *Manufacturing* and *industry* are terms from a vanished era. In an information age, who wants to talk about manufacturing? Nonetheless, at day's end, what do we as human beings keep doing? We invent things, make things, and sell things. A crucial difference in this century is that humans have a new digital toolbox at our disposal, and we are increasingly making sure the things we invent, make, and sell don't end up destroying the planet we all share.

If you are able to accept this premise—that inventing, making, and selling is the core economic activity of humans—how can we design a future to facilitate and advance our own DNA? We need to design contemporary, state-of-the-art factories and buildings that are operationally best in class, that don't damage the environment or our fellow citizens, and that deploy technology and artificial intelligence, with both firmly in the control of human beings (and *not* machines). Governments have a strong role to play in this ecosystem by developing systems that ensure that everyone in society has equal access to opportunity. *This* is how to install top-down rules taken from an industrial age and put them to work in a digital era. Better still, the Australian COVID Commission pulled up a chair and listened to what I was saying.

Ultimately, we were able to put into place a modern manufacturing initiative. The Australian government plans to devote substantial resources to building an economy for the next two or three decades. At one point I was reminded that the longer the pandemic went on, the longer Australia's economy would take to recover—and (paradoxically) the more likely the solutions I just described would endure. But it was important to be realistic too. Politicians come and go. With COVID resurgent across Australia in 2021, the government might be unable to sustain those changes, in which case we would have *wasted* a crisis.

The question remains: How can a company exist today and survive tomorrow while remaking its business model *today* to create opportunities on *behalf* of tomorrow? Reenter Lou Gerstner, who once gave a speech to Dow's management team. Asked to describe the moment that scared him the most at IBM, Gerstner said without hesitation, "It was when we began making money again."

Are you considering doing audacious, courageous things in your company? *Do them in a crisis.* Don't wait. No crisis on hand? Then step up and envision the conditions of a crisis by imagining the *content* of what you are doing and the *context* of your operating environment. If you do that, your culture and people will evolve from incumbency and unwillingness to change into something genuinely novel, daring, and future oriented. Complacency comes when leaders and companies believe they have the right to keep profiting from what they have always done. *They don't.*

Finally, just because I am advising you, as Churchill did, never to let a good crisis go to waste, that doesn't mean that managing through a crisis isn't difficult, frightening, and enervating. There are some upsides, though. When facing crisis, organizations are given an opportunity to question themselves. Some realize they need to reset and reimagine how they might look years from now. In 2030, or 2050, will Amazon, Tesla, or even Apple remotely resemble the companies they are today?

Takeaways and Tools

- CEOs must create a culture that allows an enterprise to evolve away from the company founder, or founding family, and toward the leader who will guide the business today and tomorrow. It's not about what happened in the past, or even what's taking place now. Leaders need to focus on the needs and opportunities of the *future*.

- Complacency usually happens when CEOs and enterprises assume they have the right to continue profiting from what they have always done. They don't.

- Leaders who are considering making bold or risky moves should do them in a crisis. If no crisis exists, then create crisis conditions by sketching out future hypotheticals. What will your company look like a decade, two decades, or three decades from now? Focusing on these questions will help reorient your culture and people toward the future.

- People can find it challenging to wrap their heads around potential worst-case scenarios, especially in good times. But in a scary and insidious way, "we're doing fine" means that the calcification of your enterprise is already under way. Eventually, the worst-case scenario will occur when you find that one or more of your nimbler competitors is eating your lunch.

- Creating a culture that is always on edge is the traditional domain of small companies and start-ups—but larger enterprises can also see benefits. At Dow, I kept everyone fearful they might lose their jobs if standard answers were the only thing they could produce. I insisted that everyone always be future focused on what might go wrong. Imagine X or Y scenario. Are you prepared to handle it? How?

- Having run through scenarios in the C-suite, the next step is to run test cases with consultants. In an engineering-based, process-based, and safety-based company like Dow, it's not a stretch to say that everything is fine—until it's not. Dow's goal was and is to future-proof itself against every conceivable physical, government, and market-based event. It should be every company's goal.

8

The New Role of Government

Battery-powered cars are making waves these days. In 2021, sales of all-electric vehicles, or EVs, were up dramatically in the US, Europe, and China. "Battery-powered cars are having a breakthrough moment,"[1] confirmed the *New York Times*, noting that US automakers have graduated to manufacturing all-electric versions of pickup trucks, a long-time favorite of American consumers, an evolution that "represents the biggest upheaval in the auto industry since Henry Ford introduced the Model T in 1908."[2]

With the car industry expected to pour half a trillion dollars[3] over the next five years to transition to EVs from fossil-fuel cars and trucks, the surging popularity of e-mobility has profound ramifications for US businesses, workers, and, not least, our environment. What most people don't realize is that EVs never would have happened without a strong partnership between business and government.

During the 2008 global economic crisis, the Treasury secretary under President George W. Bush worked alongside major US banks to safeguard certain key US industries, the automotive sector notable among them. The multibillion-dollar intervention and bailout offered to two of the Big

Three US carmakers—General Motors and Chrysler—weren't always smooth, but if the government hadn't intervened, the car industry would have faced bankruptcy, meaning there would be no domestic EV industry today.

The EV industry, as well as e-mobility, goes beyond cars to encompass helicopters, drones, and, eventually, airplanes. What are some of the barriers to entry?

Cost is the first. EV cars are typically more expensive than gas-fueled cars. The second hurdle is recharging and the worry that your house or garage won't generate enough power. Also, what if your car battery runs out, stranding you on the side of the road? In 2016, the Obama administration took steps to address the second of these barriers by launching a series of initiatives designed to accelerate the transition from fossil fuels to EVs, thereby reducing oil dependence, and increasing and improving access to clean energy technologies. They included creating multiple electric vehicle charging corridors along American interstates in thirty-five US states and improving EV charging technology. The Obama White House also announced that key power and utility companies nationwide and carmakers were committed to "[driving] the market transformation to electric vehicles by making it easy for consumers to drive their vehicles."[4] The key phrase embedded within the White House announcement was *collaboration between the government and industry.*

These two examples of private-public collaboration bring us to today and the massive opportunities inherent in the EV industry. Imagine if the nearly three hundred million cars in the US were replaced by electric vehicles. Everyone would want to get aboard this wave. Why shouldn't they? With technology improving and EV prices dropping, who wouldn't want to be an EV manufacturer in the twenty-first century? A complete transition from gas-fueled cars to EV vehicles may take a few decades to happen, but the day can't come soon enough when the $640 billion in incentives and subsidies that the US government gives to the fossil fuel industry annually is transferred over to the EV industry and economy.

Again, this conversation wouldn't be taking place without the help of two former presidential administrations. The first provided emergency lifeblood to the car industry. The second provided the infrastructure to charge EVs, knowing that if they didn't, there wouldn't *be* a conversion from fossil fuels to EVs. The third is happening today. The US lags China, Japan, and South Korea in the competition for energy leadership in a low-carbon world. According to the *Wall Street Journal*, the US government and the private sector are investing heavily through federal grants and private fundraising in numerous battery start-ups, a critical mission considering that US carmakers are already seeking cutting-edge, long-term suppliers for future mass production of EV cars. If batteries can't be found here, automakers will simply locate sourcing abroad.[5]

The lesson I take from this is that business and government need to put aside their old antagonisms and form a new model of partnership. This will require the birth of a new class of government worker and, not least, a new kind of politician. I once heard it said that a world fearful of change often pins its hopes on nostalgia, choosing to "march backward to the future." That option is no longer possible, nor can we extrapolate future needs based on what happened in previous centuries. The question facing both the private and public sector remains: How can we create rules and regulations in this century that benefit both government and business?

The History of Governmental Involvement in Business

Arguably the three biggest technological revolutions the world has seen took place in the years around World War I and World War II and in the 1960s with NASA. In those three periods, government spending created a flurry of innovation and development across the private sector. The first two cases involved war expenditures on behalf of military defense and offense. With NASA, the government spent money to put a man on the moon. The inventions of both air conditioning and the internet have their roots in governmental spending and development, mostly thanks to national labs staffed with top-of-the-line scientists and academics, who ultimately deserve credit for helping create enormous private sector growth and new economies.

Among the beneficiaries were early tech adapters like Hewlett-Packard, Motorola, Intel, Apple, Microsoft, Google, and IBM. Government investment in the industry during the 1960s and 1970s helped give birth to faster chips, connected computing, and computing in general. Companies that partnered with the government flourished. Dow, Boeing, DuPont, GM, Ford, and other large enterprises were behemoths that partnered with the government to manufacture the products created and developed in government labs. Back then, no one called it a "public-private partnership"—but what came out of it had a massive, positive impact on private industry. It signaled a change from the relationship between business and government that took place in the first half of the twentieth century.

Back then, government's role in business could best be described as *hands on.* Government drove, and business was in the backseat. Government provided money, skills, workforces, and, not least, ambition and optimism. Businesses and entrepreneurs like Henry Ford, George Westinghouse, Thomas Edison, and H. H. Dow took those governmental handouts and *did* extraordinary things with them.

From the late 1950s on, government began turning away from business. The new watchword was *hands off.* With business and the economy thriving, government sought to reframe its role. The new job and responsibility of government agencies was taking care of society and the constituents who voted politicians into office. Government's task was to ensure that this sizable constituency—and every product or service that came out of the business world—was properly regulated. In the case of Dow and other big companies, the "regulatory process" usually consisted of multiple congressional hearings, commissions, and a carrot-and-stick model. "Fix yourself and your industry," the government said, "or we will take away your carrots."

The change from hands-on to hands-off may have been gradual, but it felt abrupt. It created bad blood. Formerly untethered entrepreneurs and enterprises found themselves shackled overnight. Government had decided that humans needed protection from corporate shortcuts and compromises around product safety and environmental damage, and even accounting and financial fraud. This was the business environment in which I came of age. Companies and leaders soon got used to the idea of governments, who were keeping close watch on society and the greater good of humanity, laying down the law. These regulations ranged in size from draconian to medium-sized—but no such thing existed as a business environment with *no* rules.

Then and now, it's easy to infer that most businesses would resent and push back on regulations, but in the main that wasn't true. No one wanted to return to an era of no rules. Rules create certainty, after all. Like the traffic stripes on a highway, rules define where we're going. But it wasn't until the 1990s that the opportunity surfaced for business to *partner* with government.

Why? Technology. Digital monopolies had begun forming. Tech was moving so fast that governments found it hard to keep pace with the speed of change. This is still a problem today. How can the legislative and executive branches work together to keep up with the technology shifts within the enterprises the government needs to regulate? Policies around technology, which encompass cybersecurity, trade, energy, immigration, and infrastructure, needed to be placed not in an older context (tech barely existed last century) but in the context of the future.

The problem is that the government has struggled to appoint regulators who can match the speed of the companies and entrepreneurs being regulated. Is there a more vivid snapshot of a regulator and a regulatee being unable to come together (or even agree on the terms of negotiation) than the vision of today's social media warlords testifying before Senate oversight committees to discuss their capacity to manipulate and transform the behavior of billions of people worldwide? Most of the older lawmakers grilling the younger tech titans only dimly understand the impact and influence of the web. (Nor, it should be added, do the tech titans themselves.) This disequilibrium between the shared knowledge bases of business and government has made a future partnership model feel doubtful. Once, both sides might have welcomed the idea of collaboration. In short order, that thinking became "the government doesn't know what it's talking about—so why should we trust them?" Instead of partnering with government, the tech industry would start siccing interest and lobbying groups on regulators.

The distrust is mutual. Having seen the extraordinary wealth generated by big tech companies, which has squeezed the middle class even more than it was already, government officials see the tech titans as implacable enemies. Perhaps they should consider going top-down and enacting punitive measures to put the whole industry in its place.

This is where we are today. Business and government are drifting away from each other. The path wasn't always linear. During the Obama administration, a strong private-public partnership model seemed probable. The Trump administration was even more open to collaboration, and the business world hurriedly stepped in to partner on regulatory and tax policy. But the business world soon lost confidence in the administration. Today, under Biden, business interests are generally considered an afterthought. Rather than absorbing a core lesson of this century—that it's not *either/or*, it's *both/and*—and establishing frameworks made up of forward-looking government officials *and* forward-looking CEOs, we are regressing to the old model of *regulator* and *regulatee*. Among all else, this has the unintended consequence of stifling economic growth and delaying the retraining of the population for the jobs of tomorrow.

Where Does Government Fit Now?

I've often found myself working at the nexus of business and government on issues ranging from global trade to helping Washington navigate new, sometimes urgent business realities.

During the George W. Bush administration, a solid relationship existed between business and the various trade agencies around US and China policy. I was part of a strategic and economic dialogue and process, led by the secretary of the treasury and the secretary of state, who in turn worked closely with their Chinese counterparts. What should the US trade and economic relationship with China look like? Working with the two secretaries, we examined the strategic context between the US, the world's preeminent superpower, and China, an emergent and potentially antagonistic challenger. But instead of deploying last century's model—in *this* corner is the champion and in *that* corner is the up-and-comer—we asked ourselves how we could make the US-China relationship a win-win for both countries.

A half-dozen years earlier, the collapse of Enron, the Houston-based energy company (and back then the seventh largest company in the US), also led to a newfound relationship between government and business. In 2002, in the wake of Enron, Congress passed the Sarbanes-Oxley Act, tightening auditing financial responsibilities for corporations and boards. The business world resented it at first. Sarbox threw even the most reputationally pristine companies under the Enron bus. It wasn't consultative or collaborative. It was expensive and time consuming. But once the new rules of the road were established and explained, businesses grew to love Sarbox. It created a barrier to entry for noncompliant companies and established well-defined, transparent rules that were 80 percent—if not 100 percent—sensible. It was better than what we had before.

I also worked closely with the US government around one of Dow's subsidiaries, Hemlock Semiconductors, a manufacturer of polysilicon, the key raw material for creating solar cells. In 2013, the Chinese government announced it was planning on growing its own solar cell industry, one that would potentially knock all competitors out of that market and lead to the collapse of all US solar panel manufacturers. The Obama administration had no alternative but to impose a tariff on Chinese solar cells. If the Chinese government went ahead with its plans, it wouldn't just destroy every single American solar cell manufacturer; it would also prevent the US from developing any new materials.

In general, companies and CEOs dislike the idea of government intervening in the economy. Most leaders believe that the best and only way to trigger growth and jobs is by letting markets rule. Make no mistake— I'm a longtime believer in the power of free markets myself, and I'm not advocating for *bigger* government either. That doesn't mean there aren't areas where markets are out of their depth. Markets can't always ensure the soundness of our global and national economic foundations. Nor are they a substitute for the long-range, strategic thinking that is historically the responsibility of government. Government alone creates the policy frameworks that allow businesses to do what only they can do, which is creating value, jobs, and growth.

What I am proposing instead is the formation of a smarter, more thoughtful government that provides both home-grown and foreign-based companies with some degree of predictability and certainty if they choose to invest in the US. For the sake of companies' employees, communities, and stakeholders, government should be *more* involved. *Not* in the guise of overzealous regulators but as thoughtful partners to thoughtful business. Business can't do this alone—because even the most purpose-based business still has a profit motive. One of government's roles is to enable businesses to realize profits *and* be responsible citizens *and* consider every possible constituency *and* ensure no one is left disadvantaged or unprotected. I would go so far as to say that in this century, being pro-government is a prerequisite for being pro-business. Instead of hands-off or hands-on government, an ideal solution is *hands-together* government.

This requires a new mindset. Business and government must put aside their mutual suspicion and form a partnership devoted to serving the greater good and the national interest. First, the public and private sectors need to agree on what that framework might look like. Second, they need to start a dialogue in Washington, D.C., and across state capitals. Elected leaders must assume good faith on the part of business leaders and vice versa. History and countless new business models and innovations born with the help of government investment show us this makes all the difference.

For example, what role could the government play by investing in digital R&D? Government would become the earliest adopter, a bellwether that de-risks the second part of this process, that is, the commercialization of technology. At the end of the day, the government cares less about profit than it does about, say, putting a man on the moon. Tech should invite government to the table, give it free rein to hire the best people, and partner to scale the best ideas and innovations. The next innovation ecosystem opportunity in America involves the government spending money in the right areas *and* partnering with the private sector *and* finding ways for the venture capital community to shoulder the burden after launch. Let me explain.

The TRL Scale stands for the Technology Readiness Levels Scale. On the scale from one to ten, there are three phases. The first steps, one to three, are about creation. Invention without purpose. Serendipity. The mad genius throwing off sparks in his basement lab. This is where government investment should turn its focus. From seven to ten, companies like Dow or Boeing pick up those innovations, market them, commercialize them, teach customers how to use them, and scale them. You'll notice that I skipped steps four to seven. That's because four to seven is the valley of death. It's the place of maximum risk, with reward in sight. Here technology seeks a future home, not knowing what that home looks like. When the internet first appeared, it involved connecting humans from building to building. Did anyone know how it might evolve from there? No. During that period it required funding, which the government provided (not Al Gore). TRL four to seven, in short, is where the private sector, unlike the public sector, is reluctant to take risks (though the public sector doesn't know how to commercialize ideas). This public-private hands-together partnership gave us the technology of last century. It needs to step up its game in *this* century.

Today, the private sector companies who have benefited the most from the tech revolution without any help from the government are companies willing to take on all the risks, which typically means they are run by entrepreneur who are adventurers, like Elon Musk or Jeff Bezos. Today, in the US, there is, of course, Silicon Valley. There is, or was, the Boston Corridor. Where are all the other tech incubators? When I worked with the Obama administration, we created innovation clusters in the Midwest, at the University of Detroit, Case Western, Georgia Tech, and the University of Illinois. None of them really took off or endured. Unsure whether the next administration would provide ongoing investment, it was just too difficult to bring in private sector money. The epidemic of short-termism today that I discuss in chapter 5 applies equally to governments and politicians, who change regulatory frameworks every four years. In our current model, politicians target potential voters. They are less interested in what they can do for citizens by creating the next great thing.

This leaves us with another fundamental problem. How can we attract the right people to government and the right leaders to politics?

The Role of Regulation

Business and government don't understand each other. People working in the public sector don't understand business. People who work in a corporate environment only dimly understand the public sector, seeing it, at best, as a necessary evil, at worst oversized, authoritarian, chaotic, and hard to control. Wouldn't a close business-government partnership deter entrepreneurs, they ask? To form a hands-together partnership, this mindset must change.

It's fair to say that unlike most governments, the business world is forward thinking. Earlier I wrote that the word *regulation* must be coupled with the word *smart*. Unfortunately, they seldom coexist. To create a "smart regulation," a regulator needs the entity it is regulating seated at the same table. The two parties might start off by acknowledging the problem at hand. Here are the likely positives and negatives, and a few solutions. How can we work together to create regulations that move society away from the negatives and toward the positives, in a way that makes everyone smarter? What standard are we both pursuing? What is the best way to accomplish that standard? If the regulation in question is established, what is the risk-reward benefit to society? Is there a short-term cost but a long-term reward? If so, that regulation should be passed. This hands-together partnership is most critical as we seek to make sense of technology.

REGULATING TECHNOLOGY

Decades from now, when we look back on this time, the primitiveness of the gadgets we held in our hands will dumbfound us. Nascent though it is, no one needs to be reminded of the defining and dominant force tech plays in everyone's lives. But we lack any logical, pragmatic regulations about its impact and influence informed by the bigger desire to benefit the collective. To date, technology has focused on pockets, small communities, friend groups made up of acquaintances and sometimes strangers who share our interests and sometimes outrages. But as COVID showed, we are far less than the sum of our parts.

In the US, the pandemic was treated not as the crisis and health emergency it was but as an expression of democracy. Half the population saw masks as political gag orders and vaccines as existential trespasses on freedom and autonomy. Liberty mattered more than life and death or the health of neighbors. Mask regulations differed state by state, with some mandating the use of masks and others marketing themselves as "free states," resisting. But if a nuclear attack occurred in the US, we wouldn't call on, say, Oregon or Delaware to step up their defense efforts, would we? No, during wars and other periods of crisis, a country typically rallies around its value system. At stake is the safety and well-being of the citizens and the economy. This is the biggest reason why we must consider regulating—and taxing—internet service providers.

When chemistry started out in the first few decades of the twentieth century, almost no regulations were in place. Products were manufactured and shipped, polluting rivers, oceans, and our air. The pharmaceutical industry enjoyed a similarly lax early regulatory environment. Medicines containing opium, cocaine, marijuana, and alcohol were available and for sale before government wised up and tightened regulations around their use. It wasn't until the Clean Air Act was passed in the early 1970s, for example, that a serious effort to remediate toxic waste in the chemical industry was signed into law.

Why did we allow this? The answer is that we were slow to understand the effects, and we couldn't even measure them. With technology, there is no excuse. We already know many of the effects of what it means to be online all day long and exposed to disinformation and low-information opinions.

The US media is free, almost to a fault. Other Western democracies like Australia, New Zealand, Canada, England, and Japan offer far more stringent defamation regulation. The US would be smart to follow that model and strengthen the system of checks and balances in our media, especially in an era when digital media has overtaken print media and, in many cases, eliminated it. For its own survival, to secure and grow readership, print and cable television media have been obliged to replicate a digital template. The result is extreme and rancorous. Noise overtakes news, opinions trounce facts, and to date, no government has come up with any regulations or laws to distinguish between them.

We must develop new, coherent government standards that allow businesses to realize profits *only* if they adhere to accuracy. News stations and media platforms whose business model is based exclusively on disseminating opinion should be taxed at higher rates. Platforms that stir up outrage via extreme opinion mongering, no matter which political side they are on, should pay a literal price for their business model. Yes, it would be an example of government becoming more intrusive but also an example of government becoming *smarter*.

Consider how much of our infrastructure is, in fact, "free." For that matter, what does "free" even look like? We pay taxes and water and electricity bills. Why should the internet be different? Pricing the internet should be based on specific criteria. In the low-fee category would be churches and philanthropic endeavors. In the middle would be corporations. But if you are an extremist group, or a news or digital media platform whose business model is based on opinion mongering, not only will you have to pay a premium but an oversight board may very well veto you out of existence. Taxation would take us from criteria-free mass information to information that honors the privacy of its users and is regulated to the degree that it neither harms nor damages others. This is when data and information evolve from where they are today and become *knowledge*.

Consider how chaotic and unregulated the web is now, with NFTs, Bitcoin, blockchain, and augmented reality. Technology lacks even minimal control points. It will require some gutsy politicians to address this problem, but the business world, at least, is primed and ready. By now, everyone can agree that an uncontrolled Facebook, Twitter, and YouTube is toxic for society and the overall well-being of citizens.

I mentioned an oversight board. In the future, ideally, a regulatory agency will form, staffed with smart people drawn from academia, along with business leaders of unassailable credibility, who agree to serve as regulators of the national good. One of their mandates will be to determine what is true and what is false. Just as seat belts, air bags, and emissions controls should have been mandatory when the first cars appeared, the past should guide us as we create regulations around technology. The big difference being that, unlike the car industry, technology's learning curves are so steep and move so quickly that officials need to regulate them as they surface.

Until that day comes, the best solution is to find new ways to communicate accurate information to the public using the tools created by digital media. During the height of the antimask and antivaccine protests across the US, I attended the Benioff Dreamforce Summit. One of the speakers was Larry Brilliant, the US epidemiologist who worked with the World Health Organization in the mid-1970s to eradicate smallpox. He offered some ideas on the best way to overcome the then-rampant online misinformation around COVID. His frustration reached such a point, he said, that he reached out to Seth MacFarlane, creator of the TV cartoon *Family Guy*. Together they produced a public service announcement in which two of the show's characters, Brian and Stewie, explained the benefits of getting a COVID vaccine. The message, in short, was tailored to the people it was trying to convince.

This brings up a related question younger technology founders and teams must ask themselves: When should an entrepreneur absorb the responsibilities inherent in being an entrepreneur? Hasn't the time come for them to understand that part of the entrepreneur's job description means that your company exists within institutions, governments, academia, and advisory boards that will turn what you are selling into a product that *does well by doing good*?

Society, as we now know, is asking this century's enterprises to pay it forward. Tech companies are no exception. This is one reason why the Dows and the IBMs of the world are so skilled at developing and creating future managers. Dow and IBM both understand that their employees are akin to the members of a relay team. Their job as companies is to pass the baton, one that will be modified depending on the era of operation. Older tech companies like Google, Microsoft, and Apple have also stepped up to the plate. Today they are responsible digital enterprises that realize their role isn't just to harvest their products to maximize shareholder wealth but to forward-pay some of those profits to benefit the rest of society. This is the union of business, government, and society that I speak about often. It should happen more often.

Technology regulations should also encompass cybersecurity. How private is your information? Is the text or email you just received from the sender who claims it is? Which platforms, if any, do you trust? My own phone has more than half a dozen communications platforms, all with varying levels of security and protection, none of which is 100 percent safe, leaving my data vulnerable to theft.

Remember, too, that this decade will see the continuing development of quantum computing, in which governments worldwide are investing substantial sums. Quantum computing is a type of computation that creates vast multidimensional spaces to answer questions and arrive at solutions beyond the capacity even of supercomputers. When quantum computing takes hold, encryption technology will lag to such a degree that any supercomputer in government, academia, the CIA, or other agencies that depend on the mass processing of data will switch over. This transition will require new firewalls of cyber protection to defend that data against theft. Some platforms today already offer seven-step authentication, in addition to encryption codes that change every week or two weeks. It's the best we have, but it still leaves most of us vulnerable.

We ran up against this problem at Dow, when we lost reams of agricultural science technology when a Dow employee in China, whom we had just dismissed, passed along a trove of R&D reports he had downloaded onto his computer to the Chinese government. He was apprehended and taken to trial. Still, it was a wake-up call, and it happens in other companies too. Any number of technology-centric businesses are resisting transferring their most precious data onto the cloud, fearing that if they get hacked, they'll be unable to protect it.

Cybersecurity issues, ironically, have even led to widespread onshoring. Imagine you are a company that relocated overseas, seeking cheaper labor. All goes well for a few years, until your host government raises employee wages. The company decides to return to the US and onshore various elements of its business. It isn't the lack of capital that drives onshoring (capital today is ubiquitous), but the need to reduce or eliminate risks in your global supply chain and ensure supply integrity. Companies are saying, "When we onshore, we are going to build the best new gadget, semiconductor facility, or biotech entity *here*." They know they need to protect their digital ecosystems, a protection that can't be guaranteed if their factories are in China, Brazil, Russia, or even Europe. These drivers, which are a consequence of failed geopolitics and companies and nations over-relying on a flat world, are two factors behind private sector investment within many nations today.

The New Twenty-First-Century Politics

What does the résumé of the ideal twenty-first-century politician look like? The answer lies in the models established by business as they provide the template for tomorrow's political leaders.

One reason companies like Dow or IBM have survived for so long is that they keep their eyes trained on the future. The rearview mirror doesn't interest them. They focus instead on what their companies must do going forward. "Horses for courses" is a popular term in England and Australia, meaning simply that different people are best suited to different situations. For forward-thinking companies, this means appointing forward-thinking leaders. The same goes for those serving in government and running for political office.

Today's government officials should be among the best and the brightest from top universities and the private sector, so that they can educate other politicians on the agenda of today's concerns, from energy to housing. Again, the keyword is *forward thinking*—which applies to candidates running for office too.

It goes without saying that politicians require a platform to get elected. But the biggest element of that platform should be the promise of tomorrow and what those promises can yield for the electorate. Foremost among tomorrow's concerns is Globalization 3.0. What most politicians are slow to understand is that the biggest competition today isn't about selling more products of the kind business sold yesterday—it's about selling products society will need *tomorrow*. How can we compete for tomorrow's skills, innovations, and intellectual property? Small nation-states like Israel and Singapore intuitively understand the need to plan for the future, and so, to a slightly lesser extent, does Germany. The US has dominated in innovation for a century or longer. But we are at risk of falling behind unless we start electing leaders who will promote policies that provide younger generations with the best jobs of the future.

Two barriers keep us from attracting forward-thinking politicians. The first is money. Few people are willing to say no to Wall Street or Silicon Valley and risk serving their country by creating policies that benefit everyone—and even rarer are those who are invested in making a difference and creating an impact.

The second barrier is the media. Political campaigns today play out on streaming and social media and cable television. The nature of these platforms is antithetical to developing an informed citizenry. Studious, logical, thoughtful, content-rich candidates running for office need to understand how to sell sound bites without sacrificing the integrity of their policies. We also need to eradicate the gossip-mongering tendencies of the mass media that often trashes good people while hunting down skeletons, innuendos, and perceived wrongdoing that, given the nature of online data, never disappears.

When forward-thinking candidates are elected, there's another problem. There aren't enough of them. Thoughtfulness has become the domain of the few. One shortcut for politicians who want to make an impact is to forgo campaigning and get appointed, but in today's divided, contentious Congress, this happens less often than it should.

The bottom line: government and political leaders should acknowledge the past without leaning into it. Along with running future-oriented platforms, political candidates should run for office on policy platforms built around Inclusive Capitalism. (This is why mayors are usually good candidates for federal office, as they usually bring with them a broad understanding of all the stakeholders in their town or city.) This in turn would prompt voters to ask: Why is the policy of candidate A better than that of candidate B? Because the policies championed by candidate A are more inclusive of all stakeholders.

Finally, I believe everyone should volunteer three years to public service. This might be wishful thinking, but public service needs to be reframed as an essential ingredient of individual growth. Public service should happen twice during a lifetime. People in their twenties should volunteer three years, as should people in their sixties. To younger people who might ask why, I would repeat what I tell the students at the academy: You are not embarking on a professional career for the sake of profit. You are entering a career to create maximum impact. Isn't this the best time to experiment with verticals, and not just horizontals?

Someday, ideally, it won't matter whether you are a businessperson, a professor, an artist, or a cook. You are putting in time to help improve society and serving as a steward for future generations. After all, companies like Salesforce ask employees to volunteer some percentage of their time, knowing it can't help but make them more effective contributors to the enterprise. Shouldn't we all consider doing the same?

Taking Aim at Lobbyists

New government officials and political candidates won't surface unless we also transform the role of political influence. "Lobbying" refers literally to the lobby of Washington, D.C.,'s Willard Hotel, where politicians, businesspeople, and government representatives used to meet over drinks to discuss the tax on X or the tariff on Y. Today, of course, lobbying has become a billion-dollar industry deeply and, many believe, inextricably embedded in the US business and political model.

It is natural for capital to have developed self-preservation strategies and to carry out the desires of individuals who benefit most from maintaining the status quo. Nor do I fault wealthy people who want to continue making money (though they will never use it in their lifetimes) or who want to provide guardrails for generations of descendants. But why don't they consider *everyone's* descendants who will be walking this planet, breathing in oxygen, and swimming in the ocean a hundred years from today?

Getting money out of politics won't be easy. One solution is to pass legislation eliminating all interest groups, lobbying groups, and donor groups that fund political candidates directly or indirectly. Another solution (one that would generate maximum fear in political circles) is to create a centralized pool of resources that all candidates running for political office could access. Candidates would apply for that money and use it to do whatever is necessary to be seen and heard. If this system took hold, it would level the playing field, not least by placing a check on billionaires who self-fund their campaigns.

This system exists already in some countries, a big difference being that outside the US, most political campaigns are time sensitive. There are no primaries. Parties appoint candidates to run in a certain district. Candidates spend the next month running their campaigns, an election is held, and a winner is named. What prevents our doing that in the US?

Abolishing the primary system and shortening the political campaign model would put an end to the wealthy influencing politics in much larger percentages than those without the same resources. If one of my core premises is that the institutions of last century must be reimagined and reestablished for *this* century, this would represent a major, wholesale, positive change to the engine of the American political system. Even if it never happens, rules and regulations should be formed that control the access that interest groups have to politicians and political networks. At a minimum, we need to create transparent metrics so that when politicians are elected, a central registry reveals who donated to their campaigns and the degree of their access.

A Path Forward

Earlier I mentioned that business and government don't really understand each other. One good way to bridge that divide is by instituting sabbatical programs, such as the one launched during the Trump presidency where under Secretary of Labor Alexander Acosta, the administration formed a council featuring a yearlong federal program for high school and community college students, with businesses working side by side with the administration and Department of Labor. But no better example of a successful public-private partnership exists than Singapore's Economic Development Board, a government agency formed under the national Ministry of Trade and Industry, whose job it is to create strategies that enhance Singapore as a leading global destination for business, innovation, and talent. Along with facilitating investment in Singapore, the EDB also helps local companies transform their operations and increase productivity, while ensuring that they have access to government incentives. Singapore is a small nation-state, and an economic development board would be harder to set up and sustain in the US. But creating one would set the tempo for investment, and investment incentives and decisions, from coast to coast.

I'm an ardent believer that leadership models should occur in the collaborative role of what is, in essence, the triangle of the new world order of business. What does that triangle look like? At the top is society. At one apex is business. At the other apex is government. Society needs all its stakeholders—academics, people who work in unions, people subject to government policies—to play a role in this leadership model. That template is not yet in place, and this century's institutions must develop one.

During the pandemic, I got accustomed to addressing Liveris Academy students—everybody, for that matter!—remotely from my home office in Sydney. During one Zoom call, I told the students that if I were twenty years old again, the next few decades would exhilarate me. Never in my life have I seen a horizon richer and more opportunity filled than the one before them today. That optimism *does* come with a caveat. Liveris Academy students need to accept the embedded risk implicit in the act of hurling themselves into the discontinuity and failing. Then they must do it again and again and again.

A few weeks later, I had a socially distanced lunch with a thirty-year-old Greek entrepreneur who had spent his twenties working in the biomedical field. He had raised half a billion dollars to deploy his research in breakthrough medical technologies designed to cure diabetes, cancer, Alzheimer's, and other diseases of aging. At one point I asked, "What motivates you?" He told me he had never been drawn to a traditional career path.

I'm not saying anyone can do what he did, but why not at least try? This is something I advise business school students around the globe. If they insist on pursuing conventional business and money-making paths, I tell them, they are likely to wake up sometime in their forties and find themselves looking for a new career, having discovered that the Masters-of-the-Universe business track, no matter how well paying, can become an addiction without a cause or point. Using a finance degree to make money and brokering where capital is both sourced from and ends up is the career of a middleman, not an entrepreneur. Why not eliminate that step entirely?

The future leadership of this century is about leaders from the private and the public sector partnering to solve the biggest problems humanity faces. We need government to foster a policy climate that encourages investment and innovation. We need business to create growth, jobs, and a thriving economy. Leaders from both sectors need to take a seat at the table; otherwise, one or the other will find themselves on the menu. Let's join our hands together to propel the kind of change previous leaders and eras have found elusive. If the five Ds—denial, defiance, debate, dialogue, do—are in fact the stations of a natural cycle, we must begin the debate that transforms business, government, *and* society.

Takeaways and Tools

- Government and business have a long and beneficial history of collaboration, from FDR's New Deal to President Biden's 2021 bipartisan infrastructure bill.

- Government and business should endeavor to put aside their cat-versus-dog antagonisms and create new, future-based models of partnership. If older templates were *hands on*, followed by *hands off*, this century's model is *hands together*.

- This new model should be composed of forward-looking government officials and forward-looking CEOs. More than *bigger* government, this means the creation of *smarter* government.

- The *hands-together* partnership between business and government also requires a new mindset that is focused on serving the public good and the national interest. What role, for example, could the US government play in investing in digital R&D?

- The new norm should be *smart regulation*. Regulators and regulatees must sit at the same table and reach agreement on standards, benefits, short-term costs, and long-term rewards.

- New political candidates must focus on what society needs today and in the future. How can the US best compete for tomorrow's skills, innovations, and intellectual property? This also requires rethinking the roles played by big money, the media, and the political lobbying industry.

- Creating a generation of new government and political leaders will take time, but I'm hopeful. We should begin from the ground up by exposing younger generations to public service, while emphasizing that service and early learning will make them better future advisers, operators, and leaders.

- A more top-down approach requires a new engagement model spearheaded by a younger generation to rethink political candidates in every swing state. A top-down candidate may well emerge from this process who is supported by both business and society. The reelection of Emmanuel Macron in France is a strong, positive signal that Western countries actively seek similar candidates.

9

Leadership Lesson 3

Disrupt Yourself Whenever Possible

I n the late 1990s, Harvard Business School professor Clay Christensen wrote a book that has had a lasting influence on businesses. In *The Innovator's Dilemma*, Christensen pioneered the theory of "disruptive innovation," the notion that in the face of competition, a business could be doing everything right, over a long period of time too, and *still* be at risk of failing. It seems that good management, proper decision making, the right resource-allocation processes, careful listening to a customer base while tracking the competition, and investing resources into designing high-end, high-performing products aren't enough. Even great businesses falter.

You may wonder why I'm reaching back into the twentieth century, but Christensen's theories are even more relevant today than they were twenty-five years ago. To understand why, let's go back to an era when life and business were more straightforward.

Back in my CEO days at Dow, I could repeatedly enunciate a strategy. That strategy would find its way into a book the board and I would review at a preordained time, say, every six months or annually. We allowed for an error band of variability on both the high and low sides. Today that variability can be extreme on either end.

This means that today's companies can be dethroned in a second, for any number of reasons. The time-tested idea of leaders and companies learning strategy by *doing* simply cannot stand up against the realities of doing business in a VUCA (volatile, uncertain, complex, ambiguous) era. This century requires leaders who are comfortable with (if not exactly overjoyed by) Bitcoin abruptly showing up to jolt the financial markets, when two years earlier no one even knew what Bitcoin *was.* Whether related to cyber, blockchain, artificial intelligence, cryptocurrency, or augmented reality, numerous present-day concepts and the language we use to describe them didn't exist a year or two years ago. This adds complexity to what it means even to *engage* in disruptive innovation.

Today, for example, the oil and gas industries are now waking up to being disrupted in ways they couldn't have foreseen five years ago. Consider what happened in the Exxon boardroom in 2020, when an impact investor from a small, obscure hedge fund, Engine No. 1, waged a battle to install three of its directors on the Exxon board, which led to Exxon agreeing to substantially reduce its carbon footprint around the world. (Engine No. 1, it should be noted, had the support of BlackRock, Vanguard, and State Street, three of Exxon's largest institutional investors.) A similar event took place at Chevron, when a majority of company shareholders voted to support an activist proposal from Follow This, a Dutch campaign group that had launched a campaign to persuade Shell to reduce its own global carbon emissions.

Are you prepared to pivot without warning? Do you have one or more plan Bs? Earlier I mentioned I belong to a group founded by Richard Branson of former and current CEOs known as the B Team. We endorse three pillars: *sustainability* (no future beyond planetary boundaries); *equality* (no justice without respect for human rights); and *accountability* (no trust without transparency and responsibility). During the pandemic, the other members and I met virtually every month. Among the B Team's axioms, which are directed mostly to ourselves as reminders, is: Be bold and courageous. Embrace the moment you are in and change it.

It probably goes without saying that these leadership dynamics are different from the ones Professor Christensen was talking about when he wrote his book.

What should a leader or a business do to survive and thrive in *this* century? Well, whenever I mentor younger CEOs, or address the student body at Liveris Academy, the first, somewhat obvious, piece of advice I give them is to identify the problem or issue at hand. Does it relate to ESG factors, government regulation, geopolitical considerations? Recognize it. Define it.

Next, ask, "What tools, or even what toolbox, do I need to deal with this problem?" Leaders shouldn't underestimate themselves or think that companies over a certain size are too slow to wage battle against crisis or change. Consider, after all, how IBM turned itself around in the 1990s and early 2000s. More recently, Pfizer and Johnson & Johnson, two huge conglomerates, focused their resources and energy on developing COVID vaccines and boosters. When I interviewed Pfizer's chairman and CEO, Albert Bourla, he recalled being told that it would take up to a year and billions of dollars to bring the Pfizer vaccine to market. He responded that he needed a vaccine in three months. "Don't tell me what is impossible," Bourla remembered saying. "I want to know what is *possible*. And if the response is 'But the process . . . ' then it's everybody's job to *break* that process."

What does this tell us? Among other things, it reminds leaders that they should enumerate the one or two things (and not the ten or twenty things) they want to accomplish. Point to it, do it—and move on. All this to say that the twenty-first century demands a fast, almost SWAT-like response to confronting and solving crises.

Leaders also need to disrupt *themselves*. I mentioned earlier that when I was named CEO, the retirement age at the company was sixty. Today that rule is a relic of corporate archeology. The average tenure for a CEO in a Fortune 500 or 100 company today is 6.9 years. Why? Because persevering in a leadership position has never been harder. For that you can blame global competition, the pressures of financial performance, stock market expectations (complicated further by hedge funds and activist funds), the ninety-day march toward profits instead of a focus on medium- or long-term vision, and impatient boards that are unwilling to safeguard a CEO. It's little wonder many CEOs call it a day after only a few years.

But Dow also established the retirement age of sixty for a good reason, namely, *to enable refreshment*. These days, with age factors increasingly obsolete, the onus is on leaders and companies to refresh themselves. For many CEOs, there comes a point—and it happened to me too—when unless you refresh yourself, others won't bother. Remember, most CEOs are surrounded by sycophants who want only to keep their own jobs and tell you what you want to hear. Nor is the board invested in a CEO's longevity. The burden is on you to transform, refresh, and disrupt yourself, however which way you can.

One trait I was proudest of as CEO was a capacity to combine agility with resiliency and to continually test internal and external risk envelopes. These attributes went a long way toward keeping *me* fresh. Much can be said for youth, energy, and exuberance, but CEOs can refresh themselves at any age. It happened to me after the boardroom coup and during the Rohm and Haas acquisition. It happens today in the work I do at IBM, Saudi Aramco, Worley, Lucid Motors, Novonix, Sumitomo Mitsui Banking Corporation, and elsewhere.

A last piece of advice I picked up in my pre-CEO days, when I was serving as Dow's COO in the early 2000s, one that kept resurfacing when I was interviewing successful CEOs: don't shy away from creating a succession plan for yourself. Your tenure might not work out, for the company or for you. It needs to gel for both. Be realistic. No one is expendable. I am a longtime believer in "horses for courses." Maybe you are running a two-mile race. Maybe it's five two-mile races. You won't know until the race is over.

AFTER ALL THIS, who in their right mind would ever voluntarily step up to become a leader in this century? Wouldn't *any* job be easier, better, and less stressful? Not only do leaders need to be diligent about staying current while "working the intersections," they must face multiple tectonic shifts and revolutions around digitalization, the environment, geopolitics, rampant short-termism, the evolving role of boards and governments, *plus* the need to attend to every one of their stakeholders. Even if for some reason you still want the job, how do you prepare for it?

In my pre-CEO days with Dow, I was lucky to work in fifteen countries across Asia. At any time, I was twelve time zones away from Dow head-quarters in Midland. Cell phones didn't exist yet. Communication hap-pened twice daily, via telex. There was no map or manual telling me, or anyone, how to do business in Korea or China or India. We had to do our homework and custom form whatever was before us.

Those early experiences underlie a piece of advice I give Liveris Academy students, especially those about to enter the workforce. *Join something.* During my undergraduate years I became a member of every club I could and even became the chair of some, including the then nascent Chemical Engineering Students Society (all twenty of us!). I served on panels and participated in student protests. In the future, I remind Liveris Academy students, you might be invited to join the Brookings Institute or the Council on Foreign Relations, but in the meantime, try to develop the habit of elas-ticizing your brain. I don't know any better way to do that than by joining a group. A group in your community or local government or a bank board or community advisory board. The goal is to accumulate as much group experience as possible. Get uncomfortable early on. Figure out ways to learn horizontally as you ascend vertically. Identify your North Star, and always keep it in your sights, but don't be afraid to change, or course cor-rect. Don't overdetermine your lives or your career. Yes, piece together a three-year, or five-year, vision, but remember to stay entrepreneurial within that framework and start testing your own boundaries as early as possible.

The leaders of today also need to constantly adjust their binocular vision. They need to go wide and deep at the same time, and see problems from various heights and distances, from close-up to thirty thousand feet up in the air. That means learning things outside their sphere of focus. Early in my life, I developed a chafing impatience around anything I didn't understand. Instead of saying, "I don't understand," I dug in, studied, read late into the night, and networked to find answers beyond my purview until finally I *did* understand. I listened. I tried to uncover different ways of thinking. Then I built a bridge linking their perspective to mine. It wasn't about who was "right" or "wrong." My goal was to understand *all* positions and uncover a solution. In whatever job I was given, I always applied a *solution* mindset. In this or any other century, it's an evergreen approach.

The demands of today and tomorrow will be much more understandable for leaders if they work their way into them, instead of waking up ten years from today to find their companies are having issues with China they have no idea how to solve. Sure, you can contact their government affairs person who can call up someone in Washington, and maybe the Business Council can offer a decent template, but you're still getting only a one-way piece of advice. By gathering your own information and experiences, you'll be able to augment the advice you get, and improve on it.

Assess. Decide. Do. Do all three quickly. Be patient—but *be urgently patient.*

Takeaways and Tools

- At Dow, our band of error around strategy typically fell in the low to medium range. Today, that same band swings wildly to positive and negative extremes. In a VUCA era, strategy is learned by *doing.*

- The rate and pace of change in this century makes it likelier than not that unprecedented and unsettling events will occur. Consider the rise of cryptocurrency, NFTs, and augmented reality, none of which even existed five years ago. How prepared are you for disruption? What is your plan B, and your plan C?

- To borrow a leadership axiom from the B Team: *Be bold and courageous. Embrace the moment you are in and change it.*

- If you and your enterprise are jolted by external events, the first thing to do is identify the issue at hand. Is it geopolitical, governmental, or linked to ESG factors? Recognize it and define it.

- Next, ask yourself: "What tools or toolbox should I use to cope with this issue?" The size of your business is irrelevant. Witness how Pfizer produced a COVID vaccine in only three months, streamlining a process that usually takes upward of a year. If processes stand in your way, ignore them.

- What are the one or two things you want to accomplish as CEO? Do them, then move onto the next pair of things. Be SWAT-like in your approach and behaviors.

- Consider disrupting *yourself* as a leader. Taking time to refresh and transform yourself by habitually testing internal and external risk envelopes is the best way I know to continue honing your brain, EQ, intuition, and perspective.

- Create a succession plan for yourself. After all, things might not work out. The term "horses for courses" means that only time will tell whether you're running a two-mile race or a twenty-six-mile marathon.

- Joining something—a club, a society, a town hall, a bank board, your local government—can accustom younger leaders to elasticizing their brains. Gain as much group experience as possible early on. Get uncomfortable. Learn wide but also learn deep. Keep your North Star in sight but remember that course corrections often happen too.

10

The New Role
of Science

I n 2015, Rick Snyder, the then governor of Michigan, and I shared a panel
at the Forbes Talent Summit in Detroit, Michigan. Then and now, the
figures around the employee pipeline in the manufacturing sector were
cause for concern. Ninety percent of all manufacturers in the US were
experiencing a shortage of qualified workers, and more than six hundred
thousand technical jobs were going unfilled, with most fifteen- to
twenty-five-year-olds lacking the skills, experience, or interest to fill these
positions.

When I was done speaking, Governor Snyder, a self-described accoun-
tancy nerd, opened the floor to questions. The subject of chemistry came
up, and I cast my eyes over the audience. "Chemistry," I said, "is actually
really sexy."

There was general, confused laughter, but fifteen minutes later, once I
finished explaining what I meant, most of the audience seemed riveted.
Lipstick, lip gloss, foundation, eye shadow, mascara, cold cream, the hair-
styles of every man and woman present, even the light gleam on Governor
Snyder's necktie—none of those things, I said, would even *exist* without
chemistry.

Lipstick, for example, has adorned human faces for six thousand years in variations including coal, crushed gemstone, ochre, vermilion, and ground mulberries. Present-day lipstick, the kind you find in drugstores and department stores, owes its color to carmine dye, extracted from cochineal, scale insects native to Mexico and Central America that feast on cactuses. (Carminic acid, which scale insects produce naturally, keeps away predators.) These dyes combine with oils (to keep them from drying out), waxes (which mix to create the base structure of lipstick and keep it from fading), an emulsifier (which allows the ingredients to mix), a nanoparticle (to bind the lipstick to human skin), along with other pigments (for example, chemicals) including, in some cases, fragments of pearl that are blended in to create a glossy luster. Most commercially sold lipsticks are developed and tested for stability, color maintenance, and heat response for up to a year before a prototype is developed and produced on an industrial scale. And that's only lipstick. Mascara involves its own intricate chemistry set.

Among the molecules present in your typical, store-bought, water-soluble mascara are glyceryl stearate, ammonium acrylates copolymer, and polyvinyl alcohol. Pigment, usually black or brown, provides mascara its color. Waxes and oils—beeswax, mineral oil, castor oil—allow mascara to adhere to eyelashes while repelling water. The illusion of lengthening is achieved by applying short rayon or nylon fibers that cling to the lash ends and extend them artificially, like the eaves overhanging a roof or the top slice of bread on a sandwich.

These are only two examples of how chemistry underpins nearly everything we do, eat, drink, inject, ingest, wash, adorn our faces and bodies with, and wear, up to and including our shoes and sneakers and the clothes hanging in our closets. Chemistry is responsible for the swat of a tennis racket; the rotation of a golf club; the spin of footballs, baseballs, and soccer balls; the glide of bike pedals; and the texture of Ping-Pong paddles, ice skates, hockey sticks, and cleats. It forms the basis of almost everything we eat and drink, our medications, our toothpastes, our deodorants and antiperspirants, the tiles of our bath and shower, the heating system that keeps our spaces warm in the winter, and the ceiling fans and air conditioners that cool us off in the summer.

But there are more critical reasons why science needs to be restored to its rightful pole position. Today, the language of science is lost to most of the people who could benefit most from the discoveries that improve the quality of our lives, including medicine, clean water, food safety, efficient transport, the internet, and space exploration. Most if not all of these things we take for granted. We consider them our birthrights, door prizes handed to us for being human. This perspective must change.

The scientists and mathematicians of this century need to communicate better how they discover, invent, develop, scale, produce, and market products for everyday life and human progress, so that we can continue supporting our goals in areas like sustainability and the elimination of poverty. According to the *New York Times*, "In 2018, 15-year-olds in the United States ranked 18th in their ability to explain scientific concepts, lagging behind their peers in not just China, Singapore, and the United Kingdom, but also Poland and Slovenia."[1] From a competitive standpoint, the US can't just sit back and watch this happen.

Put another way, nothing would be better than if science and math managed to become aspirational, cool, and yes, even sexy.

AROUND THE SAME TIME I addressed the Forbes Talent Summit, I spoke to the graduating class of Wharton Business School at the University of Pennsylvania. At one point, I asked the three hundred or so students in the audience how many of them were thinking of going into manufacturing after graduating. Two or three hands. Next I asked how many students were going into finance. Almost every hand in the room went up.

It was clear, as if I needed reminding, that *manufacturing* had become one of those grubby, uncharismatic words from another era, one associated, if anyone bothered, with weeds, rusty train tracks, and boarded-up factories. (Did the US even manufacture things anymore? Didn't China make all our stuff?) Aside from wondering when exactly we allowed the people who manage money—the middlemen—to earn more than the people who develop products—the creators—I left Wharton convinced that *manufacturing* needed to be rebranded (*inventing* and *creating* is a lot closer to what manufacturers do), along with *all* the life sciences.

What comes to mind when you hear the words *science* and *math*? Probably every movie and television show ever made about the unpopular kids in high school. Science and math kids are seen as geeks, nerds, and outsiders, their handshakes weak, their social skills nonexistent. The social categories we get exposed to early are slow to disappear and can last a lifetime. Complicating the problem is social media, which focuses on surface popularity and desirability, traits calculated and amplified by followers, engagement and likes, versus science, which concerns itself with *insides* and *causes*—the *why* of things.

In an online world of covetable images, it's easy to understand why science and math have fallen out of favor. The lives of most people are routine, and I include my own. The opportunities for excitement, transformation, and transcendence don't come along often. We go online to escape everyday life, not have our faces rubbed in it. Social and mass media offer a continuous tasting menu of celebrity and money, images that usually show the results of hard work more than the effort it took to get there.

Rebranding science won't be easy, but it's a question of competitive advantage. As countries compete for jobs based on twenty-first-century skills, the division between the haves and the have-nots will only widen. In the next two decades, access to the digital toolbox and the development of a digital workforce will matter more and more. Among the core skills required for this century's workers is a facility in science, mathematics, and engineering. It's a race to the top, and it's winnable, but we need to start *now*.

AS A BOY, whenever I was asked what I wanted to be when I grew up, I always said that I wanted to be a teacher. Probably I was modeling what was before me at school, or else I was impressed by the long vacations my teachers were given. Then, in my midteens, I discovered science and math, and I found out I had an aptitude for both.

A passion and a career are often born when opportunity meets talent. This was true for me with science and math. The world opened, like that, as if a room in shadow had been flooded with light. The light grew only brighter as time went on. Science, I learned, explained *everything*. Life, death, the universe, not to mention how everything—buildings, devices, outer space—worked. The deeper I dug, the sharper and more understandable the world around me became. Some people like to say there's a "hard" scientific brain and a "soft" artistic brain, but that distinction is lost on me. I experienced the same passion playing with numbers or experimenting with theorems that visual artists must feel when they master brush strokes or study the paintings on the walls of a museum. In the same way their brains must light up when they discover texture or line or color theory, my brain came alive when I thought about what would happen if I added three carbons, versus one, to a benzene ring. Why was my benzene ring accepting only six couplings versus another ring that accepts four couplings, or two?

Throughout high school and university, science and math became my lens and language. Fluency followed and so did the growing desire on my part to expose others to a world that surprisingly few people had any interest in learning more about. "Everything is number," Pythagoras said, and at one point in my twenties, I understood "numbers" so well it felt exhilarating. I didn't feel sidelined, either. Popular science was ascendant in the 1950s and 1960s, and it would reach its peak in 1969 with the Apollo 11 moon landing.

But during the 1970s and 1980s, notwithstanding the strides made by NASA and the creation of Earth Day, to name a few examples of scientific progress, US students began falling behind their contemporaries from other developed economies. High school kids weren't being taught the vertical science capabilities that could be parlayed into careers in robotics, drones, or quantum computing. Many top scientists flocked instead to government-based agencies, and overall, if given a choice, most students proficient in math far preferred to study spreadsheets at Goldman Sachs over devoting long hours using their skills to help invent the next cutting-edge battery. Humans had become too successful, our lives too easy and convenient. The one-click comforts of life, from air conditioning to electricity to fast food, were treated by most people as inheritances. With the rise of the internet in the 1990s, efficiency and convenience only increased. The miraculous became commonplace, even at times tedious.

Now and then science managed to pierce the culture—*Breaking Bad*, for example, made chemistry cool, also profitable, illegal, and murderous—but these days science and math are conspicuously absent from mass culture and online media.

But I still believe that nothing is more astonishing, or has more to teach us, than science or, I might add, is anyone duller at parties on this subject than me. "Did you know that thing in your hands is made of polyethylene, and inside of that is a preservative that has a molecule that prevents oxygenation?" Growing up, my children learned to humor me during dinner. Were they aware that French fries and veggie burgers don't retain moisture when they're fried, which is why French fries and veggie burgers both have binders in them to solidify their surfaces? Did they also know that another category of binder is used to adhere tiles to the sides of buildings?

Dad—pass the salt. Yes, but did they realize that the production of salt requires a chemical process of separating out sodium chloride (which is what salt is) from sea, brine, or underground water? Did they know that the lettuce leaves and tomatoes in our salad owed their freshness and hygiene to soil and water science—and that a urea-based fertilizer derived from petroleum products ensured that the soil is fertilized properly and that a genetically modified organism defended those lettuces and tomatoes against pesticides and plant diseases?

More than just flaunting my chemistry chops, I was expressing my frustration with how little cultural attention and respect science continues to be given. Tech companies are still all the rage, credited for shipping electronics faster (and swamping humanity with a lot of useless information). Why is technology seen as "good" or "cool," compared to what chemistry gives us? Adding to my frustration was the fact that during my Dow career, I succeeded in making the company relevant by creating a material science company with the most cutting-edge innovation engine possible. Nonetheless, the public mostly sees Dow and other chemical companies as toxic, pollution-creating dinosaurs from another century. Not many people realize just how hard it would be to get through a single twenty-four-hour period without either chemistry or a Dow product. So let's do a thought experiment:

It's Monday. You wake up and stretch. The bed you're lying on, including the foam inside your mattress, contains Dow products. Your pillow does too. Your sheets and pillowcases, your bath and hand towels, the textile sizing agents in your bedspread—these, too, contain Dow products.

Your bare feet touch down on the rug. Like every swatch of carpeting in your home, your rug contains Dow products. The paint on your walls, the recessed lighting overhead, your lightbulbs, filaments, and light-emitting diodes that temper the heat coming from those filaments that allow them to be energy efficient are all Dow products. The varnish on your bedside table, your coffee table, and your kitchen counter, the liners inside your dresser drawers, the coat hangers in your closet, your clothes, your shoes— Dow products all. In your bathroom, there is not a single cosmetic, lotion, toothpaste, soap, or shampoo bottle that doesn't contain at least one Dow product, probably several, with most enclosed in Dow plastic. The screw top of your toothpaste and soap dispenser features Dow adhesives, without which, I might add, the tiles in your shower would crumble.

Having showered, you now pack a lunchbox. Glad wrap, Saran wrap, and Ziploc bags—those are all Dow inventions. Dow products can also be found in the frozen food you store in your freezer. In your fridge, every soda, spread, sauce, syrup, or condiment, including ketchup, mustard, and mayonnaise, includes propylene glycol, a Dow chemical.

Crude oil, a fossil fuel, has become a target of environmental activists, often for good reason, but what most people don't realize is that elements of crude oil are used in gasoline, diesel fuel, heating oil, asphalt, and petrochemicals. The Ranken Energy Corporation once compiled a list of roughly six thousand products that owe their lives to petroleum.[2] A day without petroleum means a day without bottled water, wristwatches, eyeglasses, wide-screen TVs, armchairs, side tables, cell phones, the photos hanging on your walls, the carpeting covering your stairs, the shoes and sneakers in your closet, the door to your house, your car, your windows, the shingles covering your roof, and, finally, the clothes covering your body.

In short, the gazes of my children at the dinner table never defeated my mission to evangelize for science and scientific innovation whenever I could.

One of the first things I noticed when I became the CEO of Dow was that our innovation and technology cupboard was barren. When I analyzed how much money the chemical industry had spent between 1980 and 2000, I realized that despite the staggering amounts of money spent chasing innovation, the entire industry had come up with only three—*three*—new billion-dollar products. Imagine identical data for, say, Google or Amazon. In other words, Dow, and the chemical industry in general, was no longer innovating.

I removed Dow's then head of R&D and appointed myself chief technology officer in charge of the R&D department. I brought in outside people like Bill Banholzer from General Electric, who completely transformed the company's R&D mindset. Dow had also become PhD averse and had mostly abandoned its once-tight relationship with universities like Princeton and Caltech. We soon began recruiting PhDs again and reanimating our partnerships with academic and other R&D pipelines, on the assumption that not every great idea Dow comes up with will come from within.

Dow's innovation journey culminated between 2005 to 2008. By investing more money in R&D, we ended up *making* more money. Once again, we were attracting top talent from the best tech-oriented universities in the US and abroad. Around that same time, I committed $300 million to build Dow's largest R&D center in Shanghai, China. Today, having created a foundation for an increase in the profits for Dow's products line, from 10 to 15 percent to 15 to 30 percent, depending on the year, the Shanghai office continues to be our most productive R&D center. This market cap increase was what made it possible for me to do the deals necessary to accelerate Dow's ongoing transformation, including the purchase of Rohm and Haas in 2008.

EARLIER I QUOTED THE disheartening statistics from the Forbes Talent Summit—namely, that 90 percent of all manufacturers in the US were experiencing a shortage of qualified workers, and more than six hundred thousand technical jobs were going unfilled, with most fifteen-to-twenty-five-year-olds lacking the skills, the experience, or the interest to fill those positions.

That was 2015. Those numbers haven't improved since then in any meaningful way. The US is a longtime global leader in educating its students in science, technology, engineering, and mathematics. But today, according to a study carried out by Deloitte and the Manufacturing Institute, the manufacturing skills gap could result in as many as 2.1 million jobs going unfilled by 2030.[3] Among the takeaways: the industry recouped 63 percent of jobs that were lost during the COVID pandemic, but that still left vacancies for almost six hundred thousand jobs, despite near-record job openings in the sector. What's more, nearly 80 percent of manufacturers surveyed said they would continue to have difficulties attracting and retaining workers in 2021 and beyond.[4]

It was a far cry from 2009, when, hoping to spur students toward STEM subjects, the Obama administration launched an "Educate to Innovate" campaign. The hope was to propel American students from the middle to the top of the pack in the international arena by investing $3.1 billion in federal programs on STEM education.[5] At the time, according to the National Assessment of Educational Progress (NAEP), only 34 percent of US fourth-grade students, 30 percent of eighth-grade students, and 21 percent of seniors were deemed "proficient" in science.[6]

Cut to today, when the US government's focus on STEM education has largely dissipated. From an anecdotal standpoint, students who received STEM-based educations at a young age became converts, but overall the STEM drive seems to have lost steam.

One solution to rebranding math and science is making them human, relatable, and all-in, as opposed to obscure, complicated, and excluding. A popular TV show when I was growing up in the 1950s and 1960s was *Watch Mr. Wizard*. Every week Mr. Wizard—a college English major and part-time actor named Don Herbert—and a cast of child volunteers performed a short, hands-on, kitchen-science experiment. Mr. Wizard plunged a hot dog, an apple, and a length of rubber tubing in a bowl of liquid nitrogen. He built an ammonia fountain. He made a mini hydrogen bomb and a home-made record player. He explained the science behind drinking straws, fuses, sirens, motors, Styrofoam, static electricity, centrifugal force, and convection currents. With its bangs, flashes, and clouds of smoke, *Watch*

Mr. Wizard, and a follow-up show, *Mr. Wizard's World*, made science thrilling, risky, and hypnotic, and inspired five thousand Mr. Wizard science clubs across the US.

Despite the ongoing efforts of Bill Nye, Neil deGrasse Tyson, Hank and John Green, and others, what will it take for math and science to regain that same level of joy, curiosity, and wonder?

First, it would be instructive to pose a few hypothetical questions to understand better what drives human beings emotionally. How do most of us choose to spend our time? What are some of the things we enjoy doing most? In most Western cultures, the answers tend to revolve around leisure activities—cooking, exercising, relaxing, and spending time with the people we love.

Enter science, which needs to explain, as I have already, that the existence of almost everything—a baseball or Frisbee as it leaves our hands, the shirt or blouse we put on in the morning, the prescription medications inside our kitchen cabinets, the food inside our fridges and freezers—wouldn't exist without science, math, and technology. Science needs to elucidate properly the link between the life sciences and our everyday habits, behaviors, and preferences, from a football to blue jeans to aspirin to the taste and texture of our food. The concepts and the language need to be made simple. Science, it should be emphasized, cures disease, is responsible for the freshness and safety of what we put inside our bodies, and underpins everything with which we come into contact every day.

Gamification could also help science regain its standing. When I was at Dow, I came up with the idea of partnering with Dean Kamen, the inventor of the Segway, the iBOT, and the technology used in portable dialysis machines, and will.i.am, the rapper, songwriter, music producer, founder of the Black Eyed Peas, and today an immensely successful technology entrepreneur. They had created FIRST Robotics, a competition among high-school robot teams, and Dow became a partner. By transforming robotics into a sport, the goal was to make science and technology *exciting*. Dow provided mentors to launch and support 70 new FIRST Robotics teams across the US in the hope we could eventually expand that sponsorship overseas. Our first robotics competition took place at H. H. Dow High

School in Midland. With more than forty teams competing and over a thousand spectators, it was a huge success.

The word *robotics* alone might cause some people to throw up their hands. What they don't realize is the variety of roles that are available to play on a robotics team, ranging from design to operation. What if they're still not persuaded and say they would rather go surfing? Then I would remind them that surfboards, which begin their lives with a polyurethane foam core, an outer shell made of fiberglass, and polyester resins, wouldn't even exist without chemistry.

The FIRST Robotics experience was a reminder that one company can't go it alone. Business, government, and civil society need to work together to elevate the sciences. With a targeted focus and a comprehensive approach, the US can recover its position as an incubator for the discovery and development of the world's most innovative technologies. We have the toolbox, the talent, and the will. The only thing left is reestablishing chemistry, math, and science at the center of learning. That means redefining the meaning of a high school education in this century.

For starters, it's imperative that schools teach the essentials of science, chemistry, physics, biology, and math. Schools then need to teach—and demonstrate—how using these skills can address and solve the world's most challenging problems with the help of artificial intelligence and cognitive computing. Insights and solutions around curing the big four diseases—cancer, heart disease, diabetes, and Alzheimer's. Solving aging. Targeting environmental issues, pursuing space exploration, and doing everything we can to improve the quality of life for everyone on the planet. Content comes first, followed by context. This will necessitate an overhaul of our entire educational system and a marketing effort that rebrands science in the psyches of educators, parents, and students.

Dow was among the first companies to recognize that ensuring workforce competitiveness begins long before an individual enters the workforce. Knowing how inconsistent and resource-poor many statewide educational systems can be, we decided to fill that gap. As CEO, I was eager to ensure that the children of employees in all Dow's US locations had access to first-class elementary, middle, and high school educations. Using our philanthropic arm, we began rebuilding the schools in Dow communities across the country and, among other tools, introducing an international baccalaureate standard. With our workforce in Lake Jackson, Texas, Dow also created a mini school focused on training employees and local high school students, including a community center retraining program to teach workers how to operate robots and drones.

Among the most innovative models of advancing economic opportunities for workers, while meeting the talent needs of today's economy, is Social Finance, based in Boston, a national impact finance and advisory nonprofit. In association with two training partners, Year Up and Merit America, and supported by a $100 million gift from Google in 2022, Social Finance offers wraparound support for twenty thousand learners from underserved communities to earn a Google Career Certificate to prepare for in-demand, entry-level jobs in fields ranging from data analytics to IT support, project management, and UX design—with no upfront costs to them. Google's gift is expected to drive wage gains estimated at $1 billion in aggregate over the next decade.[7]

Restoring science and math to their rightful place also means retraining high school teachers. Unlike their colleagues in high-performing countries like Korea and Finland, high school STEM teachers in the US aren't required to earn a bachelor's degree in a science discipline before they qualify to teach high school science. Today, only 35 percent of all US high school chemistry teachers hold a bachelor's degree in chemistry and/or have a chemistry certification.[8] This means most American high school chemistry, physics, and biology teachers are accredited to teach before they've mastered their own subject. That's not acceptable.

We can't control VUCA, but we *can* change how the US competes in the next few decades. Math, chemistry, biology, astronomy, and quantum physics don't need to change, but we *do* need to change how they are represented in the media and our understanding of the roles they play in our day-to-day lives.

ALONG WITH EVERYTHING ELSE, the COVID-19 pandemic served as a proof point, one that can't help but make me optimistic. By stress-testing almost every aspect of their lives, younger generations were obliged to acknowledge the part they play in their own survival and the survival of Earth. At Liveris Academy, many students asked me what they could do to help get our planet on a better path in the future. When the pandemic fades into memory, many people will return to old, familiar behaviors, habits, and rituals. But by offering both crisis and opportunity, the pandemic has also reset our pathways, which I hope will lead to top-down policies to establish a trajectory for *this* century to help solve some of humanity's most challenging problems.

In the interim, the front lines of science should rivet anyone who is paying attention.

The consumption of meat is a prime contributing factor to humanity's current "sixth extinction." Among the environmental effects that are linked to meat production are pollution caused by fossil fuels, animal methane, and effluent waste. The livestock sector is one of the world's largest sources of greenhouse gases and water pollution, and it's a causal factor in the global erosion of biodiversity. Thanks to companies like Beyond Meat and Impossible Foods, supermarket freezers are filling up with meat substitutes that mimic the taste, texture, and consistency of hamburgers, chicken, and sausages, minus the associated environmental damage caused by excessive global meat consumption.

Another serious problem in many areas of the world, and even the direct source of global conflicts, pertains to water shortages. Fruits and vegetables are rich in water, most of which is eliminated as waste during conventional processing. Scientists at an Australian company called Plant Botanical have learned to extract and purify that water, a process that allows fruits and vegetables to retain their nutrients and obliterates the need for the desalination that takes place when water is extracted from aquifers and oceans. The hope someday is that fruit and vegetable runoff can provide water for the world's most arid regions and water-poor populations.

Even more exciting, scientists are closer than they have ever been to beating the big four—cardiovascular disease, cancer, diabetes, and Alzheimer's. Recently, for example, an AI software program at the Stevens Institute of Technology in New Jersey diagnosed Alzheimer's in study subjects with

95 percent accuracy.[9] How? It seems that patients in the early stages of the disease use language in different ways than unafflicted people do. "The girl is eating the sandwich" becomes "She is eating it." The Stevens research team is currently training its AI software to detect Alzheimer's based on text fragments, from grocery lists to emails, and have expanded their research to focus on the ways language correlates with strokes and depression.[10] Finally, a shortened loop between patients and physicians has accelerated the growth of biosimilars, medications that mirror those already approved by the FDA that can be fast-tracked, one of which could very well become the next miracle drug against cancer or heart disease.

This triangulation is happening in the private sector, without any governmental assistance. How can governments fast-track things more? First, the US hospital system needs to be linked and aggregated. This would allow millions of pieces of patient data to be shared and to create a protocol for exchanging information that the government—and not private businesses or insurance companies who make money out of *not* sharing—can regulate. The drivers of this system will ideally be patients, patient data, hospitals, and the leveraging of all this information thanks to artificial intelligence.

Equally promising are the implications that scientific advancements have on human longevity.

The average life span for men today is 76.4 years, and for women 81.2 years.[11] By 2050, that life span will be in the nineties, and by 2100, it could be as much as 130 years.[12] More than a fact of life we need to put up with, aging is a *disease*, scientists believe. With scientists now able to manipulate the cell structures of genomes, it is becoming more and more evident that people can continue living healthy and pain-free until the end of their lives. In other words, humans won't "age" as the word is now defined. This means that the problems commonly associated with "aging"—hypertension, atherosclerosis, osteoporosis, macular degeneration, cerebrovascular disease, and cognitive deterioration—may eventually become diseases of the past.

Think about it. If science succeeds in eliminating cancer, cardiovascular disease, diabetes, and Alzheimer's disease, while eradicating the physical and cognitive degeneration linked to aging, in the end what will do us in? I can't help but reflect on the words of will.i.am.

The two of us were on the same panel one year at the World Economic Forum when the subject of machines doing human work came up. When that day arrived, someone in the audience asked, what will humans do? "Human will be *happy*," will.i.am answered. He took this idea further, adding, "Humans will be *intoxicated* with happiness." Being born, dying, and spending our time in between working, sounds, to an alien ear, brutal and joyless. Where is it written that humans exist solely for the purpose of performing thousands of hours of labor? Couldn't it also be argued that humans exist to emote, create, love, and, echoing will.i.am, be happy? If scientific and human ingenuity can collaborate to create the molecules that go into creating smart machines that can do the menial tasks most of us would rather not do—with humans, and not machines, in charge of the production and economics—who wouldn't want that? Wouldn't everybody's lives be significantly improved?

Could we go so far as to redefine what "being alive" means? By eliminating all the stressors endemic to doing menial tasks, wouldn't our brains be freed up to focus on the roles we play in our world? Don't we all want to live longer, healthier lives, surrounded by all the people we love? If anyone believes *happiness* and *science* are contradictory terms, that one is "soft" and the other "hard," they should think again. The inventors, scientists, and engineers of our world are the people ultimately equipped to solve humanity's most challenging problems, and that includes the problem of happiness. Wouldn't it make sense to invest in science and the potential for the greater happiness of humanity *now*?

Takeaways and Tools

- Science needs to be restored to its proper place in our culture. To do this, we need new ways of highlighting products and activities most humans take for granted, from bicycles and air conditioning to clothing, shoes, and cosmetics.

- Unless we focus on STEM education, the US risks losing its global competitive advantage in innovative new technologies. Today's workplace suffers from a critical shortage of qualified workers in the tech industry, with hundreds of thousands of jobs going unfilled. This could result in close to two million positions remaining unfilled by 2030.

- The reinvigoration of STEM education must begin with the private sector. Today's biggest wealth creators, for example, tech companies, should create a committee or leadership group focused on improving STEM education. Tech enterprises have the most to lose if they can't meet the supply side or onboard future talent. With immigration issues remaining problematic in the US, the talent pipeline—which begins with science-based education and teacher training—must be fixed at the community level, via community colleges and high schools.

- Companies should understand that future competitiveness begins today. Dow introduced an international baccalaureate standard in our community high schools, and in one Texas community retrained our workforce to operate robots and drones.

- Among the most innovative models to advance economic opportunities and meet today's talent needs is Boston-based Social Finance. Thanks to a $100 million gift from Google, Social Finance is helping twenty thousand learners prepare for well-paying entry-level jobs in data analytics, IT support, project management, and UX design.

11

The New Tomorrow

A few years ago, I participated in a fireside chat at the New York Stock Exchange, the discussion encompassing everything from corporate boards to the state of the global markets. When it was over, a man who introduced himself as Larry Senn, a business consultant, joined my chief of staff and me in the elevator and handed me a book he had written. I should take the time to read it, he said, adding that my temperament struck him as being on or near the top of the framework set out in his book. Well, I ended up liking the book so much, I begin quoting from it.

The premise of *The Mood Elevator* is that our thoughts and perspectives rise and fall on a moment-by-moment basis the same way an elevator does. We go from anxious, angry, self-righteous, impatient, and depressed on the lowest floors to adaptive, appreciative, resourceful, and optimistic on the uppermost floors. Having always been fascinated by the human capacity for flexibility, and how and in what ways leaders continually adjust to new situations and circumstances, I did the self-diagnosis exercise in the back of the book. Senn was right. My average daily mood hovered on and around the very top of the mood elevator. *Curious* and *grateful* were the two adjectives the book said described me.

Both words resonated. I've always been inquisitive and driven to see all sides of a subject. I have a huge store of gratitude, goodwill, and love for my wife, children, and grandchildren, and my close friends in and out of business. I believe that people who spend all their time complaining, hating, criticizing, or assuming the worst about others (people, in other words, who inhabit the lowest floors of the mood elevator), don't understand how miraculous and magnificent life is. Every day brings new discoveries, ideas, and perspectives. The only thing required of us is that we listen and pay close attention to our surroundings.

"History never repeats," Mark Twain said (purportedly), "but it rhymes." Some of those rhymes are forming before us today. We need to recognize them as they take shape and remember that relative to infinity, we are here in our bodies and on this Earth for only a few seconds. I can't speak for anyone else, but I'm determined to make sure *my* few seconds here are as good as possible. Good for me, yes, and good for my circle—my family, my friends, my work colleagues—but also good for society and our planet. As my recent election to the presidency of the Brisbane Olympics 2032 shows, I gravitate toward the intersections of business, government, academia, the nonprofit sector, and civic society. Unlike many of the subjects in these pages, where business is called upon to respond to negatives, with the Olympics these elements can come together in the most positive way possible.

Curiosity and gratitude are also what motivates me to leave behind an imprint and a legacy and what drives me to work as closely as I do with the faculty and students of Liveris Academy. My goal is to do everything possible to help ensure and expand the possibilities (and bandwidth) of their future leadership. My experience with these incredible students is in large part responsible for the optimism I feel as we face down the most challenging issues of this century.

With that in mind, let us close out this book with a thought experiment. Imagine that it is 2050, roughly three decades from now. Who will lead? What will society look like? What will leadership look like? Starting today, can we rebuild a world order that *works*, one strengthened by new businesses, new governments, new institutions? In 2050, today's twenty-five-year-olds will be pushing fifty-five. Today's sixty-five-year-olds probably won't be around anymore. In the roughly three decades standing between now and then, can we create a new way forward?

JANUARY 2050. You are on your morning commute, a passenger in an accident-free car that drove itself to your workplace and, with no help from you, found its way to its own parking space. (Refueling is unnecessary since whatever power you need is delivered wirelessly while driving.) You board the elevator and get off at your floor. Your colleagues include recent graduates who, when they weren't studying, were playing videogames that were neither videos nor games. Instead, they leverage hologram technologies synced to artificial intelligence to physically move 3-D Tetris blocks. When they're not doing that, they are connecting with their friends in real time via virtual worlds, generated from their social networks.

If you live in a city, the buildings around you will generate their own power and return energy to an interconnected (but localized) grid that is 100 percent smart and efficient. At the same time, new devices will have been invented that continuously draw carbon from the air and transform it into feedstocks for advanced materials—things like self-healing polymers that automatically repair their own tears, cuts, and cracks. Overhead, uncrewed spacecraft will be busy harvesting the earth's rarest elements from asteroids—creating a universe that has virtually unlimited access to raw materials like platinum and palladium. Where scarcity exists today, technology will create abundance tomorrow, helping us break free even from the leashes of our own Earth.

Back at home, your dishwasher is set to operate at the time of night when electricity costs are lowest. That goes for all your other appliances, too, which have evolved to regulate themselves and give or draw power to and from a localized grid. By the way, your refrigerator knows when you are out of frozen pizza and will automatically order more—frozen pizza, I should add, that, using newly engineered ingredients, is both delicious *and* good for you.

Most if not all work is automated and driven by artificial intelligence. Humans steer AI machines as they carry out daily tasks and strategic work. Work, at least as we define the word today, no longer exists. With *happiness* taking its place as the foremost barometer of life, leisure and fulfillment will take their natural places as essential reasons for and drivers of existence. Terminal illnesses are in the past. In my office is a thick packet spelling out how scientists will be able to cure all the various diseases linked to aging. By 2050, you will be able to pop a pill and live until 150, not in a decrepit, lingering condition but in a continuously healthy state.

We will continue to see the evolving merger of digital and human. Today, Elon Musk is funding work to implant chips into the brain to allow humans to be smarter while expanding the bandwidth of our brains. A merger of AI and humanity is often perceived to be impossible, but even the most doubting or regressive thinkers believe it is imminent. By 2050, we will be halfway there. Think about it: if you wed antiaging advances with human biology, and artificial intelligence with biology, you will have dreamed up a completely new human being. It may sound science fiction–like, but it's not. Accept it as a vision born of the technology revolution that none of us could have imagined even thirty years ago.

Looking wider, by 2050 we will see the advent of new global institutions and stronger regional alliances. More of the world's population will have access to food, water, and shelter, with the quality of life in advanced nations more equitably distributed. A new cadre of global leaders will be in office, their mandate being to create new values-driven, socially and morally conscious blueprints for humanity to continue living on our planet. Society will drive the economy, not the other way around. Money and its middlemen will be more highly regulated and tightly controlled. An as-yet unimagined successor to the UN's Sustainability Development Goals will be the only KPIs by which leaders and enterprises are measured.

All this means is that right now we should be thinking ahead. What will be the policies corralling this technological evolution? How can we spread advances evenly across humanity, from rich countries to the poorest areas of the world? How will global institutions work? This 2050 vision also makes clear that any corporation or enterprise that hasn't incorporated digitalization and modernity into its processes will be left in the dust. Unless you are digitally efficient and automation efficient and have a highly trained, skilled workforce, your business will vanish.

Over the past two decades, the UN and its security council have failed to prevent regional conflicts. The idea that the twenty largest economies in the world will embrace the subjects I've covered in this book not just for themselves but for the rest of the world is almost zero. If we can't get the global world order to work with our global institutions, then we need to create new ones. The first step is to embrace this reality.

The second step involves making conscious choices, while recognizing that these decisions can't be extrapolated from the present day. Transforming and re-creating our current institutions may not be possible in a top-down way, which leaves us no alternative but to begin from the bottom up.

By 2050, new alliances must be led by business, which, as I mentioned before, tops the Edelman Trust Barometer for the first time ever as the most trusted institution on Earth. Those enterprises that believe in the vision of the world being one with opportunities must build a case and distribute that vision across other institutions, enterprises, and governments. Think back to what happened after World War II when Churchill won the war *and* won peace. Through the Marshall Plan and the occupation and rehabilitation of Japan, the US gave both countries new life, creating two extraordinary societies that endure today. Today countless institutions, or "summits," are being formed by people in their twenties and thirties, sponsored by key thought leaders like Richard Branson and Hank Paulson and institutions like the World Economic Forum. I hold tight to the vision of millions of young people coming together to acknowledge the world's most pressing problems and exchanging the best ideas and solutions to change and solve them.

Liveris Academy may well be one example of such a summit. But I'm just one person who from my vantage point is seeing what will drive the future of business and government and who has a few ideas about what shape the future will take. I spend an enormous amount of time and energy driving toward what our world *could* be. Maybe I'll be among those who play a role in turning what *could* be into what *will* be. At least that's my hope.

But in the next few decades, my advice is to seek out opportunity because these days it's everywhere, especially in a VUCA era. Consider the results of an eight-year, twenty-five-hundred-company study done by Bain & Company that found that economic turmoil, contrary to popular belief, created vast opportunities for companies to move forward into leadership positions. During the last great economic downturn in 2001, for example, 24 percent more firms moved from laggards to leaders than took place in earlier, more economically predictable periods. In fact, the companies that made acquisitions during a downturn generated *tripled* the returns of companies making acquisitions during the boom cycle.[1] This confirms a lesson from the Great Depression of the early 1930s, namely, that more millionaires were created during those few dark years than during any other time in American history.

Both times, individuals and companies saw opportunities and acted on them. VUCA will continue to take its toll on everyone, especially affecting companies with shaky balance sheets. In uncertain times, most companies are tempted to shed businesses and retrench with their products, services, and geographies. But assuming a company's balance sheet is healthy, now would be an excellent time to speed up the implementation of your strategy.

A DECADE OR SO AGO, I had the honor and privilege of sitting down for a meal with an American hero. General Colin Powell, who died in 2021, served four US presidents at the highest levels of government. He could have chosen to spend his retirement years looking back over his career or reminiscing about being central to so many world events. Instead, he said something to me that I will paraphrase.

"Do not stare in the rearview mirror. Do not glance at the side mirrors. Focus intensely through the front windshield—because *that* is where the future is—*that* is where the better days are—and *that* is where the better ways are found."

I think of those words a lot, especially today, when change moves at the speed of "live," and there is relentless pressure to respond instantaneously to every development. Today's business leaders understand the temptation of focusing exclusively on whatever challenge is before them—the next earnings report or the upcoming election. That pull is more potent than it's ever been. It is also more potentially disastrous, with the consequences, ranging from economic volatility to political stasis, all around us.

It would be equally shortsighted to focus on long-term challenges while excluding short-term concerns. If you can, see if you can adapt the perspective of an airline pilot. Your job is to keep one eye on the controls and the instruments in front of you—these blinking lights are analogous to short-term challenges—and the other eye trained on the horizon, representing longer-term objectives and solutions. To my mind, this is the *only* way for twenty-first-century leaders to proceed safely to their destinations.

First, leaders lead, but leaders also follow. They listen and learn. Intellectual (and emotional) curiosity is or should be a lifelong habit and journey. It's worth repeating the Confucian adage I cited earlier: two ears and one mouth.

Second, leaders have humility and a genuine identification with their roots and histories, and those of their colleagues.

Third, leaders embrace reality, make conscious choices, and lead by building collaborative teams and embracing fellowship.

Fourth, leaders live by inspiration, aspiration, and perspiration. To lead, you need a vision, a strategy, a purpose, motivation, and the willingness to work hard. Leaders should lead from the front and set an example. This will drive better outcomes, for you and humanity in general.

Finally, live your life on the numerator, not the denominator. For those who don't have a background in science or engineering, this one probably requires a short explanation.

Experience has taught me that there are two ways to approach any situation. You can be part of the denominator—a mindset in which whatever you bring to the table divides or subtracts from the goal and makes the outcome worse than before. Or you can be part of the numerator—meaning that your contributions are additive and multiplying and are enhanced by your presence and contributions.

Whenever I find myself in a tough situation, I always ask myself: How can I be part of the *numerator*? How can I be an optimist, a solutions enabler, a creative problem solver, someone who contributes his judgment, energy, smarts, and passion?

As the challenges of the upcoming century mount, we need everyone, using all their talent and wisdom, to step up and do their part to lead us forward. My hope is that this book will be a call for millions of people to constantly seek out opportunities for progress, using every tool at their disposal. No one said it better than the novelist, playwright, poet, and social critic James Baldwin. "The world is before you," he said, "and you need not take it or leave it as it was when you came in."

When I retired from Dow in 2018, I left my act one behind and transitioned into act two. This has made me relatively unique among my business peers, as few of them have chosen to reinvent themselves as broadly as I have tried. But my act two has begun to yield some valid and (I hope) valuable ideas, namely, that we are living within intersections amid paradigm shifts, which in turn means that future trajectories we could have once extrapolated from the past no longer work. We need new paradigms, new catalysts, and new role models.

It's worth repeating: the institutions of this century that need to be changed are unlikely to change from within. The incitement for change must come from business, from business leaders, and from youth and communities. In turn, these leaders need to aggregate and accumulate their capabilities in different mechanisms, in the same way business and government came together to propel forward the infrastructure bill.

I leave you with one last reminder, namely, to learn the context of what is happening, whether you do that through books or through Google. Lead with context, using the expanded bandwidth that technology has placed at everyone's disposal. Do not squander the unprecedented ability you have in this century to lead with context *and* content. It is a privilege.

ANDREW LIVERIS

ENDNOTES

INTRODUCTION

1. Manyika, James, Susan Lund, Michael Chui, Jacques Burghin, Jonathan Woetzel, Parul Batra, Ryan Ko,and Saurabh Sanghvi. "Jobs Lost, Jobs Gained; What the Future of Work Will Mean for Jobs, Skills, and Wages." McKinsey & Company, November 28, 2017. https://www.mckinsey.com/featured-insights/future-of-work/jobs-lost -jobs-gained-what-the-future-of-work-will-mean-for-jobs-skills-and-wages.

CHAPTER 1

1. Graham, Flora. "COP26: Glasgow Climate Pact Signed into History." *Nature*, November 13, 2021. https://www.nature.com/articles/d41586-021-03464-9.
2. Nidumolu, Ram, C. K. Prahalad, and M. R. Rangaswami. "Why Sustainability Is Now the Key Driver of Innovation." *Harvard Business Review*, September 2009. https:// hbr.org/2009/09/why-sustainability-is-now-the-key-driver-of-innovation.
3. https://thehill.com/opinion/civil-rights/400602-why-companies-need-discussion -debate-even-defiance-in-the-workplace/.
4. https://clintonwhitehouse3.archives.gov/PCSD/Overview/.
5. Boudette, Neal E., and Coral Davenport. "G.M. Announcement Shakes Up US Automakers' Transition to Electric Cars." *New York Times*, January 29, 2021. https:// www.nytimes.com/2021/01/29/business/general-motors-electric-cars.html.
6. Ibid.
7. "Larry Fink's 2021 Letter to CEOs." BlackRock, 2021. https://www.blackrock.com /corporate/investor-relations/larry-fink-ceo-letter.
8. Sorkin, Andrew Ross, and de la Merced, Michael J. "It's Not 'Woke' for Businesses to Think beyond Profit, BlackRock Chief Says," *New York Times*, January 17, 2022.
9. Nicas, Jack. "New iPhones Fuel Strong Profit for Apple." *New York Times*, January 28, 2020. https://www.nytimes.com/2020/01/29/business/dealbook/coronavirus -apple-starbucks.html.
10. Haddon, Heather, and Micah Maidenberg. "Starbucks Closes Half of China Stores amid Coronavirus Outbreak." *Wall Street Journal*, January 28, 2020. https://www .wsj.com/articles/starbucks-closed-half-of-china-stores-amid-coronavirus-outbreak -11580247048.
11. "Net Zero Takes Off." State Street Global Advisors, n.d. https://www.ssga.com/us/en /institutional/ic/capabilities/esg.
12. https://www.salesforce.com/news/press-releases/2021/09/21/salesforce-achieves -net-zero-across-its-full-value-chain/.

13. Rep. *The Coca-Cola Company: 2020 Business & Environmental, Social and Governance Report.* Coca-Cola Company, 2020. https://www.coca-colacompany.com/content /dam/journey/us/en/reports/coca-cola-business-environmental-social-governance -report-2020.pdf.

14. https://www.unilever.com/planet-and-society/protect-and-regenerate-nature/zero -deforestation/.

15. Abuljadayel, Fahad, and Jana Salloum. "'Let the Unicorns Come!' PIF Advisor Says Saudi's Economic 'Pie' Is Growing." *Arab News*, October 26, 2021. https://www .arabnews.com/node/1955626/business-economy.

CHAPTER 2

1. Tankersley, Jim. "Biden Signs Infrastructure Bill, Promoting Benefits for Americans." *New York Times*, November 15, 2021. https://www.nytimes.com/2021/11/15/us /politics/biden-signs-infrastructure-bill.html.

2. Ibid.

3. Friedman, Milton. "The Social Responsibility of Business Is to Increase Its Profits." *New York Times*, September 13, 1970.

4. Ibid.

5. Dealbook. "Greed Is Good. Except When It's Bad." *New York Times*, September 13, 2020. https://www.nytimes.com/2020/09/13/business/dealbook/milton-friedman -essay-anniversary.html.

6. Ibid.

7. Ibid.

8. Ibid.

9. "Rethinking the Future of Capitalism in America." November 12, 2020. https://www .mckinsey.com/featured-insights/long-term-capitalism/rethinking-the-future-of -american-capitalism.

10. Ibid.

11. Ibid.

12. Congressional Budget Office, October 25, 2011. https://www.cbo.gov/publication /42729.

13. Hess, Abigail Johnson. "In 2020, Top CEOs Earned 351 Times More Than the Typical Worker." CNBC Make It, September 15, 2021. https://www.cnbc.com/2021 /09/15/in-2020-top-ceos-earned-351-times-more-than-the-typical-worker.html.

14. Hinshaw, Drew. "Omicron Variant Highlights Risks of Low Vaccination Rates in Poor Countries." *Wall Street Journal*, November 26, 2021. https://www.wsj.com /articles/omicron-variant-highlights-risks-of-low-vaccination-rates-in-poor -countries-11637960558.

15. "Ten Richest Men Double Their Fortunes in Pandemic While Incomes of 99 Percent of Humanity Fall." Oxfam, January 17, 2022. https://www.oxfam.org/en/press -releases/ten-richest-men-double-their-fortunes-pandemic-while-incomes-99 -percent-humanity.

16. Saslow, Eli. "The Moral Calculations of a Billionaire." *Washington Post*, January 30, 2021. https://www.washingtonpost.com/nation/2022/01/30/moral-calculations -billionaire/.

17. Ibid.

18. Ibid.

19. Business Roundtable. "Promote 'an Economy that Serves All Americans.'" August 19, 2019. https://www.businessroundtable.org/business-roundtable-redefines-the-purpose-of-a-corporation-to-promote-an-economy-that-serves-all-americans.

20. Benioff, Marc. "Marc Benioff: We Need a New Capitalism." *New York Times*, October 14, 2019. https://www.nytimes.com/2019/10/14/opinion/benioff-salesforce-capitalism.html.

21. Ibid.

22. Ibid.

23. Edelman Trust Barometer 2022, https://www.edelman.com/sites/g/files/aatuss191/files/2022-01/2022%20Edelman%20Trust%20Barometer_FullReport.pdf.

24. Ibid.

25. Buffett, Warren E. "Stop Coddling the Super-Rich." *New York Times*, August 14, 2011. https://www.nytimes.com/2011/08/15/opinion/stop-coddling-the-super-rich.html.

26. Report, "55 Corporations Paid $0 in Federal Taxes on 2020 Profits." Institute on Taxation and Economic Policy, April 2, 2021. https://itep.org/55-profitable-corporations-zero-corporate-tax/.

27. Wessel, David. "Who Are the Rich, and How Might We Tax Them More?" Policy 2020 Brookings, October 15, 2019. https://www.brookings.edu/policy2020/votervital/who-are-the-rich-and-how-might-we-tax-them-more/.

28. "The Digital Skills Gap: What Workers Need for the Jobs of the Future." The RAND Blog, March 1, 2022.

29. Goldstein, Dana. "After 10 Years of Hopes and Setbacks, What Happened to the Common Core?" *New York Times*, December 6, 2019. https://www.nytimes.com/2019/12/06/us/common-core.html.

30. Ibid.

31. The Dow Chemical Company, "Dow Named One of America's Most JUST Companies for the Third Year by JUST Capital," Cision PR Newswire, January 11, 2022. https://www.prnewswire.com/news-releases/dow-named-one-of-americas-most-just-companies-for-the-third-year-by-just-capital-301458441.html.

32. https://www.prnewswire.com/news-releases/dow-named-one-of-the-worlds-most-admired-companies-by-fortune-301474115.html.

33. Buss, Dale. "Which School Has Most Fortune 500 CEOs?: Not Harvard, It's Wisconsin." *Chief Executive*, March 19, 2019. https://chiefexecutive.net/fortune-500-ceos-wisconsin/.

CHAPTER 4

1. Nostrant, Rachel. "US, China Lead List of Top Defense Spenders in 2021." *Military Times*, September 23, 2022. https://www.militarytimes.com/news/your-military/2022/09/23/us-china-lead-list-of-top-defense-spenders-in-2021/.

2. Davidson, Helen. "China's Act of 'Hostage Diplomacy' Comes to End as Two Canadians Freed." *The Guardian*, September 25, 2021. https://www.theguardian.com/world/2021/sep/25/canadian-pm-trudeau-says-detained-citizens-michael-kovrig-and-michael-spavor-have-left-china.

3. Zhong, Raymond. "In Halting Ant's I.P.O., China Sends a Warning to Business." *New York Times*, November 6, 2020. https://www.nytimes.com/2020/11/06/technology/china-ant-group-ipo.html.

4. Benveniste, Alexis. "China Bans Didi, Its Biggest Ride-Hailing Service, from App Stores." CNN, July 4, 2021. https://www.cnn.com/2021/07/04/tech/china-app-store -didi/index.html.

5. Swartz, Spencer, and Shai Oster. "China Tops US in Energy Use." *Wall Street Journal*, July 18, 2010. https://www.wsj.com/articles/SB10001424052748703720504575376712353150310.

6. Ayoub, Joseph. "Today in Energy." US Energy Information Administration, May 14, 2014. https://www.eia.gov/todayinenergy/detail.php?id=16271.

7. Braw, Elisabeth. "Don't Let China Steal Your Steel Industry." *Foreign Policy*, May 19, 2020. https://foreignpolicy.com/2020/05/19/dont-let-china-steal-your-steel-industry/.

8. Zhai, Keith. "China Set to Create New State-Owned Rare-Earths Giant." *Wall Street Journal*, December 3, 2021. https://www.wsj.com/articles/china-set-to-create-new -state-owned-rare-earths-giant-11638545586.

9. "Inside China's Plan to Create a Modern Silk Road." Morgan Stanley, March 14, 2018. https://www.morganstanley.com/ideas/china-belt-and-road.

10. Higgins, Andrew. "A Pricey Drive Down Montenegro's Highway 'From Nowhere to Nowhere.'" *New York Times*, August 14, 2021. https://www.nytimes.com/2021/08/14 /world/europe/montenegro-highway-china.html.

11. Abi-Habib, Maria. "How China Got Sri Lanka to Cough Up a Port." *New York Times*, June 25, 2018. https://www.nytimes.com/2018/06/25/world/asia/china-sri-lanka -port.html.

12. Reuters. "China Theft of Technology Is Biggest Law Enforcement Threat to US, FBI Says." *The Guardian*, February 6, 2020. https://www.theguardian.com/world/2020 /feb/06/china-technology-theft-fbi-biggest-threat.

13. Liu Jie. "Official Data Confirm China as World's Biggest Auto Producer, Consumer, Challenges Remain." Embassy of the People's Republic of China in the United States of America, November 1AD, https://www.mfa.gov.cn/ce/ceus//eng/gyzg /t650880.htm.

14. Obama, Barack. "Remarks by President Obama at APEC CEO Summit." The White House, 2014. https://obamawhitehouse.archives.gov/the-press-office/2014/11/10 /remarks-president-Obama-apec-ceo-summit.

15. Moses, Claire. "China's Crackdown on Hong Kong." *New York Times*, June 23, 2021. https://www.nytimes.com/2021/06/23/briefing/china-hong-kong-apple-daily -closure.html.

16. Woo, Stu, and Liza Lin. "The China-US 5G Battle Upends a Telecom Industry Consortium." *Wall Street Journal*, October 12, 2021. https://www.wsj.com/articles /china-us-5g-battle-11634000482.

17. Kaplan, Robert D. "Opinion: The Biden Administration Just Stalled China's Advance in the Indo-Pacific." *Wall Street Journal*, October 21, 2021. https://www .washingtonpost.com/opinions/2021/09/21/biden-administration-just-stalled -chinas-advance-indo-pacific/.

18. Ibid.

19. Lieber, Dov, and Nick Kostov. "Ben & Jerry's Decision to Stop Sales in West Bank Puts Unilever in Tough Spot." *Wall Street Journal*, July 20, 2021. https://www .wsj.com/articles/ben-jerrys-decision-to-stop-sales-in-west-bank-puts-unilever-in -tough-spot-11626799596.

20. "Airbnb Reverses Ban on West Bank Settlement Listings." BBC, April 10, 2019. https://www.bbc.com/news/world-middle-east-47881163.

21. "We Now Use 100% Renewable Grid Electricity Globally." Unilever, January 30, 2020. https://www.unilever.com/news/news-search/2020/we-now-use-100-renewable-grid-electricity-globally/.

22. "Sanitation and Hygiene for Better Health." Unilever, n.d. https://www.unilever.com/planet-and-society/health-and-wellbeing/sanitation-and-hygiene-for-better-health/.

23. "Pledge 1%." Salesforce, n.d. https://www.salesforce.org/pledge-1/.

24. Kessler, Glenn. "The 'Very Fine People' at Charlottesville: Who Were They?" *Washington Post*, May 8, 2020. https://www.washingtonpost.com/politics/2020/05/08/very-fine-people-charlottesville-who-were-they-2/.

25. Gelles, David. "The C.E.O. Who Stood Up to President Trump: Ken Frazier Speaks Out." *New York Times*, February 19, 2018. https://www.nytimes.com/2018/02/19/business/merck-ceo-ken-frazier-trump.html.

26. Ramzy, Austin. "How China Tracked Detainees and Their Families." *New York Times*, February 17, 2020. https://www.nytimes.com/2020/02/17/world/asia/china-reeducation-camps-leaked.html.

CHAPTER 5

1. Barton, Dominic. "Capitalism for the Long Term." *Harvard Business Review*, March 2011. https://hbr.org/2011/03/capitalism-for-the-long-term.

2. Biden, Joseph. "How Short-Termism Saps the Economy." *Wall Street Journal*, September 27, 2016. https://www.wsj.com/articles/how-short-termism-saps-the-economy-1475018087.

3. Ibid.

4. Barton, Dominic. "Capitalism for the Long Term." *Harvard Business Review*, March 2011. https://hbr.org/2011/03/capitalism-for-the-long-term.

5. Iacurci, Greg. "Money Invested in ESG Funds More Than Doubles in a Year." CNBC, February 11, 2021. https://www.cnbc.com/2021/02/11/sustainable-investment-funds-more-than-doubled-in-2020-.html.

CHAPTER 6

1. Barton, Dominic. "Capitalism for the Long Term." *Harvard Business Review*, March 2011. https://hbr.org/2011/03/capitalism-for-the-long-term.

2. Ibid.

3. Barton, Dominic, and Mark Wiseman. "Where Board Rooms Fall Short." *Harvard Business Review*, January 2015. https://hbr.org/2015/01/where-boards-fall-short.

CHAPTER 7

1. Lagace, Martha. "Gerstner: Changing Culture at IBM—Lou Gerstner Discusses Changing the Culture at IBM." Harvard Business School: Working Knowledge, December 9, 2002. https://hbswk.hbs.edu/archive/gerstner-changing-culture-at-ibm-lou-gerstner-discusses-changing-the-culture-at-ibm.

CHAPTER 8

1. Ewing, Jack, and Boudette, Neal E. "Why This Could Be a Critical Year for Electric Cars." *New York Times*, February 8, 2022. https://www.nytimes.com/2022/02/08/business/energy-environment/electric-cars-vehicles.html.

2. Ibid.

3. Ibid.

4. Mooney, Chris. "This Is Obama's Plan to Line the Country's Roads with Electric Vehicle Chargers." *Washington Post,* July 21, 2016. https://www.washingtonpost .com/news/energy-environment/wp/2016/07/21/this-is-obamas-plan-to-fill-the -countrys-roads-with-electric-vehicle-chargers/.

5. Patterson, Scott. "US Bets on Faster-Charging Battery in Race to Catch Energy Rivals." *Wall Street Journal,* February 26, 2022.

CHAPTER 10

1. Madavilli, Apoorva. "The US Is Getting a Crash Course in Scientific Uncertainty." *New York Times*, August 22, 2021. https://www.nytimes.com/2021/08/22/health /coronavirus-covid-usa.html.

2. https://www.ranken-energy.com/index.php/products-made-from-petroleum/.

3. "US Manufacturing Skills Gap Could Leave as Many as 2.1 Million Jobs Unfilled by 2030, Deloitte and the Manufacturing Institute Study Finds." Deloitte, May 4, 2021. https://www2.deloitte.com/us/en/pages/about-deloitte/articles/press-releases /deloitte-manufacturing-skills-gap.html.

4. Ibid.

5. "Office of the Press Secretary: President Obama Launches 'Educate to Innovate' Campaign for Excellence in Science, Technology, Engineering & Math (STEM) Education." The White House: President Barack Obama, November 23, 2009. https:// obamawhitehouse.archives.gov/the-press-office/president-obama-launches-educate -innovate-campaign-excellence-science-technology-en.

6. "Reading 2011: National Assessment of Educational Progress at Grades 4 and 8." 2011. https://nces.ed.gov/nationsreportcard/pdf/main2011/2012457.pdf.

7. "Google Career Certificates Fund." Social Finance, https://socialfinance.org/project /google/.

8. "The American Chemical Society: A Force for Good." American Chemical Society, n.d. https://www.acs.org/content/acs/en/about/aboutacs/force-for-good.html.

9. "A.I. Tool Promises Faster, More Accurate Alzheimer's Diagnosis." Stevens Institute of Technology, August 27, 2020. https://www.stevens.edu/news/ai-tool-promises -faster-more-accurate-alzheimers-diagnosis.

10. Ibid.

11. "Life Expectancy at Birth, at Age 65, and at Age 75, by Sex, Race, and Hispanic Origin: United States, Selected Years 1900–2016." 2017. https://www.cdc.gov/nchs /data/hus/2017/015.pdf.

12. "Maximum Human Life Span Could Reach 130 Years by 2100." Medical News Today, n.d. https://www.medicalnewstoday.com/articles/maximum-human-lifespan-could -reach-130-years-by-the-end-of-this-century.

CHAPTER 11

1. Zook, Chris, James Allen, and Dunigan O'Keeffe. "The Engine 2 Imperative: New Business Innovation and Profitable Growth under Turbulence." Bain & Company, December 17, 2020. https://www.bain.com/insights/engine-2-imperative-new -business-innovation-and-profitable-growth-under-turbulence/.

INDEX

ABOUT THE AUTHOR

One of the world's most admired business leaders, ANDREW N. LIVERIS is the former CEO and chairman of The Dow Chemical Company, the former executive chairman of DowDuPont, a former chairman of the Business Council, and an advisor to three US presidents. He currently serves as chairman of Lucid Motors and The Hellenic Initiative, and is a director on the boards of IBM, Saudi Aramco, and Worley, among others. Liveris is an advisor to Salesforce, Sumitomo Mitsui Banking Corporation, and PIF, the sovereign wealth fund of Saudi Arabia. He founded the Liveris Academy at his alma mater, the University of Queensland, and serves as an executive committee member of Richard Branson's B Team. Most recently, Liveris was named president of the Organizing Committee for the Brisbane 2032 Olympic and Paralympic Games. The author of the widely acclaimed book *Make It In America*, Andrew resides with his wife, Paula, in Palm Beach, Florida, and spends time in Australia and Greece.